W9-DBY-264

SHIKIMORI'S
Not just a cutie

8

KEIGO MAKI

Characters

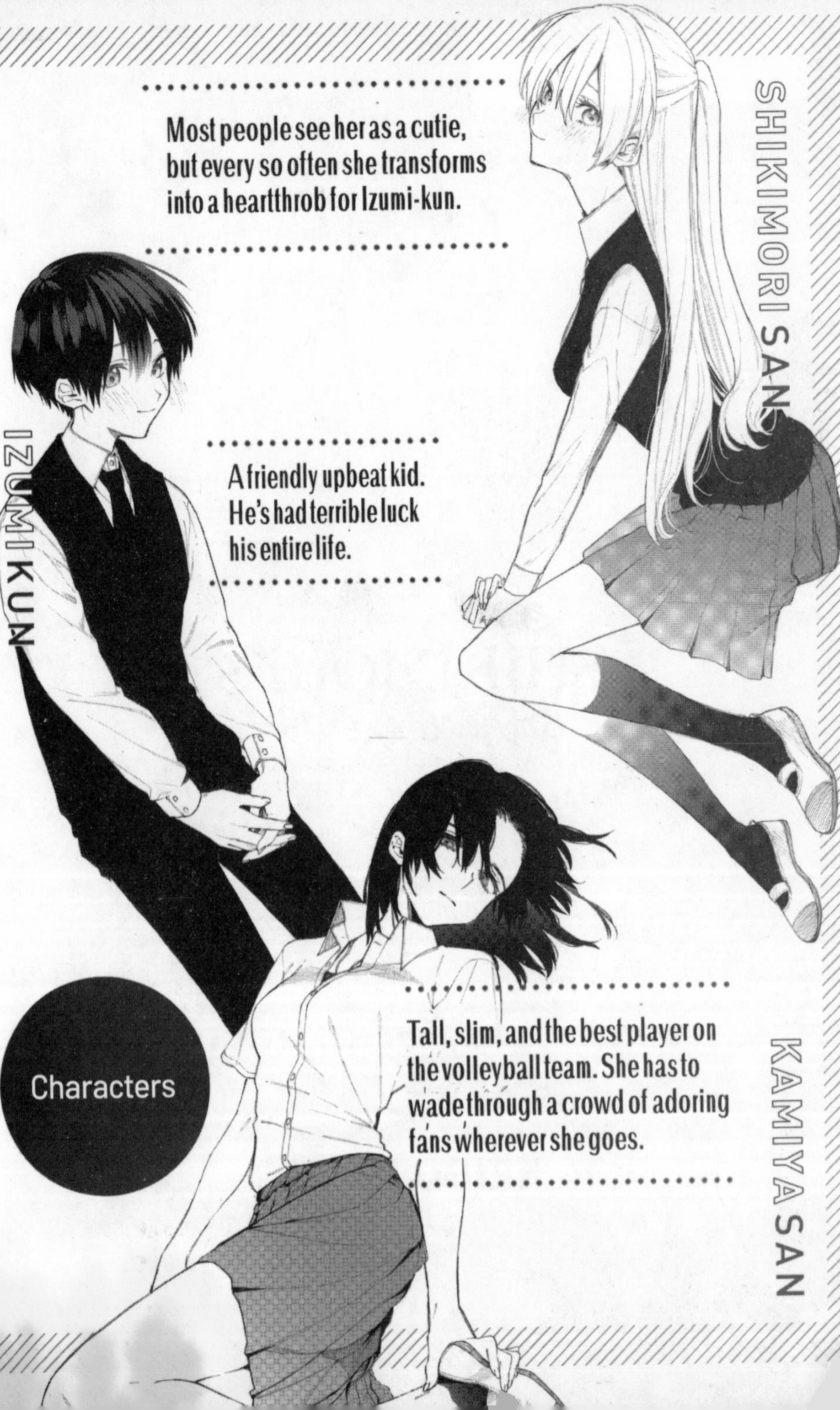

SHIKIMORI SAN

Most people see her as a cutie, but every so often she transforms into a heartthrob for Izumi-kun.

IZUMI KUN

A friendly upbeat kid. He's had terrible luck his entire life.

KAMIYA SAN

Tall, slim, and the best player on the volleyball team. She has to wade through a crowd of adoring fans wherever she goes.

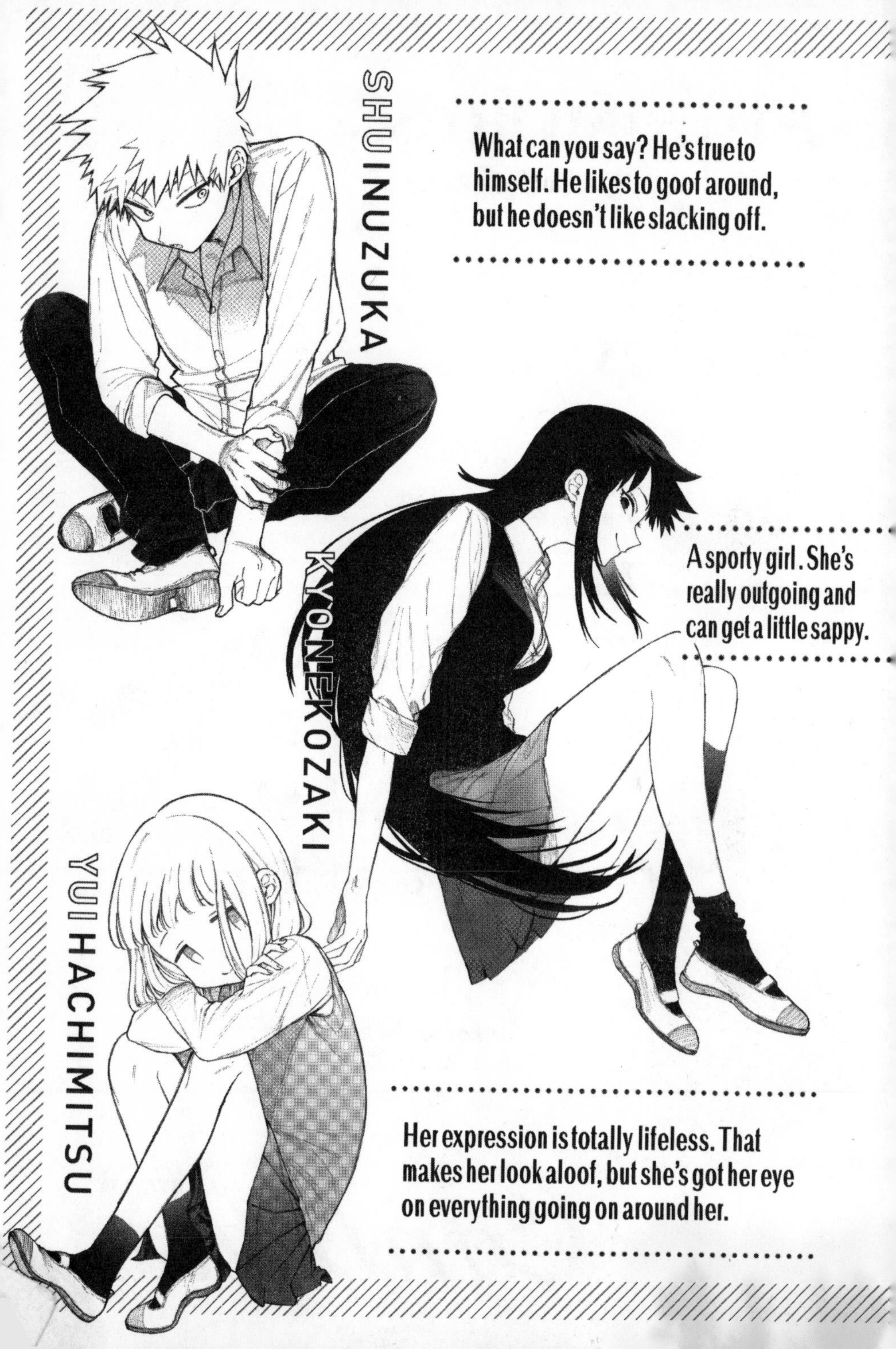
SHU INUZUKA
What can you say? He's true to himself. He likes to goof around, but he doesn't like slacking off.
KYO NEKOZAKI
A sporty girl. She's really outgoing and can get a little sappy.
YUI HACHIMITSU
Her expression is totally lifeless. That makes her look aloof, but she's got her eye on everything going on around her.

SHIKIMORI'S
not just a cutie

volume.8

Contents

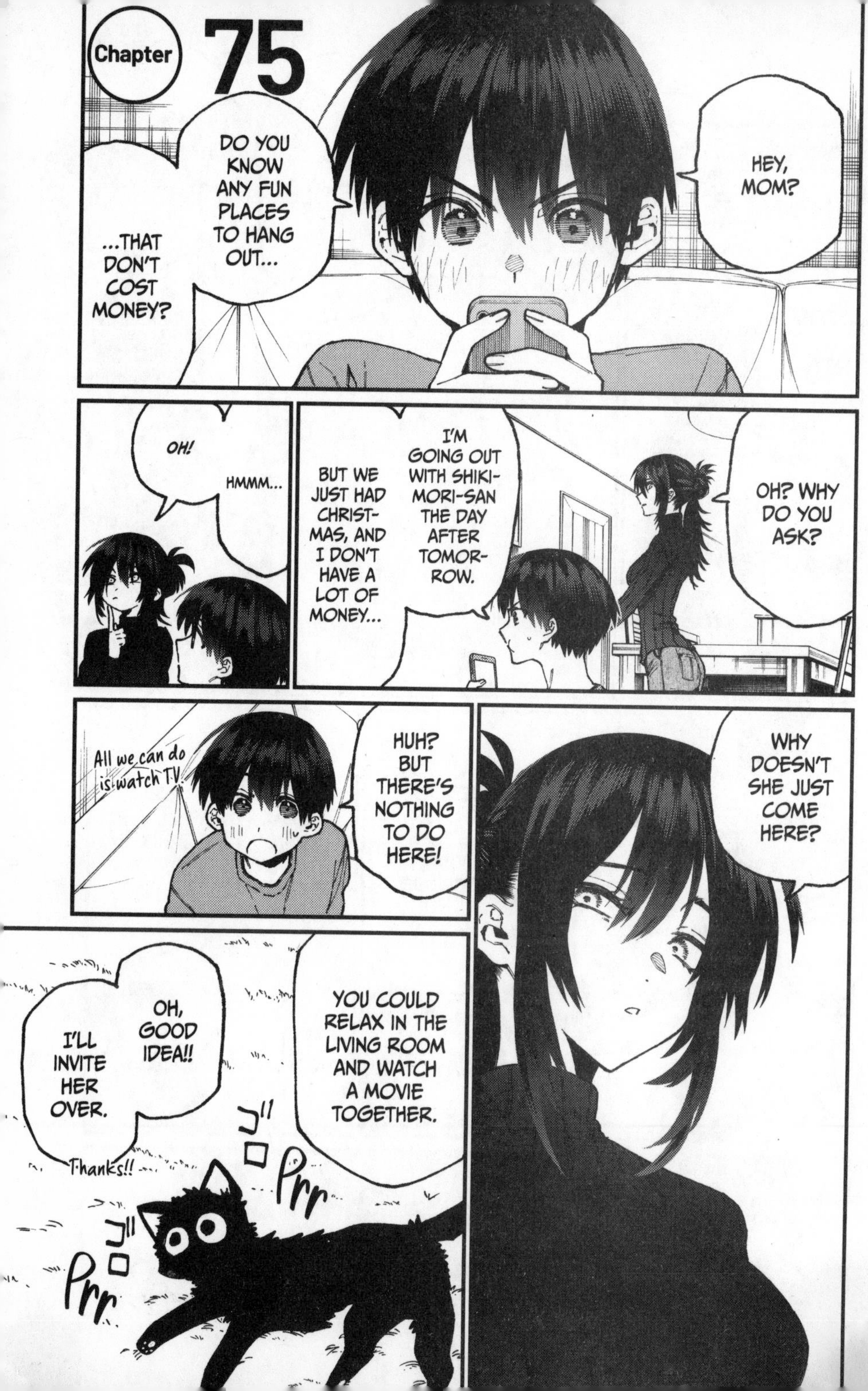
Chapter 75
HEY, MOM?
DO YOU KNOW ANY FUN PLACES TO HANG OUT...
...THAT DON'T COST MONEY?
OH? WHY DO YOU ASK?
I'M GOING OUT WITH SHIKIMORI-SAN THE DAY AFTER TOMORROW.
BUT WE JUST HAD CHRISTMAS, AND I DON'T HAVE A LOT OF MONEY...
OH!
HMMM...
WHY DOESN'T SHE JUST COME HERE?
HUH? BUT THERE'S NOTHING TO DO HERE!
All we can do is watch TV.
YOU COULD RELAX IN THE LIVING ROOM AND WATCH A MOVIE TOGETHER.
OH, GOOD IDEA!!
I'LL INVITE HER OVER.
Thanks!!
Prrr
Prrr

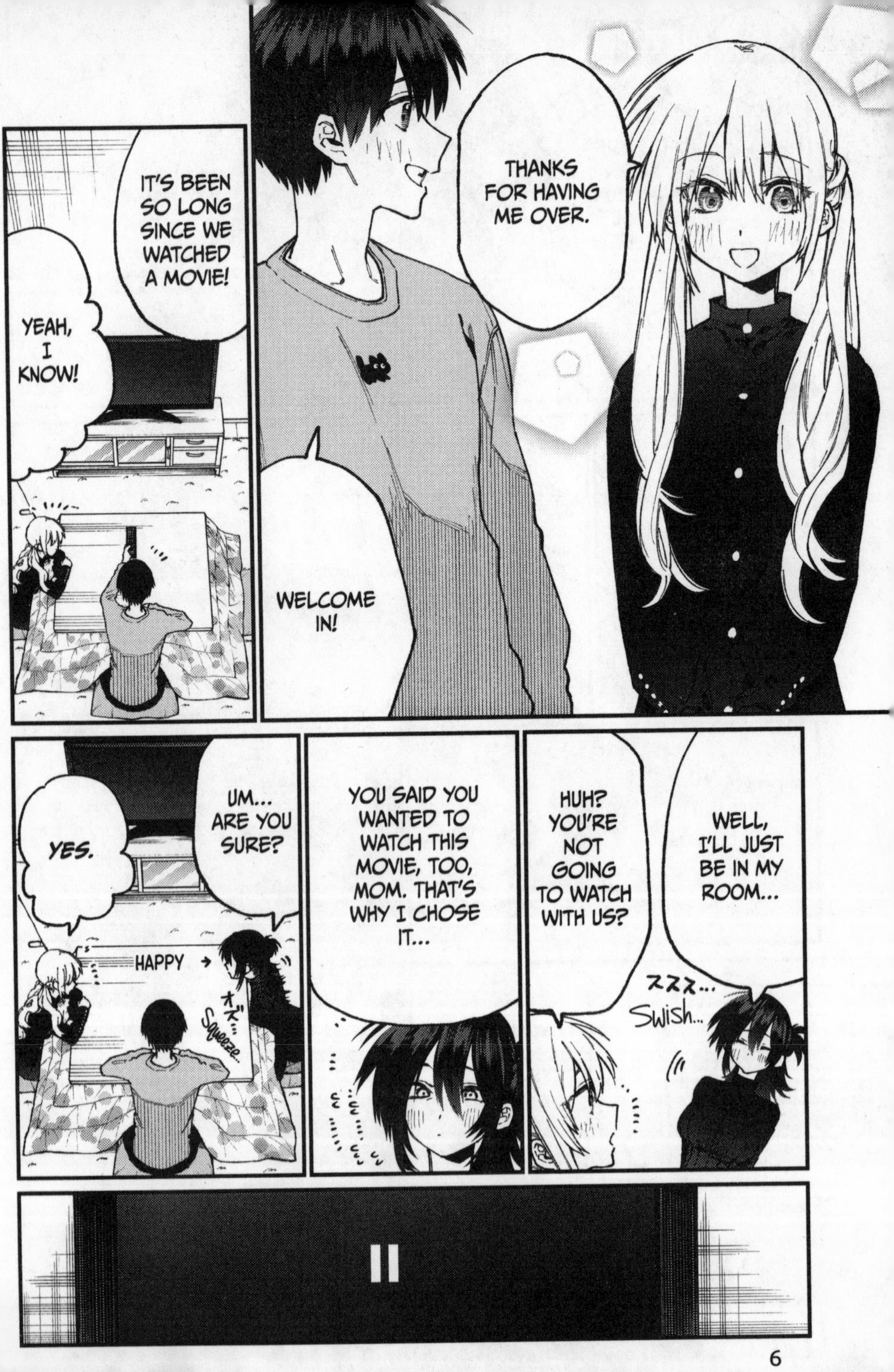
THANKS FOR HAVING ME OVER.
WELCOME IN!
IT'S BEEN SO LONG SINCE WE WATCHED A MOVIE!
YEAH, I KNOW!
WELL, I'LL JUST BE IN MY ROOM...
スス... Swish...
HUH? YOU'RE NOT GOING TO WATCH WITH US?
YOU SAID YOU WANTED TO WATCH THIS MOVIE, TOO, MOM. THAT'S WHY I CHOSE IT...
UM... ARE YOU SURE?
YES.
HAPPY →
オズ... Squeeze...

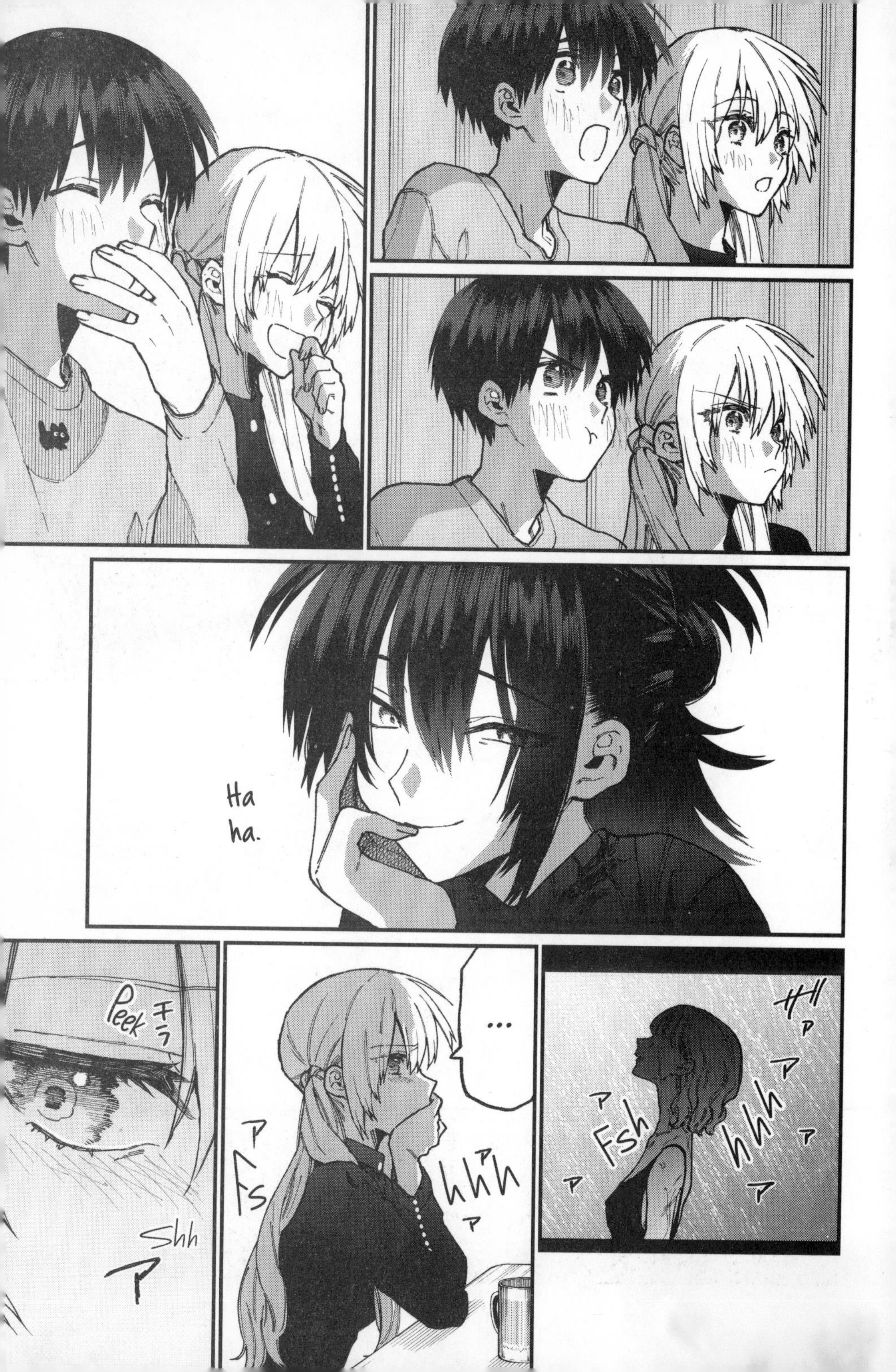
Ha ha.
Fsh
hhhh
...
Fs
hhhh
Peek
チラ
Shh

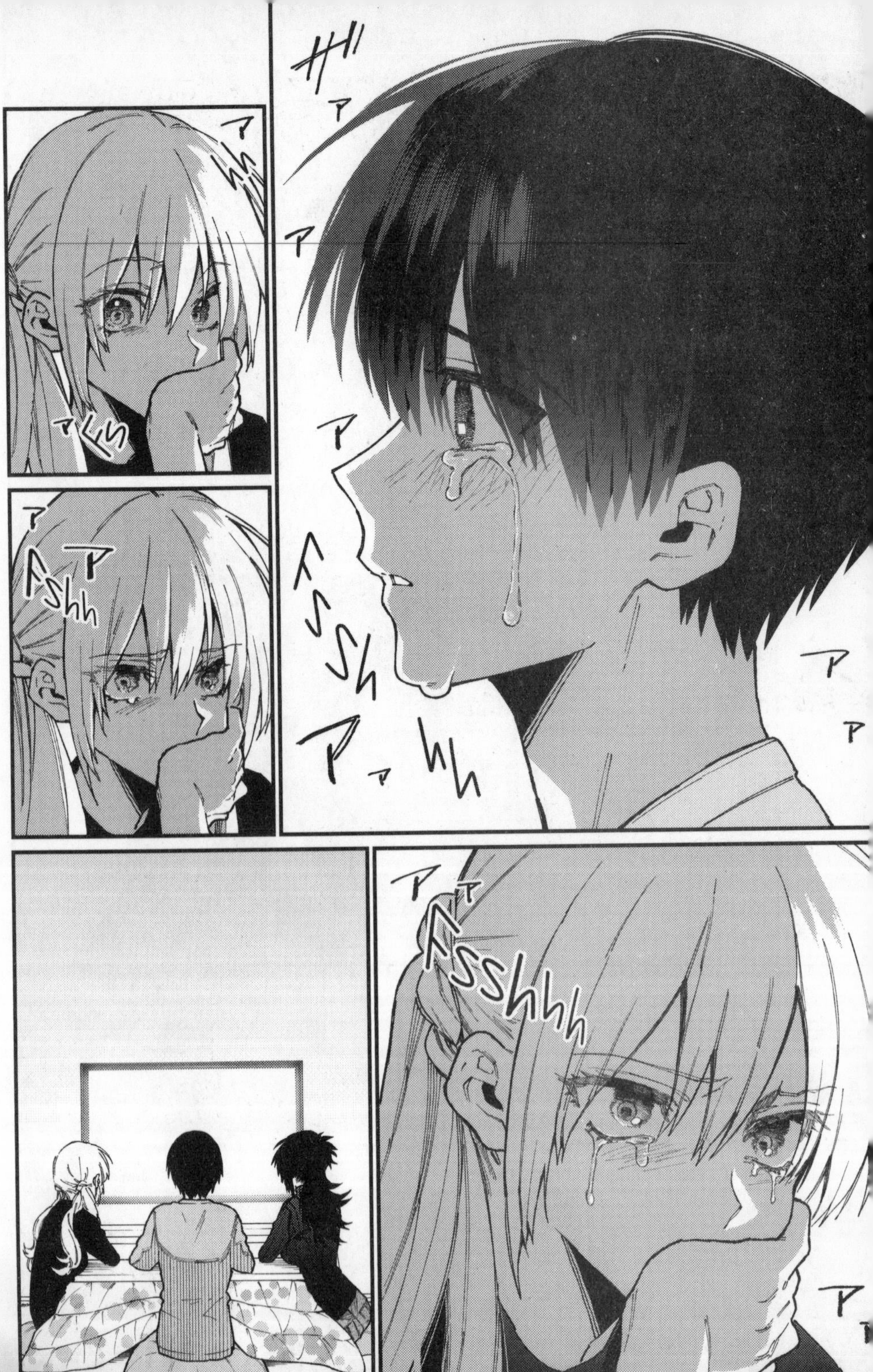
Fsshhh
Fshh
Fsshhh

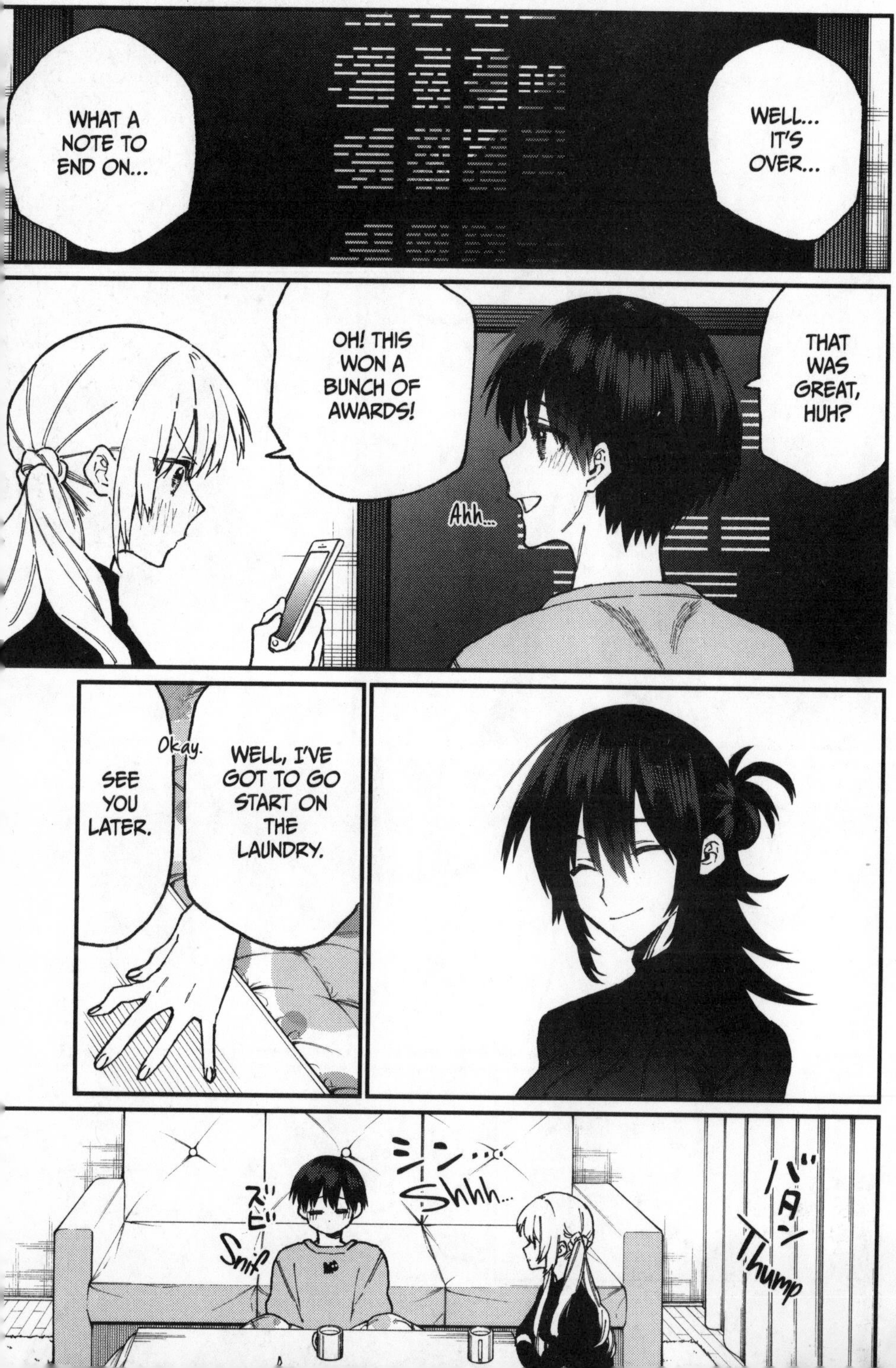
WELL... IT'S OVER...
WHAT A NOTE TO END ON...
THAT WAS GREAT, HUH?
Ahh...
OH! THIS WON A BUNCH OF AWARDS!
WELL, I'VE GOT TO GO START ON THE LAUNDRY.
Okay.
SEE YOU LATER.
バタン
Thump
シーン...
Shhh...
ズビ
Snif

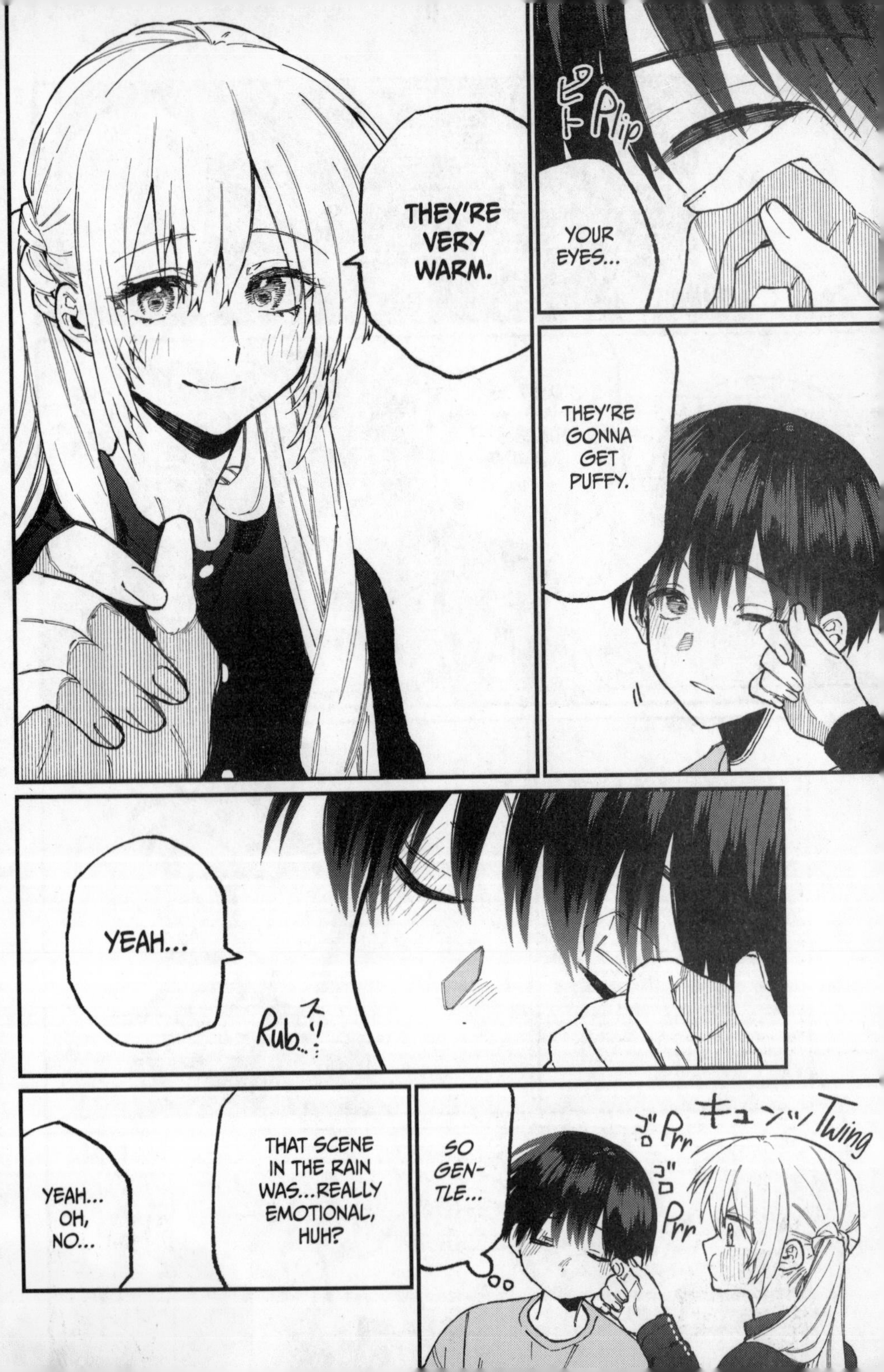
ピト Plip
YOUR EYES...
THEY'RE GONNA GET PUFFY.
THEY'RE VERY WARM.
YEAH...
スリ Rub...
キュンッ Twing
ゴロ Prrr
ゴロ Prrr
SO GEN-TLE...
THAT SCENE IN THE RAIN WAS...REALLY EMOTIONAL, HUH?
YEAH... OH, NO...

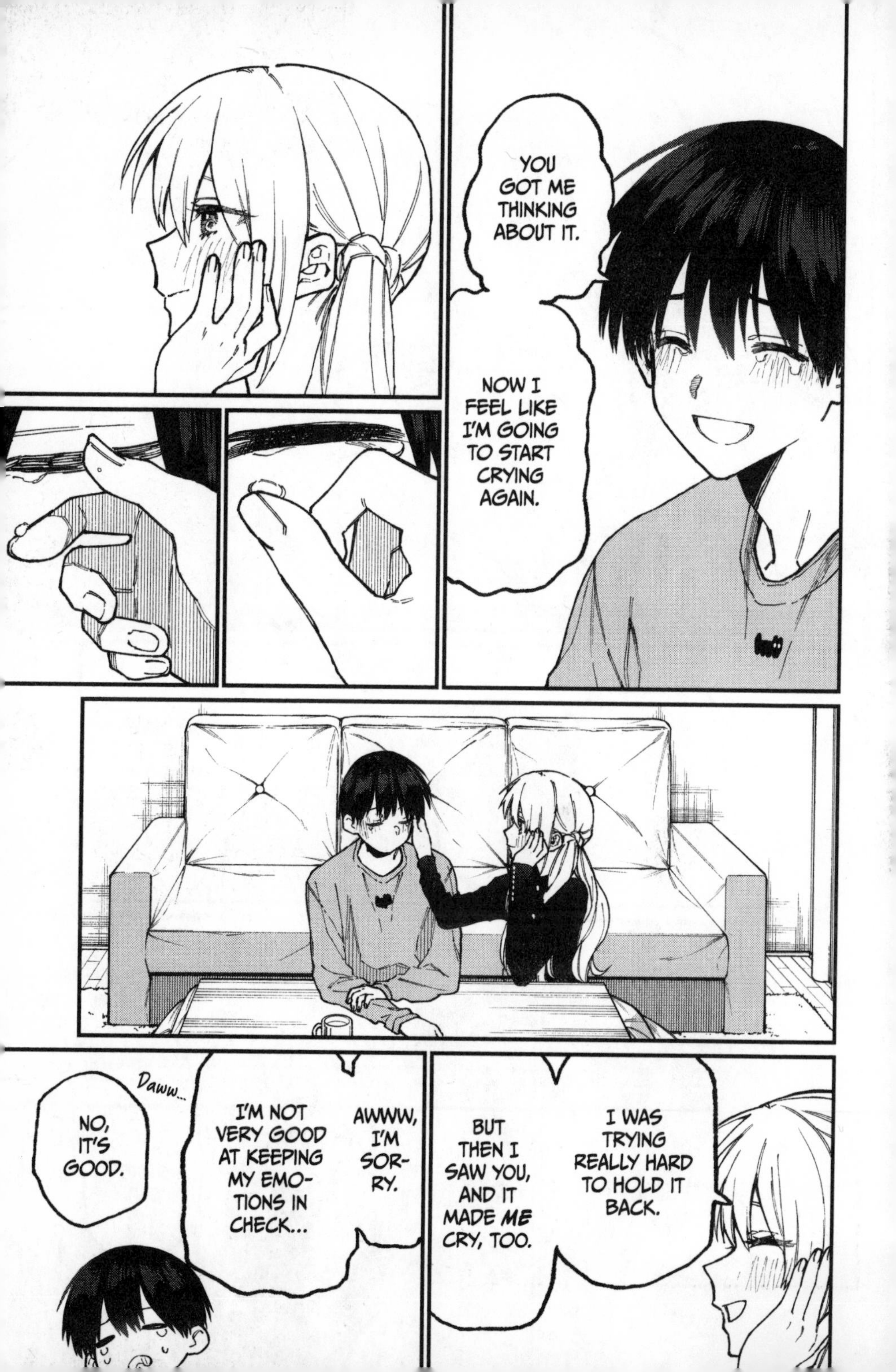
YOU GOT ME THINKING ABOUT IT.
NOW I FEEL LIKE I'M GOING TO START CRYING AGAIN.
I WAS TRYING REALLY HARD TO HOLD IT BACK.
BUT THEN I SAW YOU, AND IT MADE *ME* CRY, TOO.
AWWW, I'M SORRY.
I'M NOT VERY GOOD AT KEEPING MY EMOTIONS IN CHECK...
Daww...
NO, IT'S GOOD.

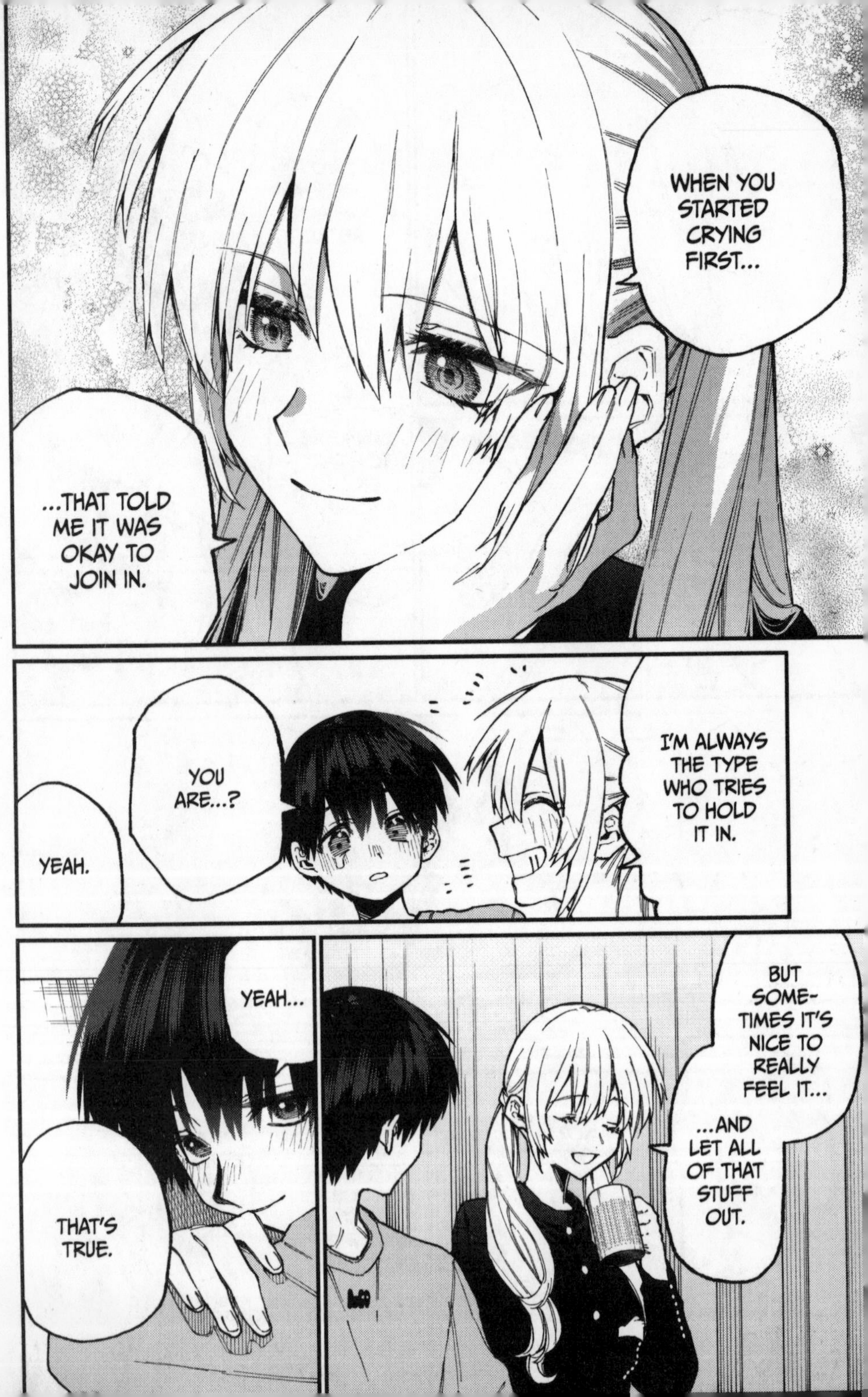
WHEN YOU STARTED CRYING FIRST...
...THAT TOLD ME IT WAS OKAY TO JOIN IN.
I'M ALWAYS THE TYPE WHO TRIES TO HOLD IT IN.
YOU ARE...?
YEAH.
BUT SOME-TIMES IT'S NICE TO REALLY FEEL IT...
...AND LET ALL OF THAT STUFF OUT.
YEAH...
THAT'S TRUE.

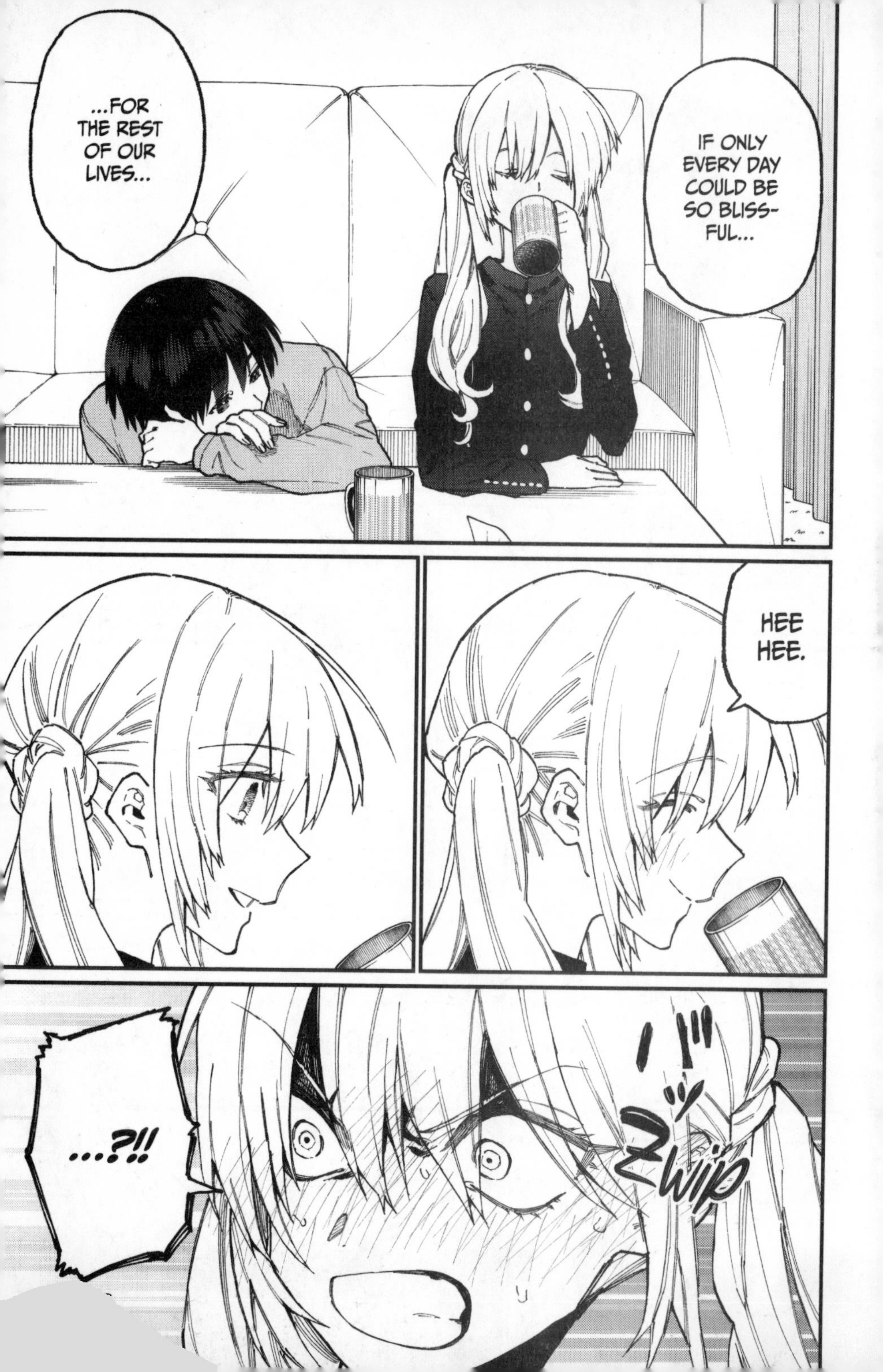
IF ONLY EVERY DAY COULD BE SO BLISS-FUL...
...FOR THE REST OF OUR LIVES...
HEE HEE.
ZWIP
...?!!

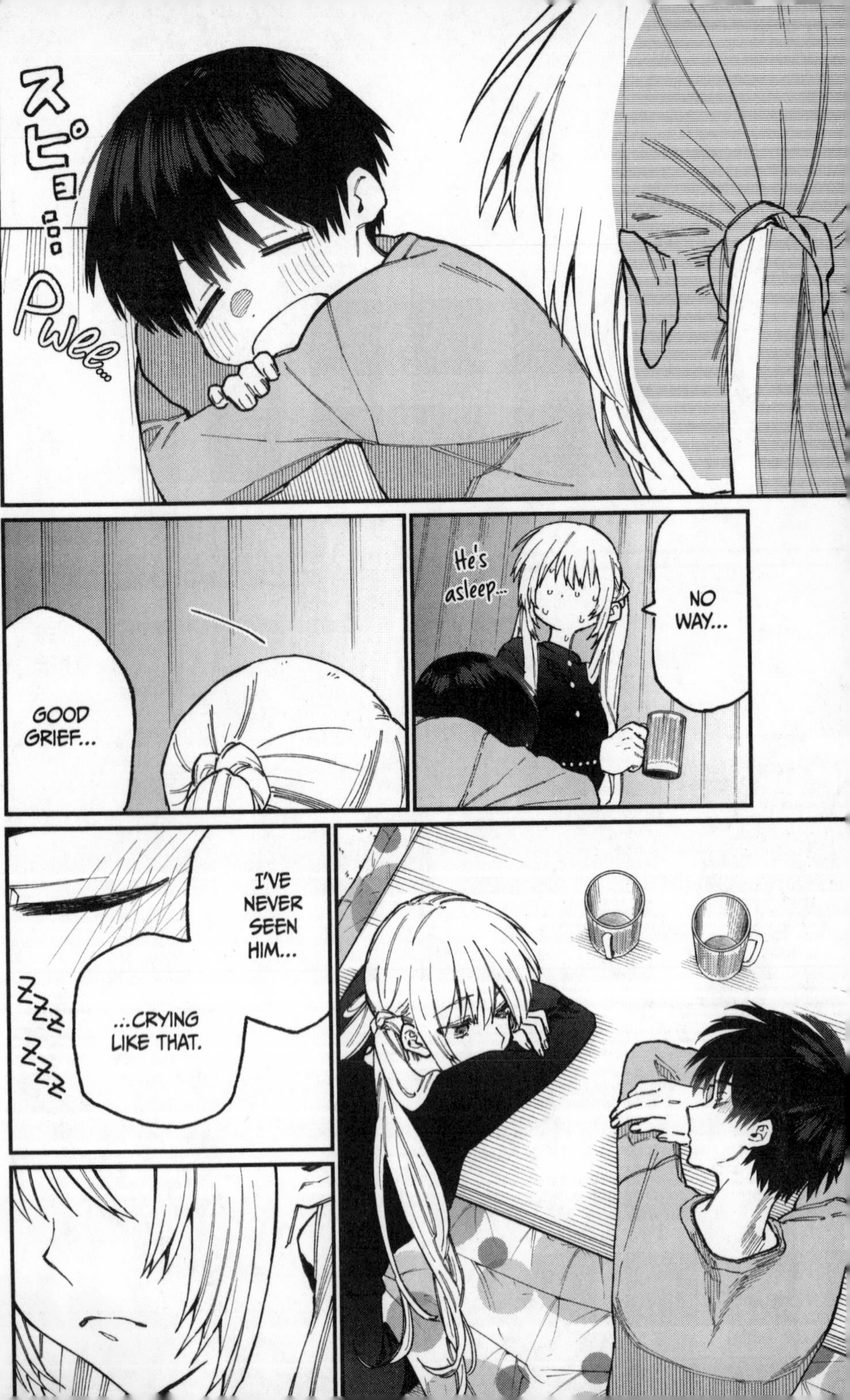
スピョ
Pwee...
NO WAY...
He's asleep...
GOOD GRIEF...
I'VE NEVER SEEN HIM...
...CRYING LIKE THAT.
ZZZ
ZZZ

I THINK... I PREFER IT...

...WHEN HE'S SMILING...

...WHAT'S THIS?

WELL, I'M DONE.

ﾊﾞﾁｬ Click

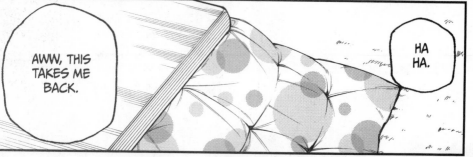

AWW, THIS TAKES ME BACK.

HA HA.

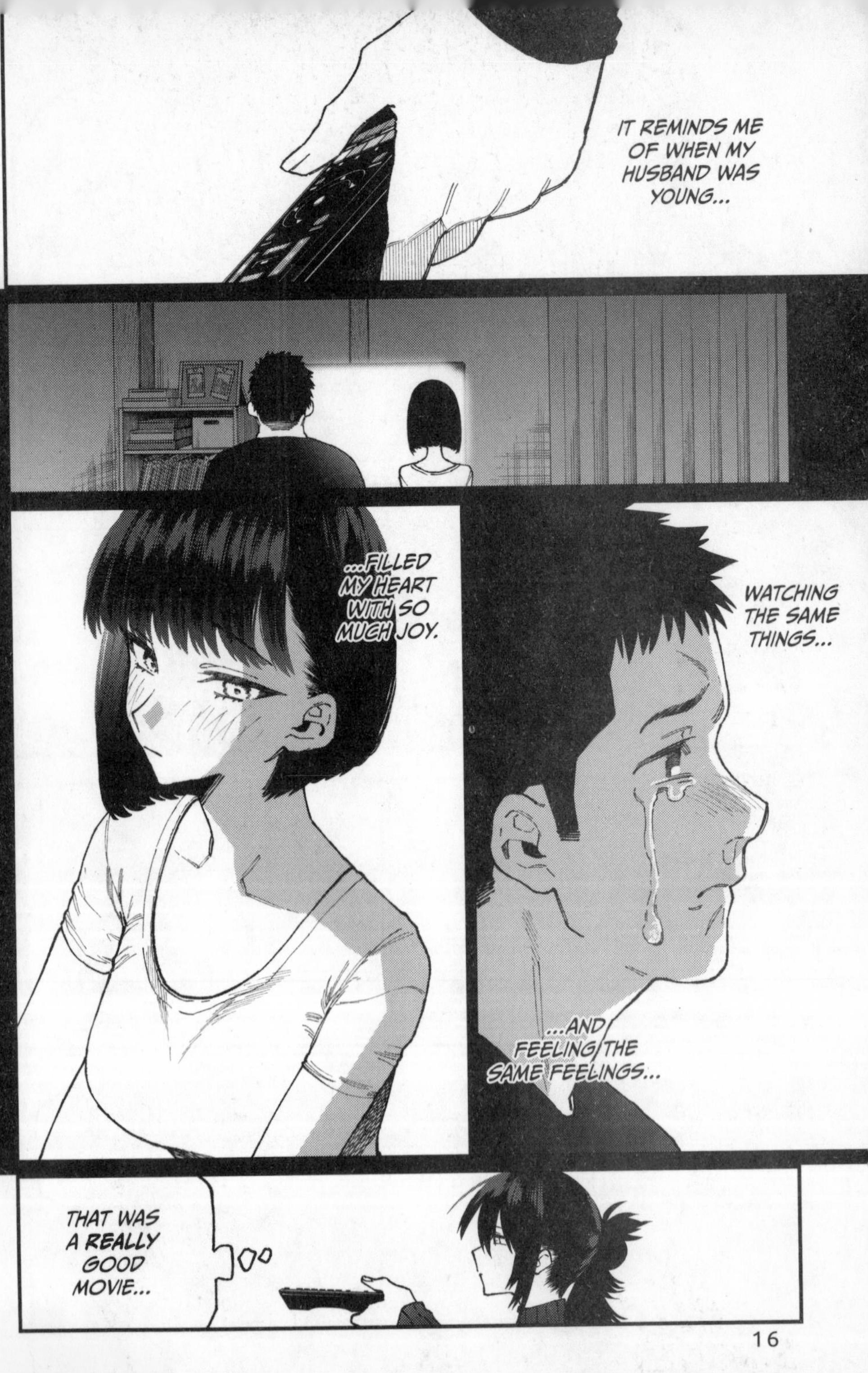
IT REMINDS ME OF WHEN MY HUSBAND WAS YOUNG...
WATCHING THE SAME THINGS...
...AND FEELING THE SAME FEELINGS...
...FILLED MY HEART WITH SO MUCH JOY.
THAT WAS A REALLY GOOD MOVIE...

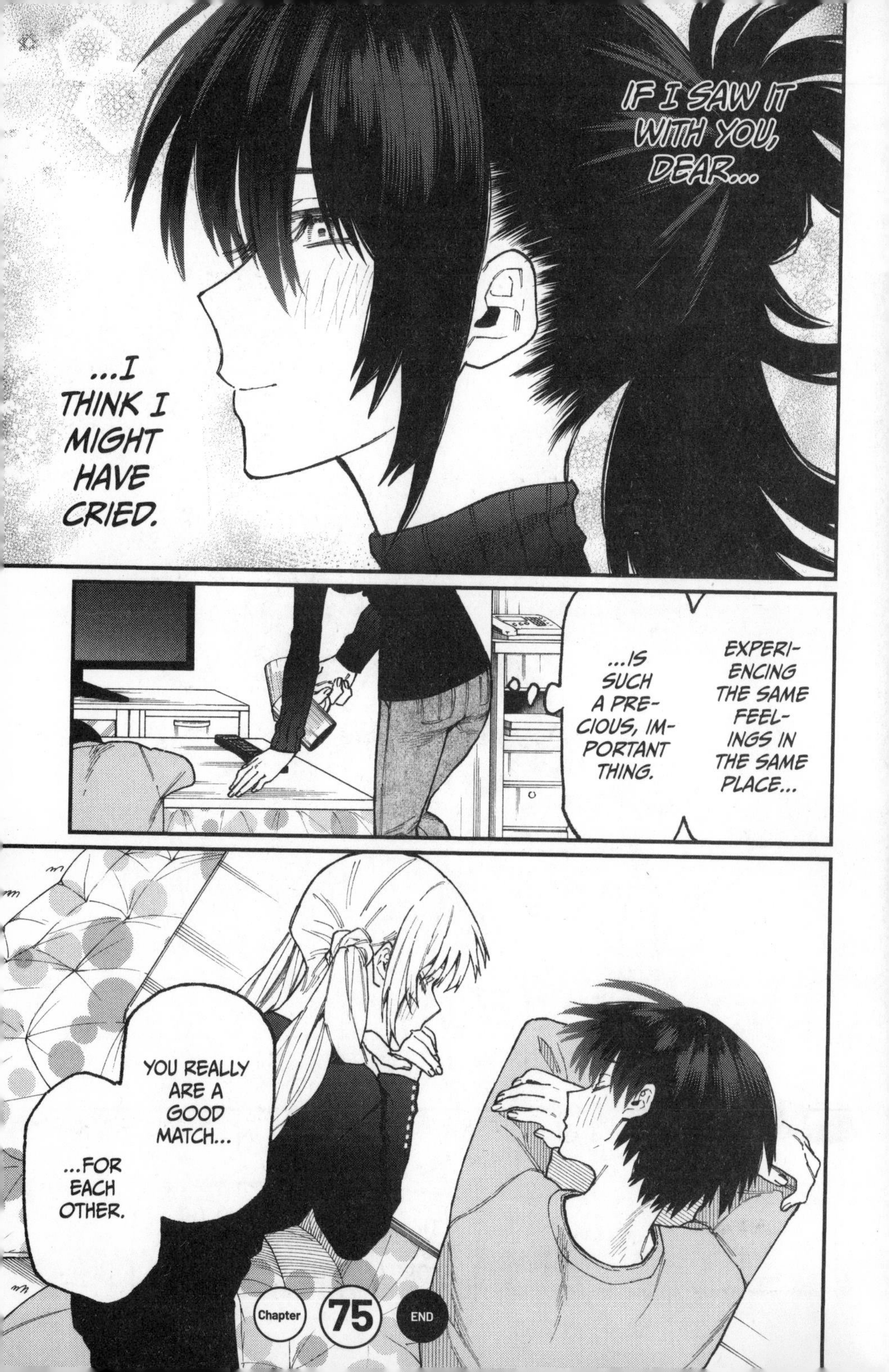
IF I SAW IT WITH YOU, DEAR...
...I THINK I MIGHT HAVE CRIED.
EXPERIENCING THE SAME FEELINGS IN THE SAME PLACE...
...IS SUCH A PRECIOUS, IMPORTANT THING.
YOU REALLY ARE A GOOD MATCH...
...FOR EACH OTHER.
Chapter 75 END

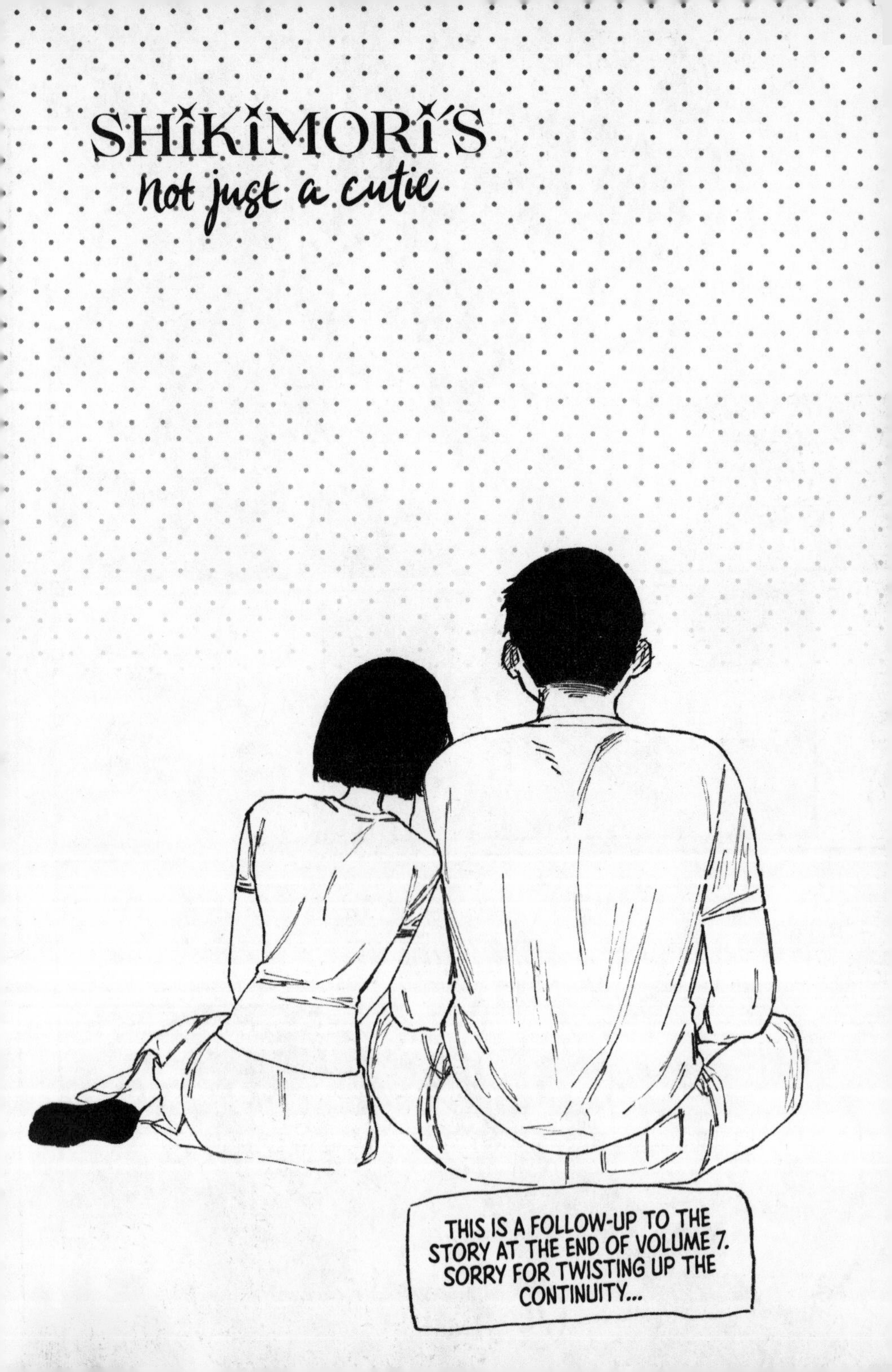
SHIKIMORI'S
not just a cutie
THIS IS A FOLLOW-UP TO THE STORY AT THE END OF VOLUME 7. SORRY FOR TWISTING UP THE CONTINUITY...

Chapter 76

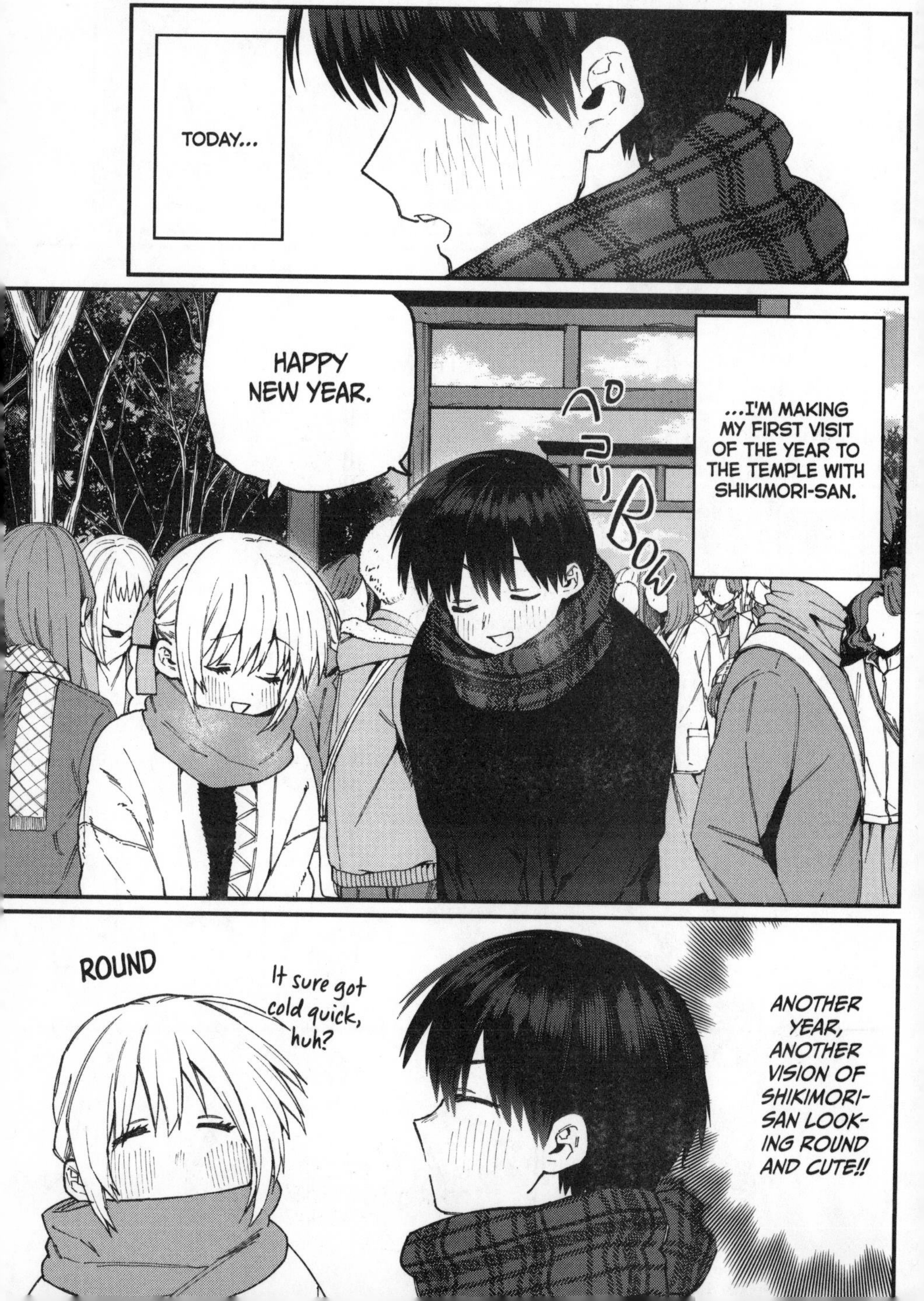
TODAY...
...I'M MAKING MY FIRST VISIT OF THE YEAR TO THE TEMPLE WITH SHIKIMORI-SAN.
ペコッ
BOW
HAPPY NEW YEAR.
ANOTHER YEAR, ANOTHER VISION OF SHIKIMORI-SAN LOOKING ROUND AND CUTE!!
It sure got cold quick, huh?
ROUND

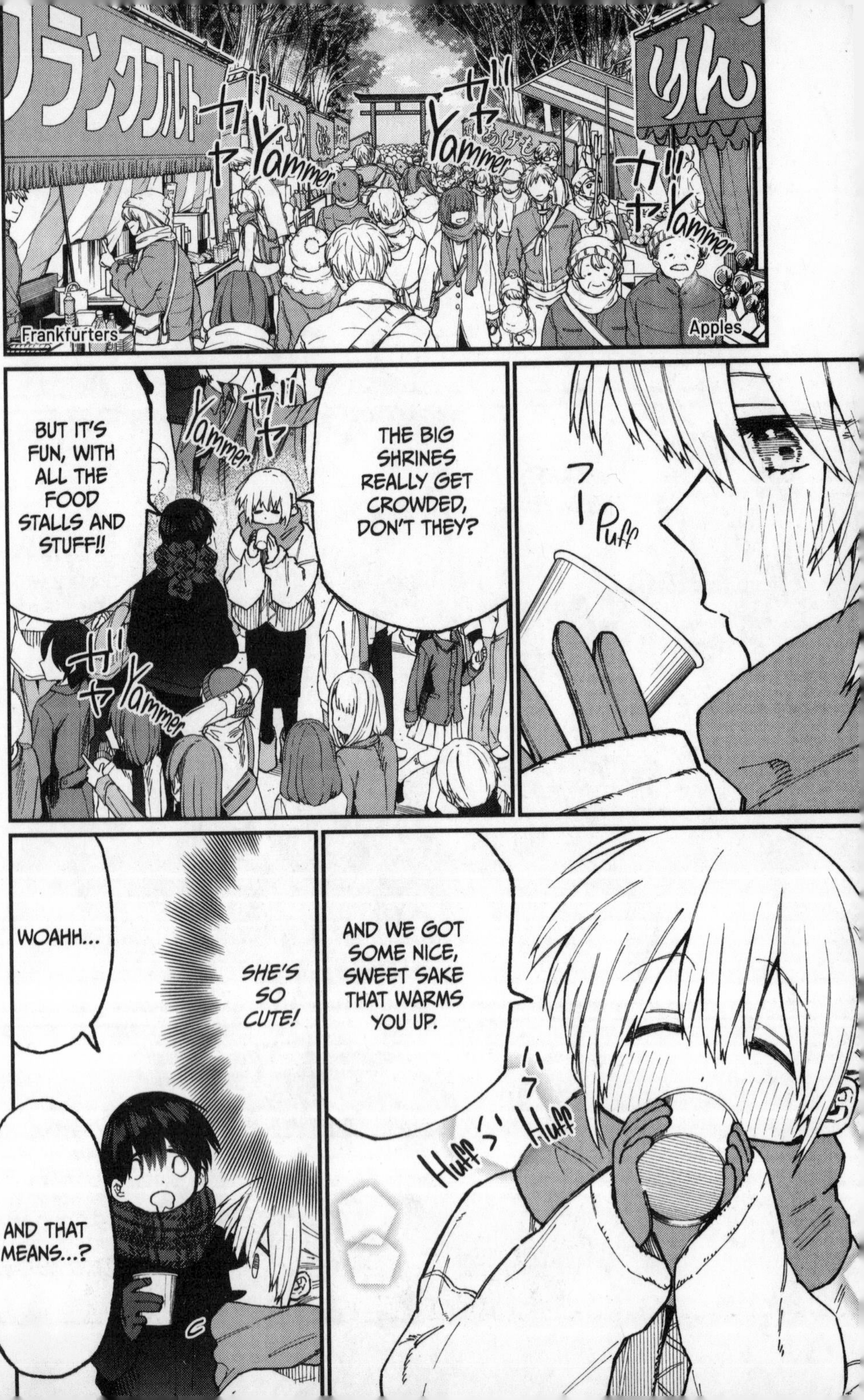
Apples
Yammer
Yammer
Yammer
Frankfurters
Puff
THE BIG SHRINES REALLY GET CROWDED, DON'T THEY?
Yammer
BUT IT'S FUN, WITH ALL THE FOOD STALLS AND STUFF!!
Yammer
AND WE GOT SOME NICE, SWEET SAKE THAT WARMS YOU UP.
Huff
Huff
WOAHH...
SHE'S SO CUTE!
AND THAT MEANS...?

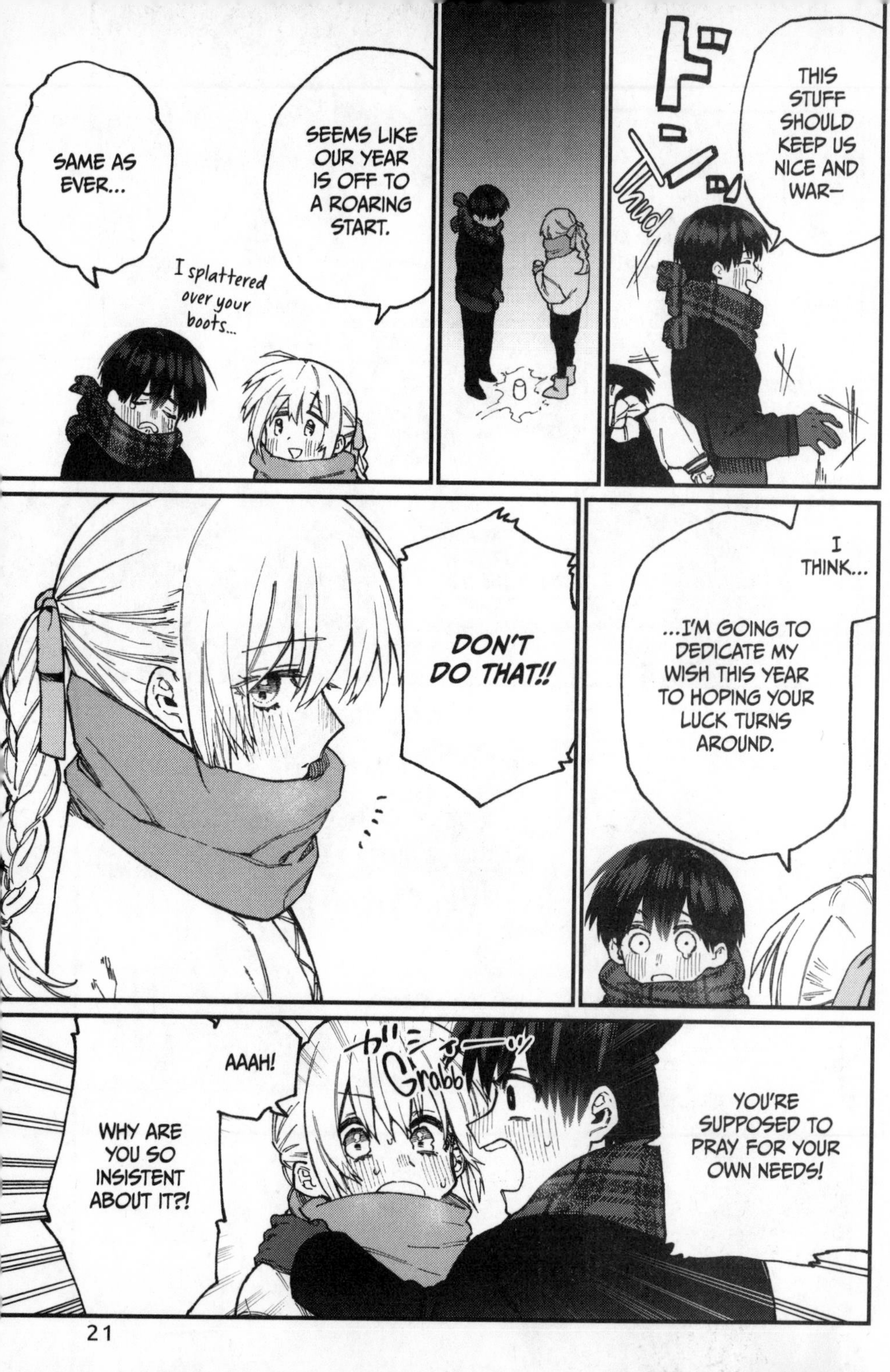
Thud
THIS STUFF SHOULD KEEP US NICE AND WAR—
SEEMS LIKE OUR YEAR IS OFF TO A ROARING START.
SAME AS EVER...
I splattered over your boots...
I THINK...
...I'M GOING TO DEDICATE MY WISH THIS YEAR TO HOPING YOUR LUCK TURNS AROUND.
DON'T DO THAT!!
......
YOU'RE SUPPOSED TO PRAY FOR YOUR OWN NEEDS!
Grabb
AAAH!
WHY ARE YOU SO INSISTENT ABOUT IT?!

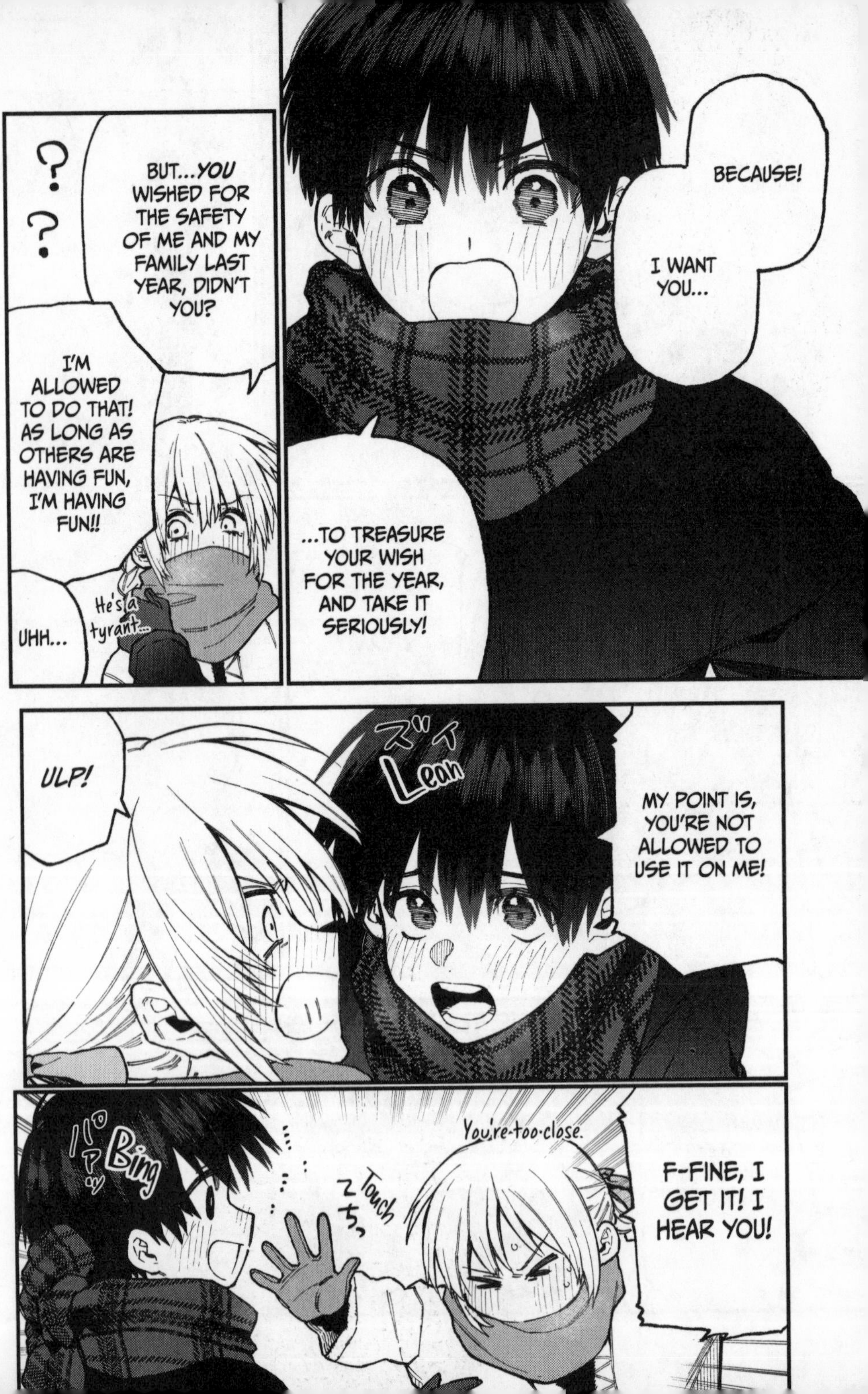
BECAUSE!
I WANT YOU...
...TO TREASURE YOUR WISH FOR THE YEAR, AND TAKE IT SERIOUSLY!
BUT...*YOU* WISHED FOR THE SAFETY OF ME AND MY FAMILY LAST YEAR, DIDN'T YOU?
??
I'M ALLOWED TO DO THAT! AS LONG AS OTHERS ARE HAVING FUN, I'M HAVING FUN!!
He's a tyrant...
UHH...
MY POINT IS, YOU'RE NOT ALLOWED TO USE IT ON ME!
ズイ
Lean
ULP!
F-FINE, I GET IT! I HEAR YOU!
You're-too-close.
こちっ
Touch
...
...
パァッ
Bing

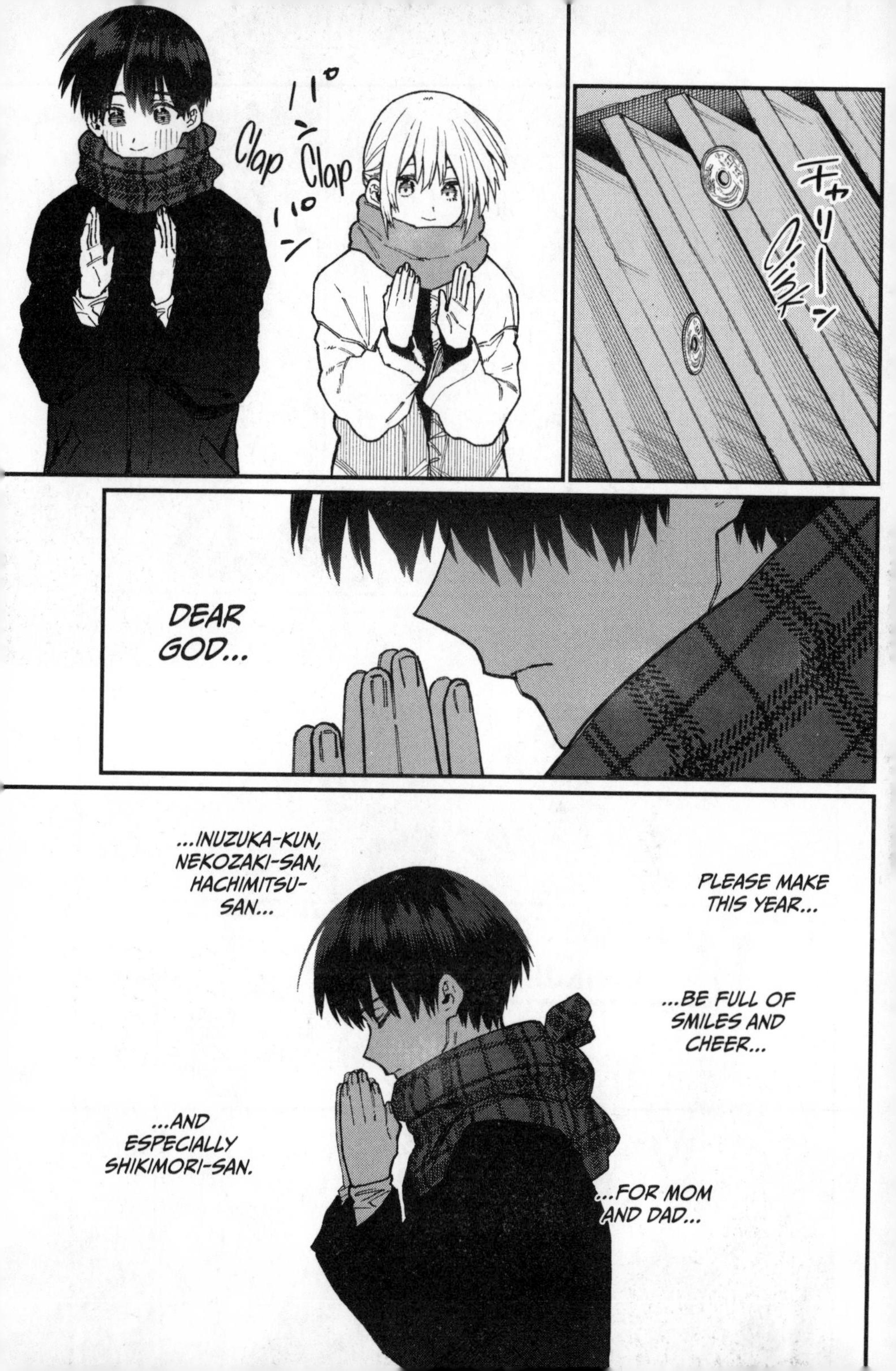

チャリーン
Clink
Clap
Clap
DEAR GOD...
PLEASE MAKE THIS YEAR...
...BE FULL OF SMILES AND CHEER...
...FOR MOM AND DAD...
...INUZUKA-KUN, NEKOZAKI-SAN, HACHIMITSU-SAN...
...AND ESPECIALLY SHIKIMORI-SAN.

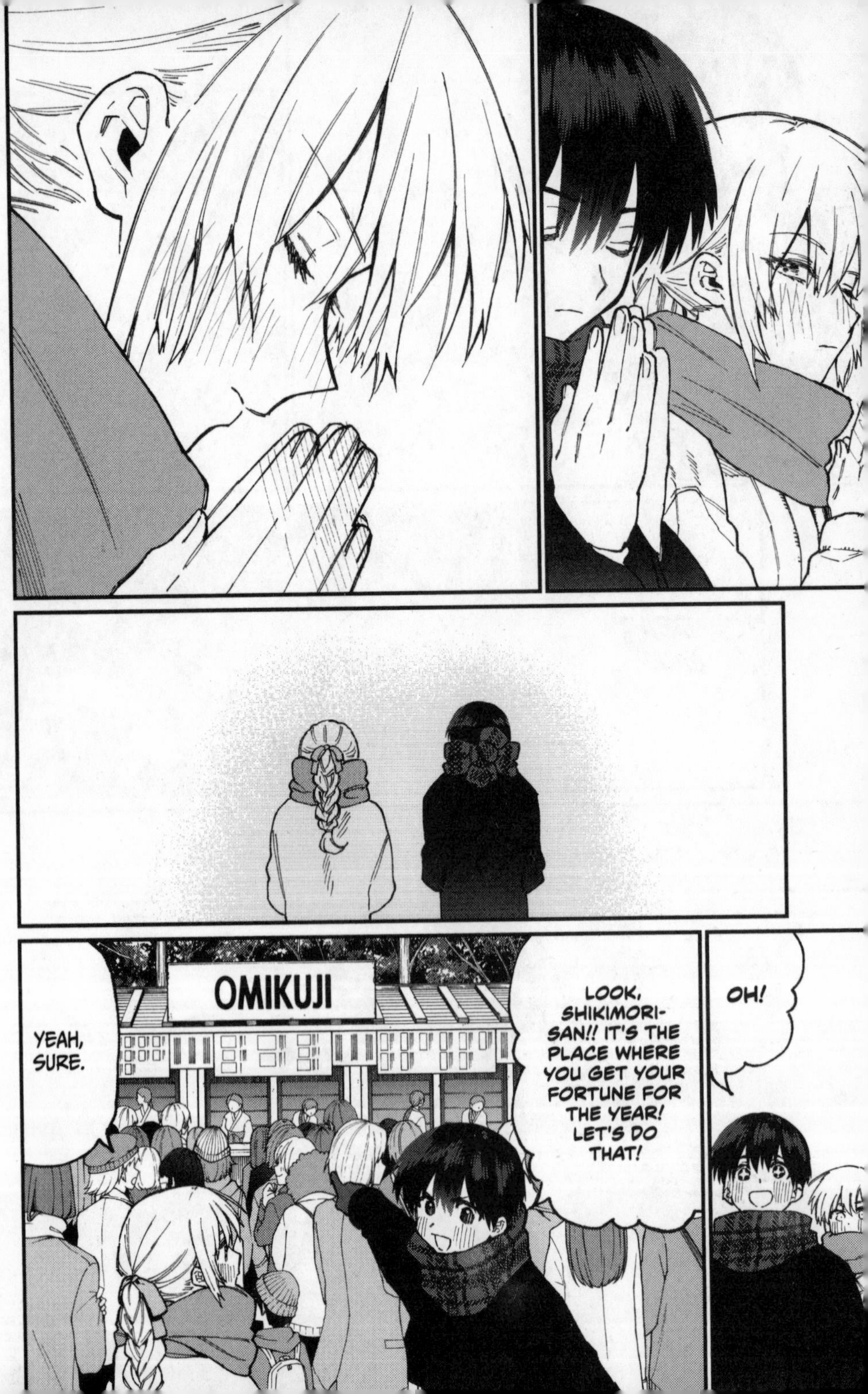

OH!
LOOK, SHIKIMORI-SAN!! IT'S THE PLACE WHERE YOU GET YOUR FORTUNE FOR THE YEAR! LET'S DO THAT!
OMIKUJI
YEAH, SURE.

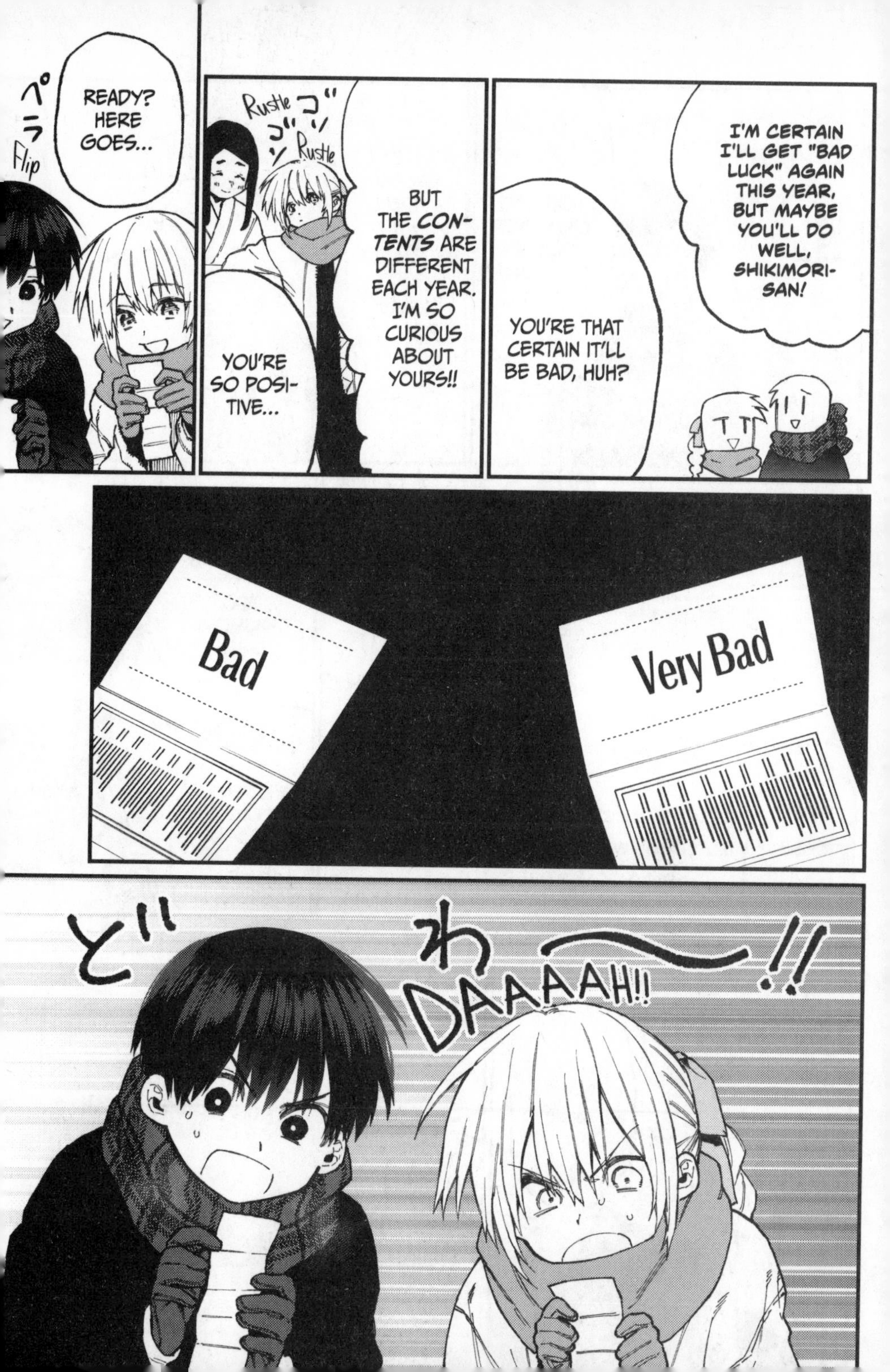
I'M CERTAIN I'LL GET "BAD LUCK" AGAIN THIS YEAR, BUT MAYBE YOU'LL DO WELL, SHIKIMORI-SAN!
YOU'RE THAT CERTAIN IT'LL BE BAD, HUH?
Rustle
Rustle
BUT THE CONTENTS ARE DIFFERENT EACH YEAR. I'M SO CURIOUS ABOUT YOURS!!
YOU'RE SO POSITIVE...
READY? HERE GOES...
Flip
Very Bad
Bad
DAAAAH!!

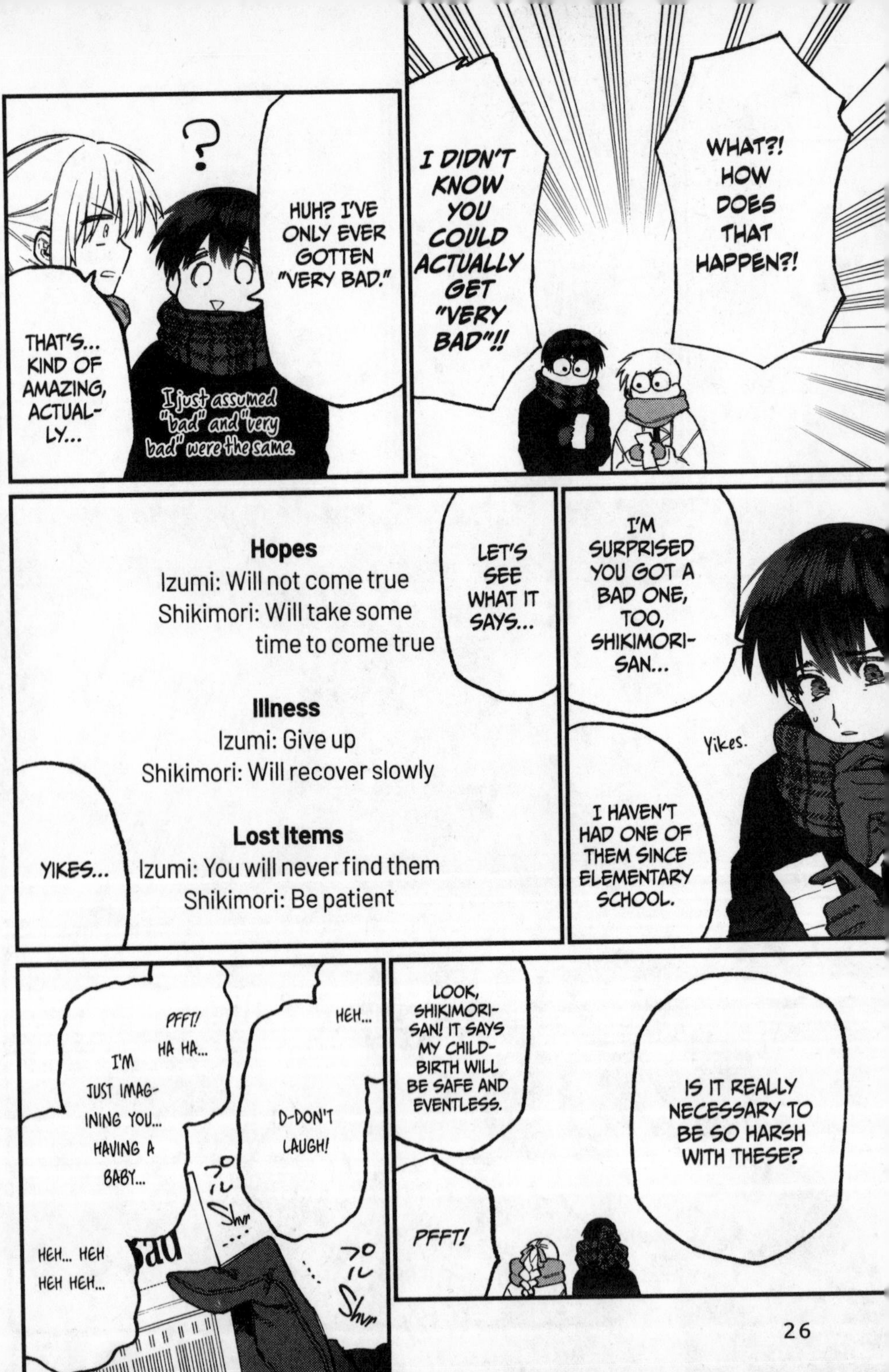
WHAT?! HOW DOES THAT HAPPEN?!
I DIDN'T KNOW YOU COULD ACTUALLY GET "VERY BAD"!!
HUH? I'VE ONLY EVER GOTTEN "VERY BAD."
I just assumed "bad" and "very bad" were the same.
THAT'S... KIND OF AMAZING, ACTUAL-LY...
I'M SURPRISED YOU GOT A BAD ONE, TOO, SHIKIMORI-SAN...
Yikes.
I HAVEN'T HAD ONE OF THEM SINCE ELEMENTARY SCHOOL.
LET'S SEE WHAT IT SAYS...
Hopes
Izumi: Will not come true
Shikimori: Will take some time to come true
Illness
Izumi: Give up
Shikimori: Will recover slowly
Lost Items
Izumi: You will never find them
Shikimori: Be patient
YIKES...
LOOK, SHIKIMORI-SAN! IT SAYS MY CHILD-BIRTH WILL BE SAFE AND EVENTLESS.
IS IT REALLY NECESSARY TO BE SO HARSH WITH THESE?
PFFT!
HEH...
D-DON'T LAUGH!
PFFT! HA HA...
I'M JUST IMAG-INING YOU... HAVING A BABY...
HEH... HEH HEH HEH...
Shvr
Shvr

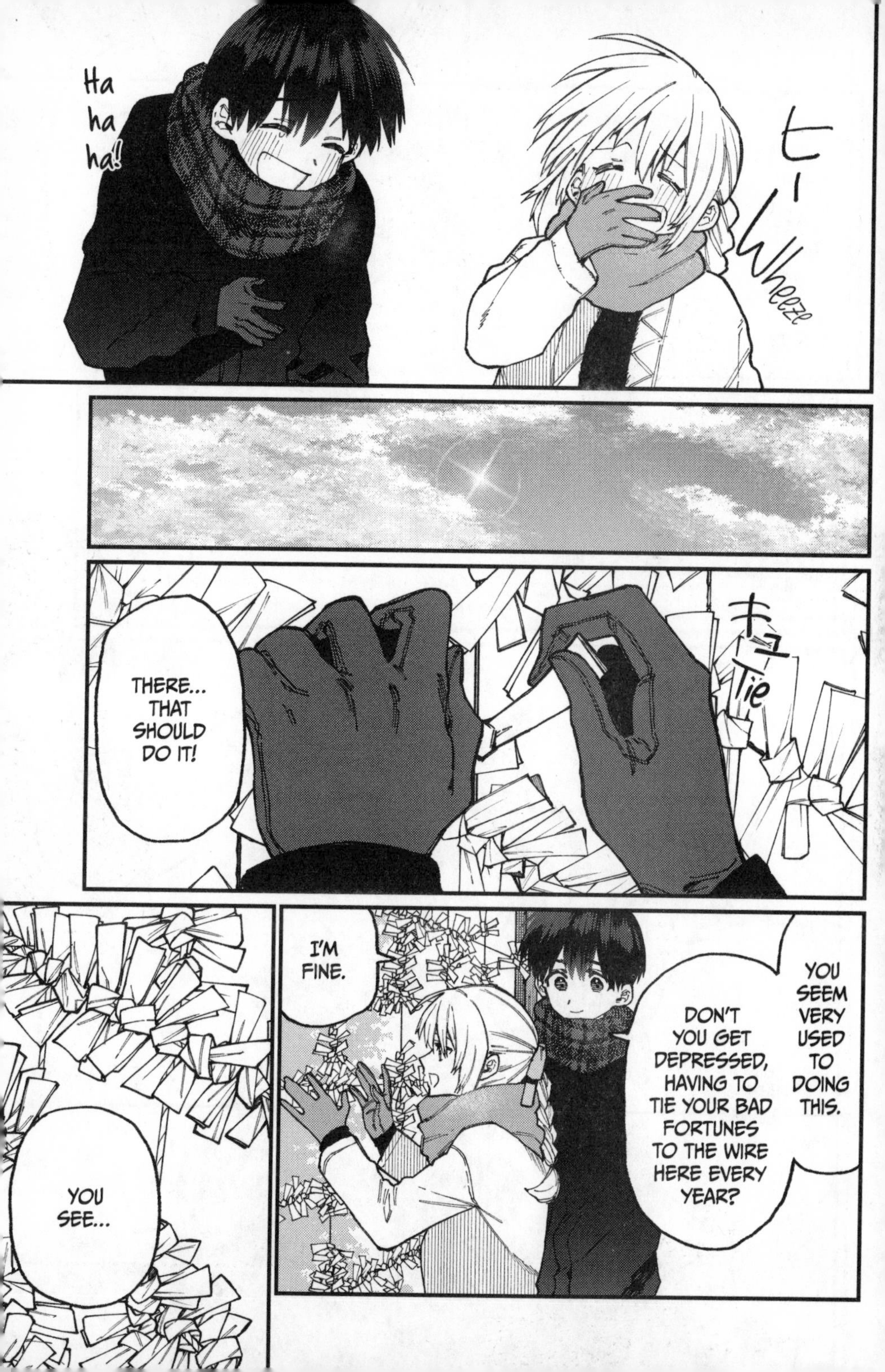
ヒー
Wheeze
Ha ha ha!
キュ
Tie
THERE... THAT SHOULD DO IT!
YOU SEEM VERY USED TO DOING THIS.
DON'T YOU GET DEPRESSED, HAVING TO TIE YOUR BAD FORTUNES TO THE WIRE HERE EVERY YEAR?
I'M FINE.
YOU SEE...

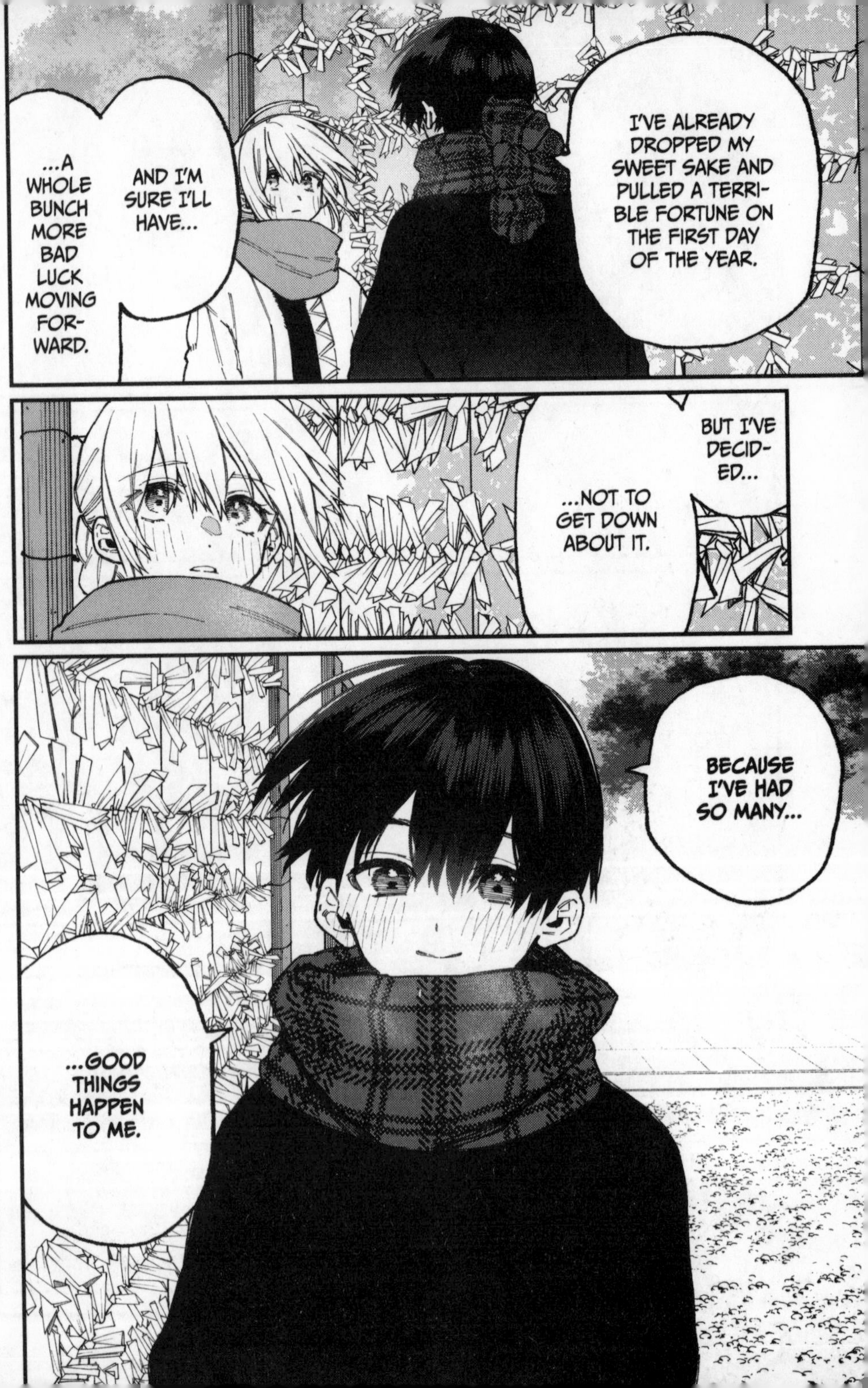
I'VE ALREADY DROPPED MY SWEET SAKE AND PULLED A TERRIBLE FORTUNE ON THE FIRST DAY OF THE YEAR.
AND I'M SURE I'LL HAVE...
...A WHOLE BUNCH MORE BAD LUCK MOVING FORWARD.
BUT I'VE DECIDED...
...NOT TO GET DOWN ABOUT IT.
BECAUSE I'VE HAD SO MANY...
...GOOD THINGS HAPPEN TO ME.

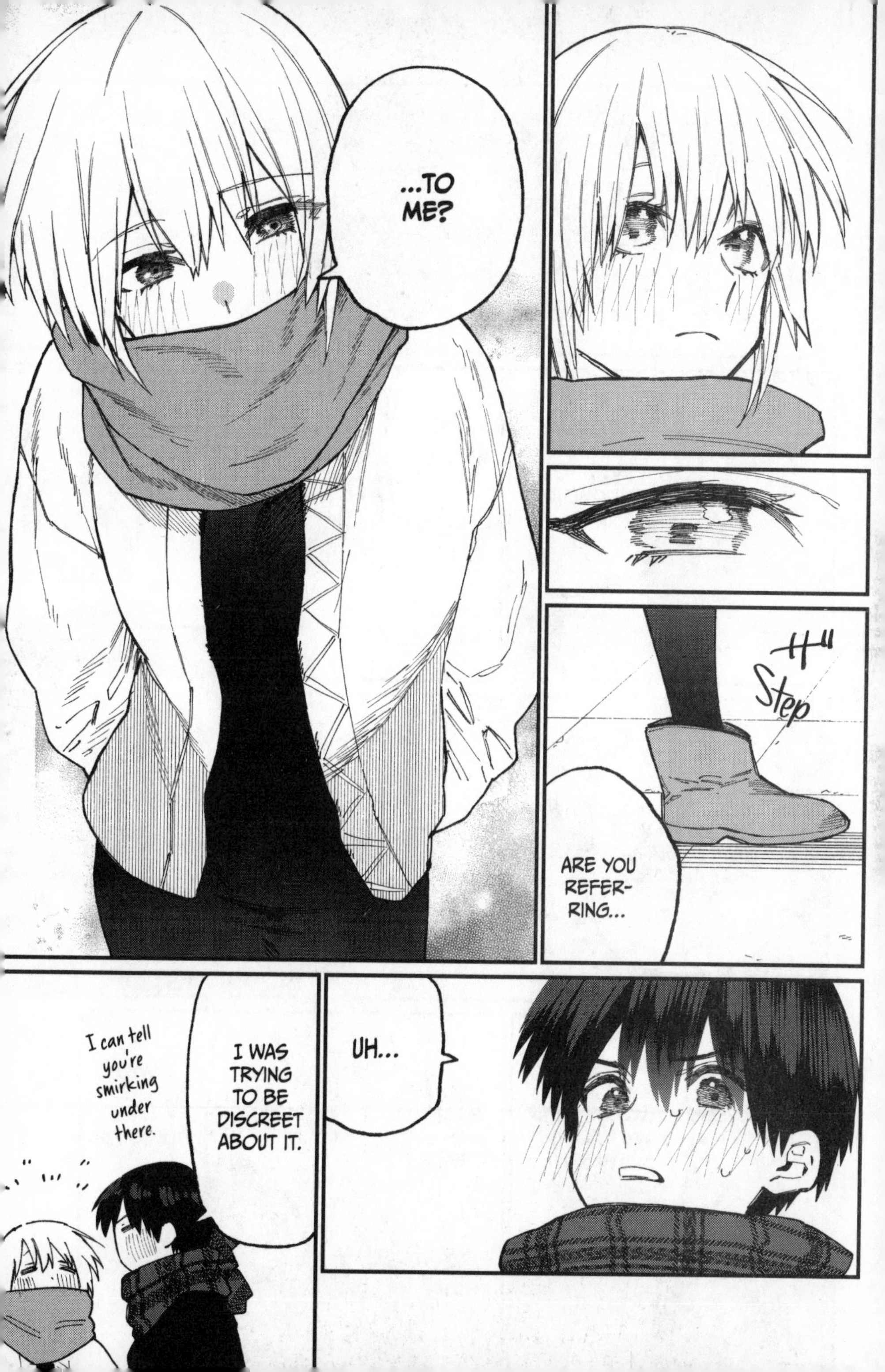
Step
ARE YOU REFER-RING...
...TO ME?
UH...
I WAS TRYING TO BE DISCREET ABOUT IT.
I can tell you're smirking under there.

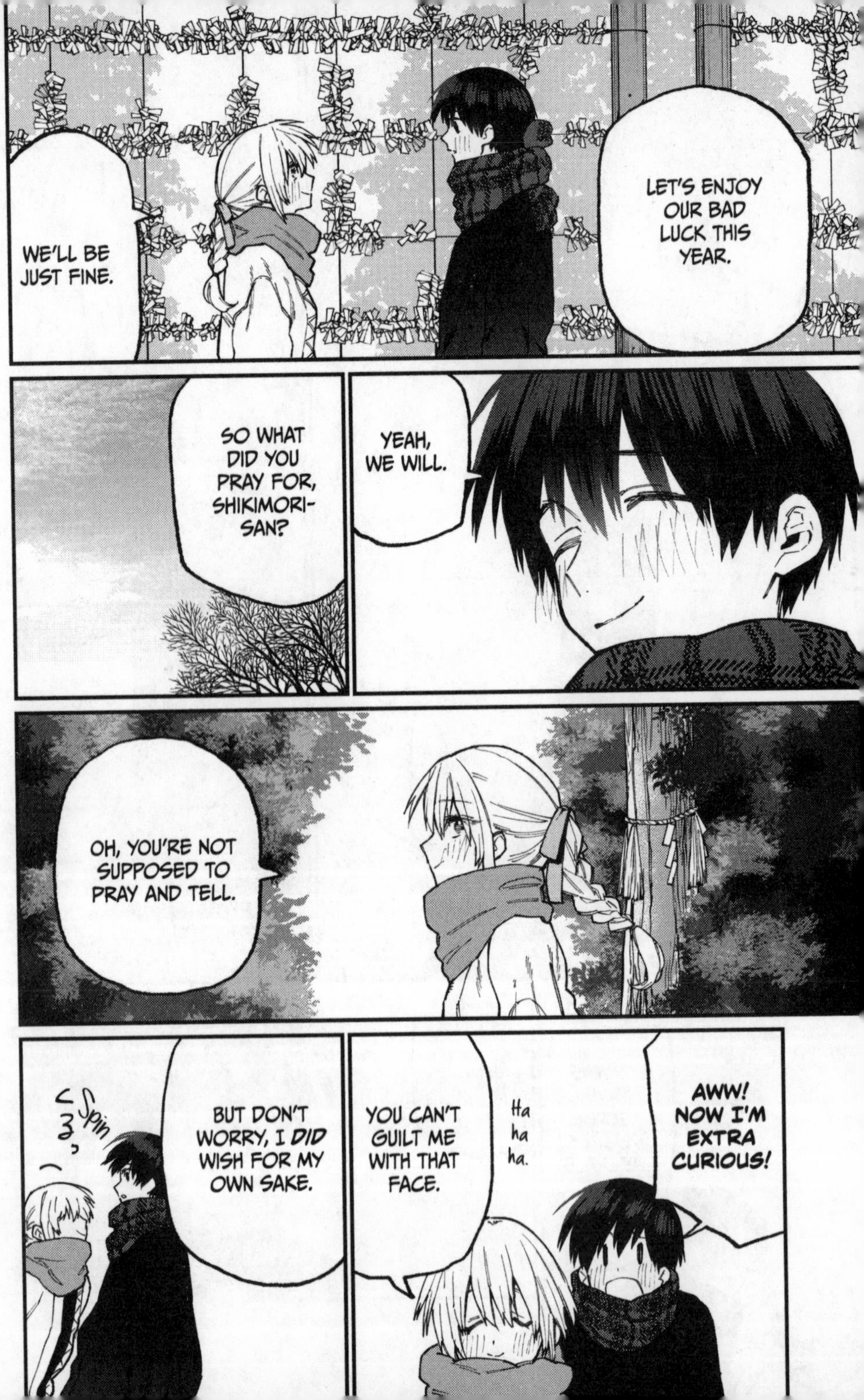
LET'S ENJOY OUR BAD LUCK THIS YEAR.
WE'LL BE JUST FINE.
YEAH, WE WILL.
SO WHAT DID YOU PRAY FOR, SHIKIMORI-SAN?
OH, YOU'RE NOT SUPPOSED TO PRAY AND TELL.
AWW! NOW I'M EXTRA CURIOUS!
Ha ha ha.
YOU CAN'T GUILT ME WITH THAT FACE.
BUT DON'T WORRY, I *DID* WISH FOR MY OWN SAKE.
Spin

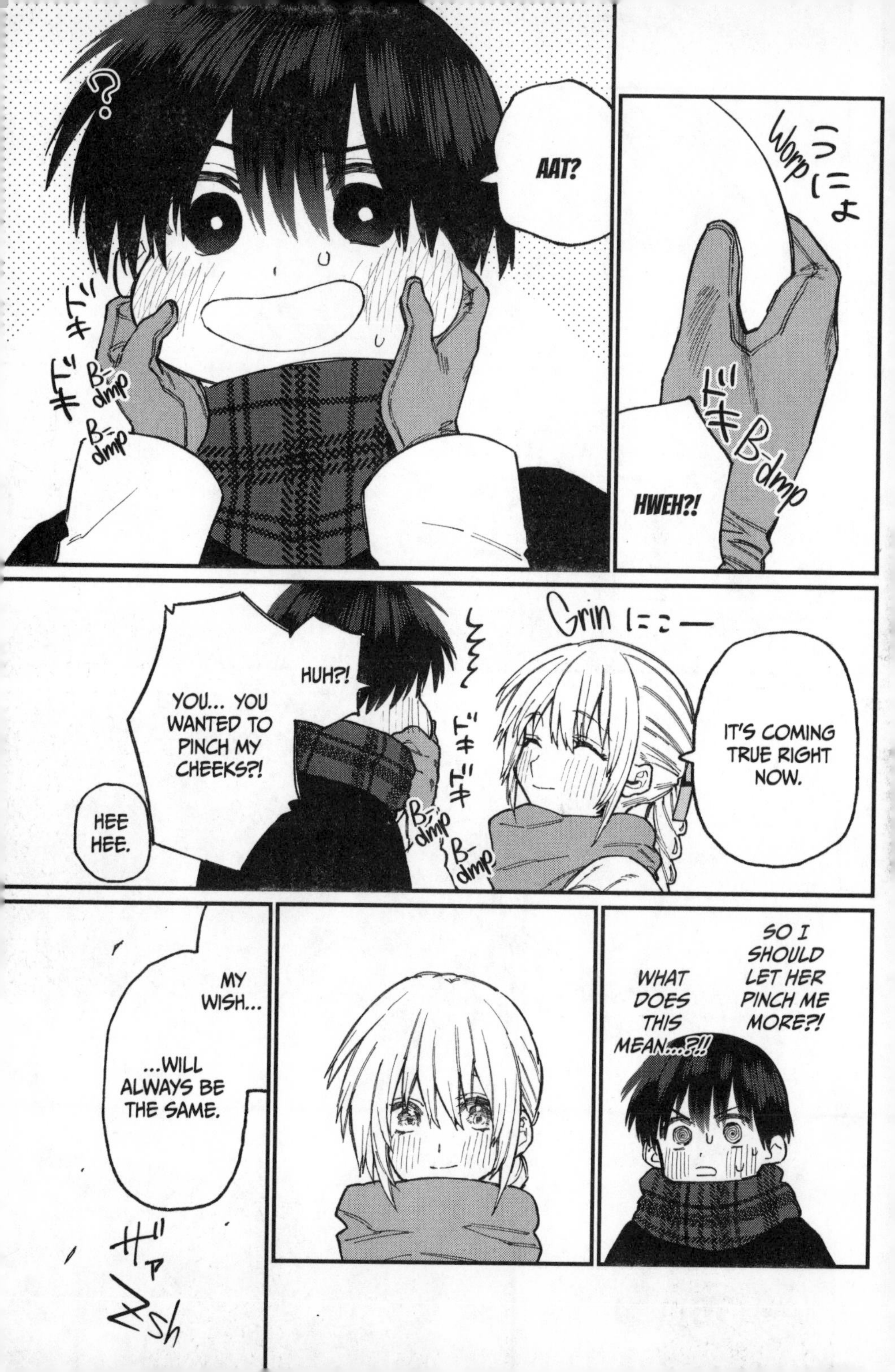
うにょ Worp
ドキ B-dmp
HWEH?!
AAT?
?
ドキ B-dmp
ドキ B-dmp
Grin にこー
IT'S COMING TRUE RIGHT NOW.
ドキ B-dmp
ドキ B-dmp
HUH?!
YOU... YOU WANTED TO PINCH MY CHEEKS?!
HEE HEE.
SO I SHOULD LET HER PINCH ME MORE?!
WHAT DOES THIS MEAN...?!!
MY WISH...
...WILL ALWAYS BE THE SAME.
ザッ Zsh

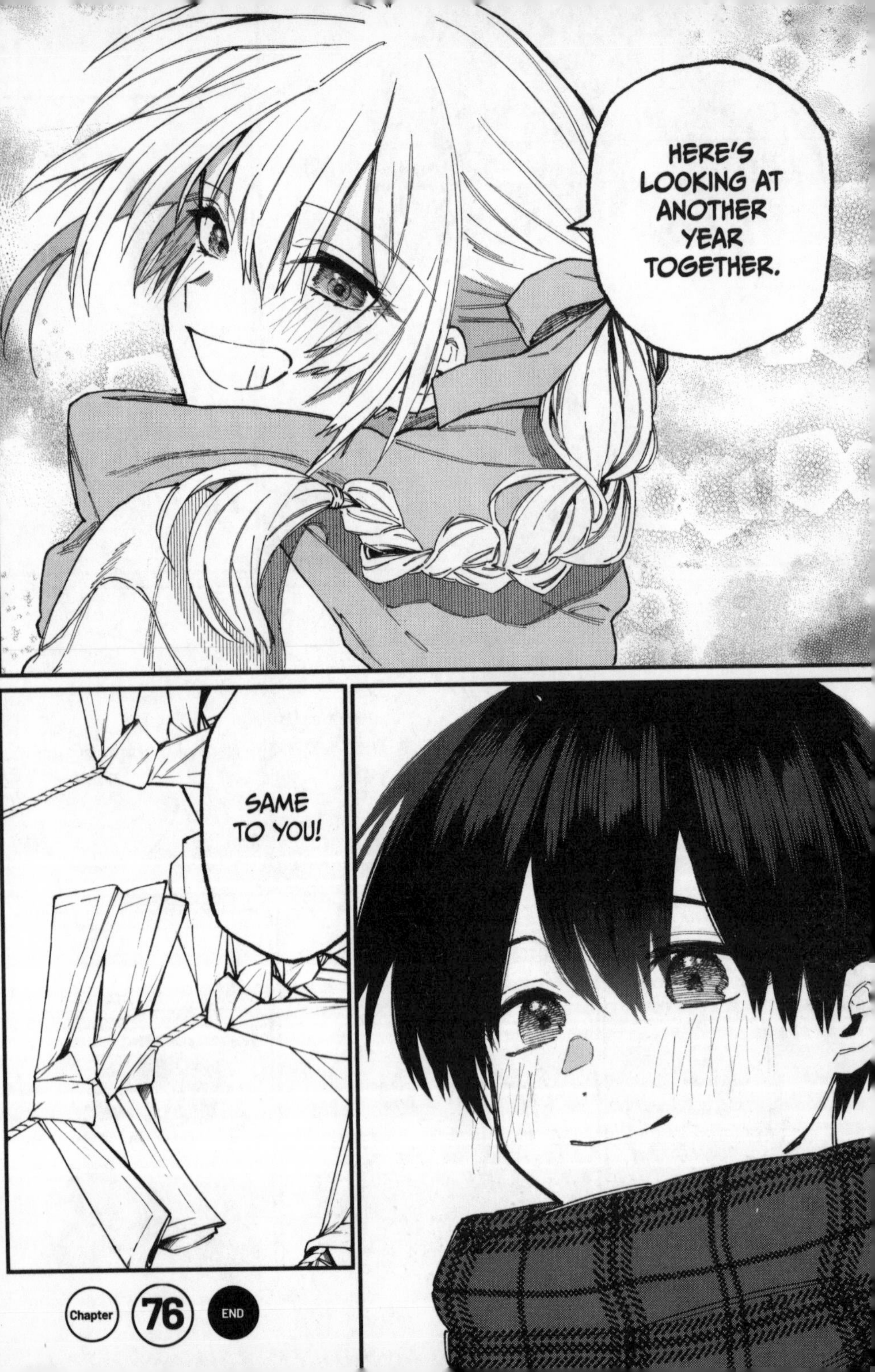
HERE'S LOOKING AT ANOTHER YEAR TOGETHER.
SAME TO YOU!

Chapter 76 END

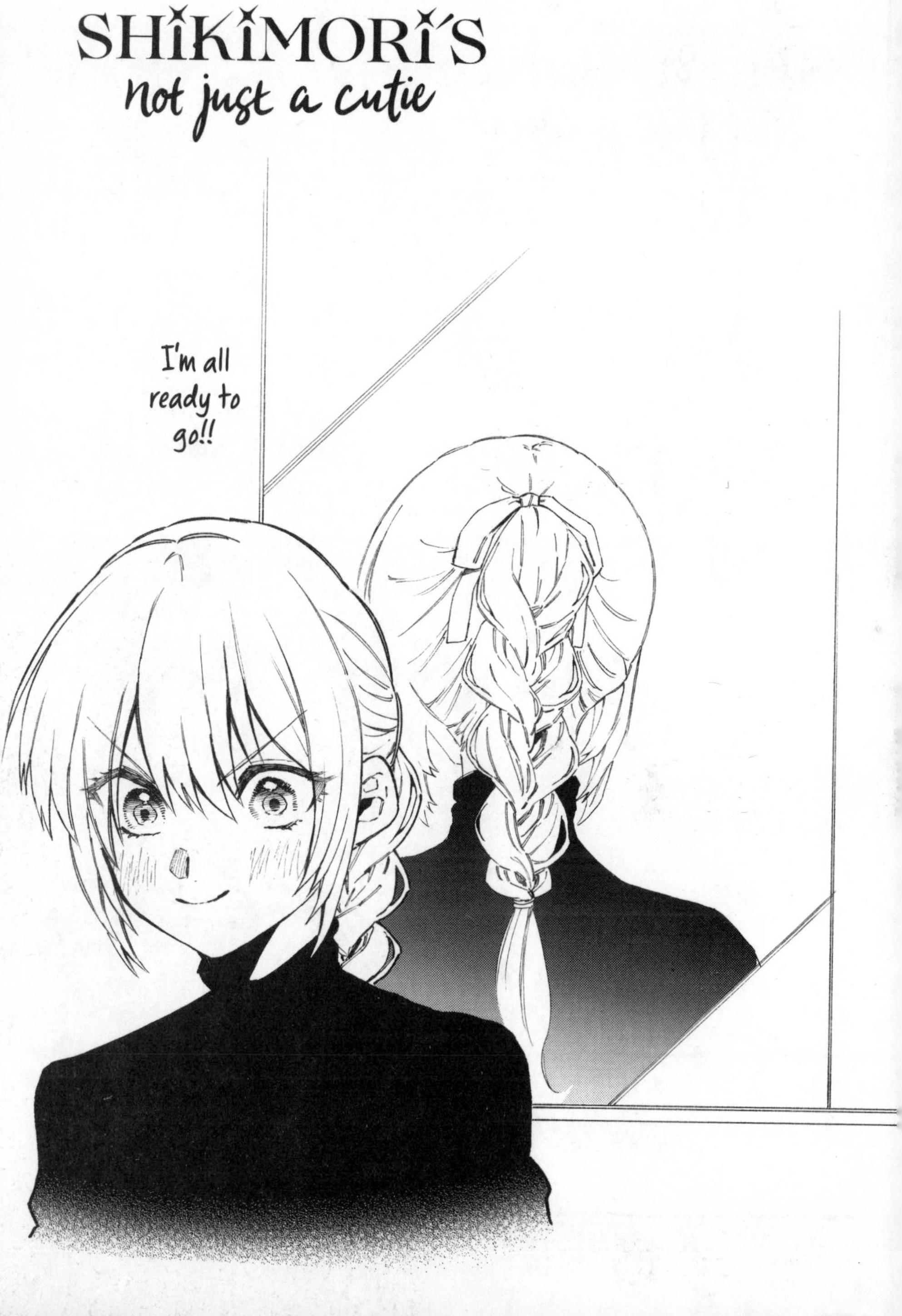
SHIKIMORI'S
Not just a cutie
I'm all ready to go!!

SHIKIMORI'S
not just a cutie

HOPPING BAD LUCK VAMPIRES

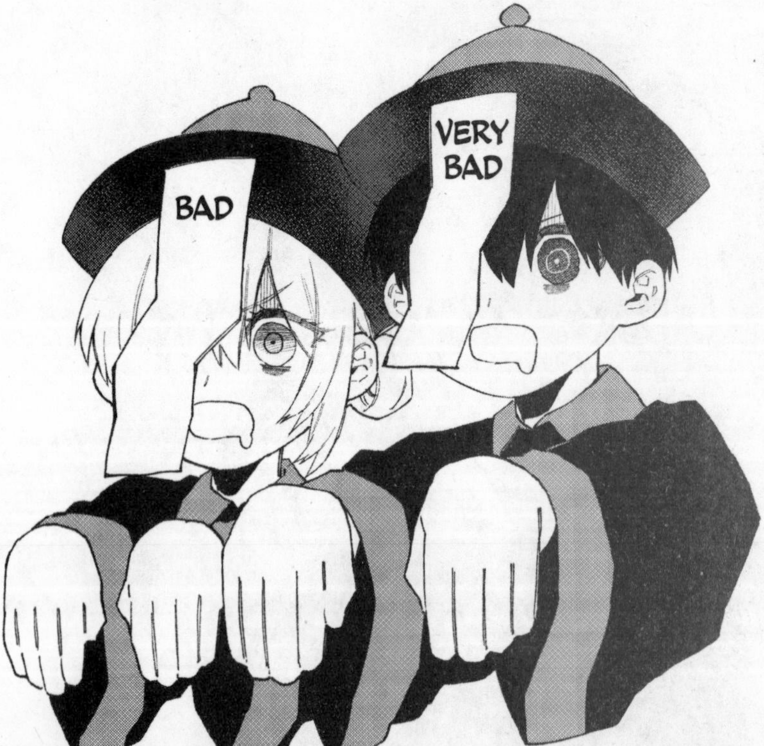
VERY BAD
BAD

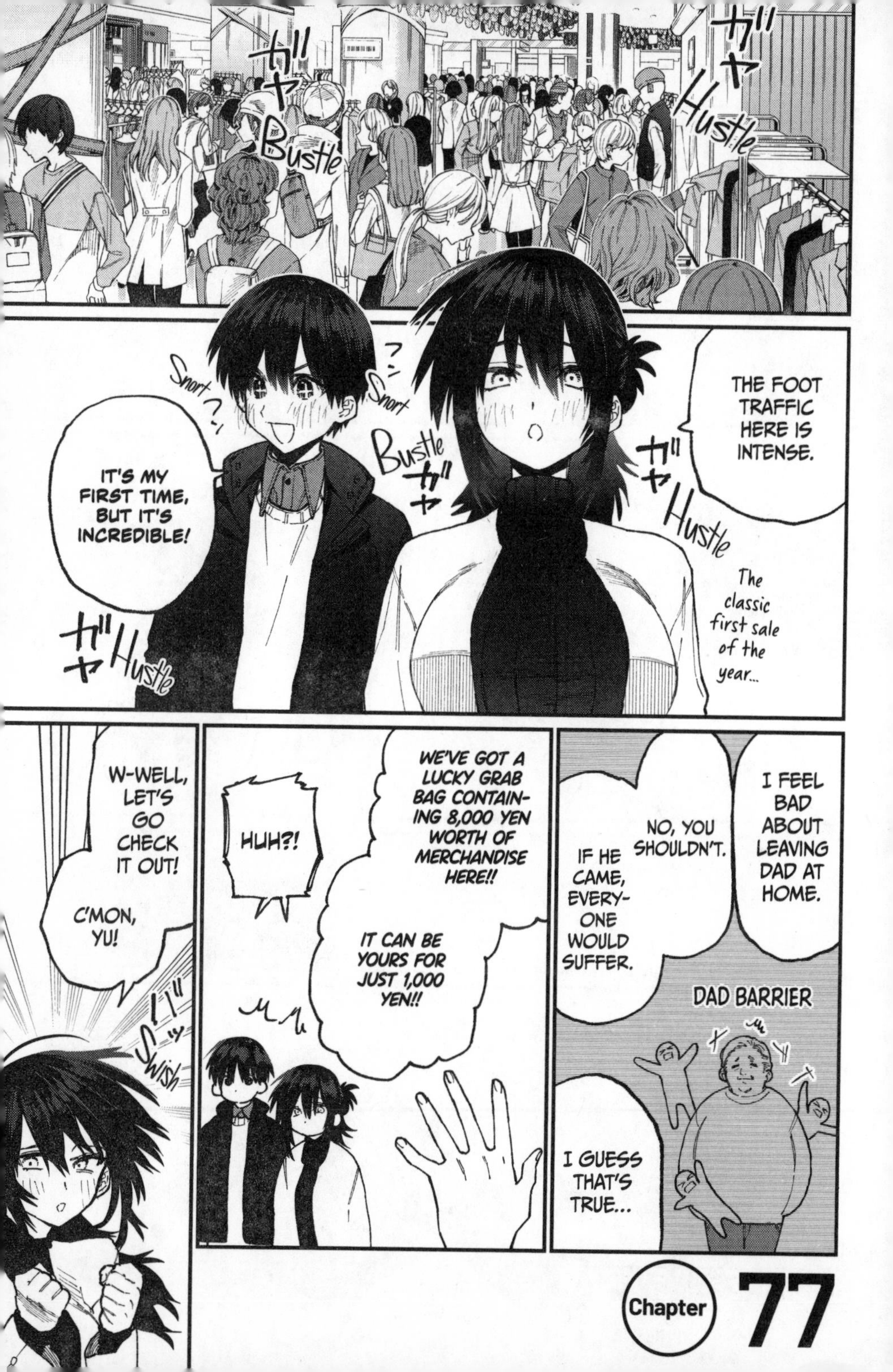
ガヤ Hustle
ガヤ Bustle
THE FOOT TRAFFIC HERE IS INTENSE.
ガヤ Hustle
The classic first sale of the year...
Bustle ガヤ
Snort Snort
IT'S MY FIRST TIME, BUT IT'S INCREDIBLE!
ガヤ Hustle
I FEEL BAD ABOUT LEAVING DAD AT HOME.
NO, YOU SHOULDN'T.
IF HE CAME, EVERYONE WOULD SUFFER.
DAD BARRIER
I GUESS THAT'S TRUE...
WE'VE GOT A LUCKY GRAB BAG CONTAINING 8,000 YEN WORTH OF MERCHANDISE HERE!!
HUH?!
IT CAN BE YOURS FOR JUST 1,000 YEN!!
W-WELL, LET'S GO CHECK IT OUT!
C'MON, YU!
Swish

Chapter 77

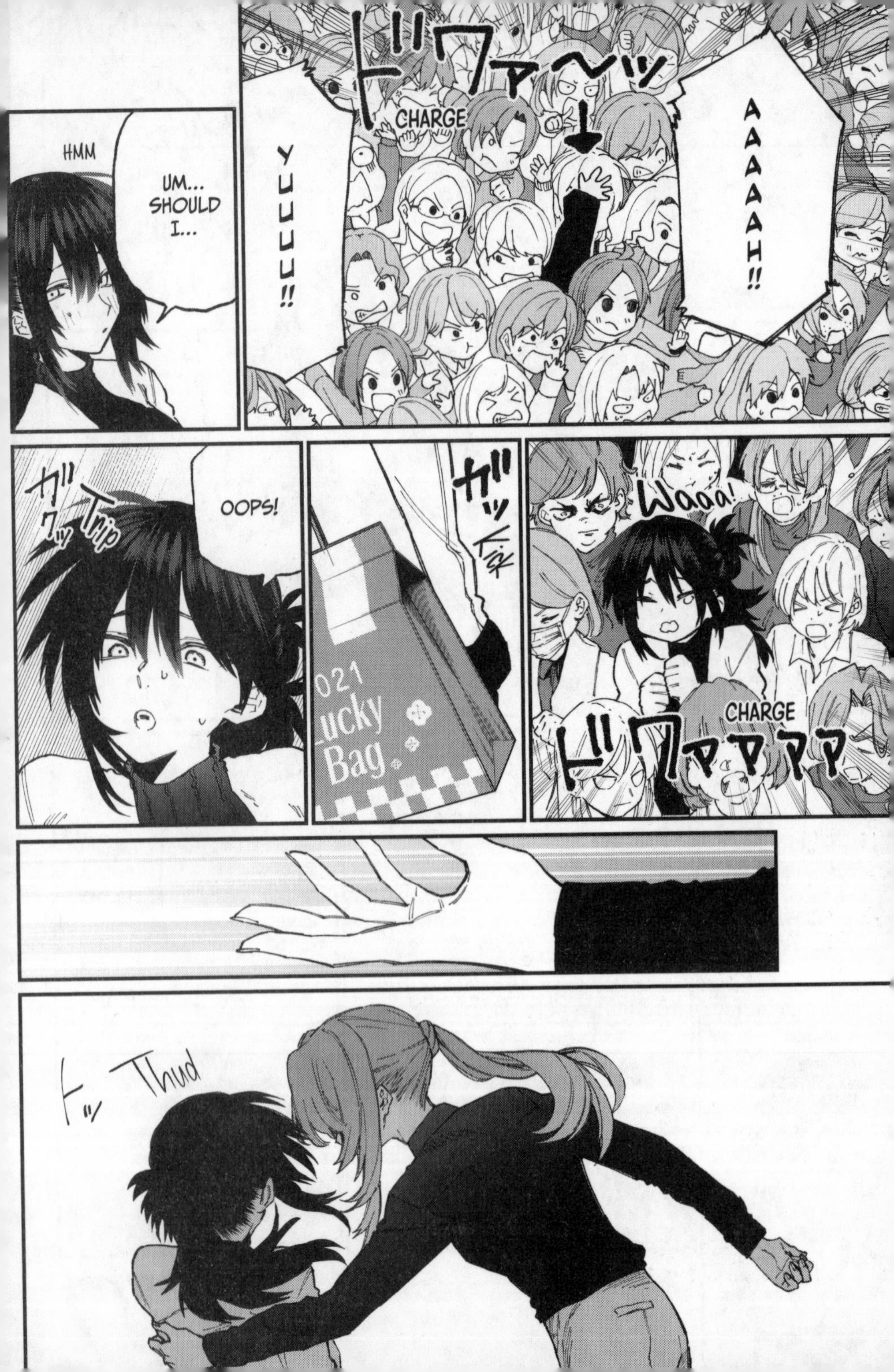

AAAAAAH!!
ドワァヘッ
CHARGE
YUUUUU!!
UM... SHOULD I...
HMM
Waaa!
ドワァァァァ
CHARGE
ガッ
Kick
021
ucky
Bag
OOPS!
ガクッ
Trip
トッ
Thud

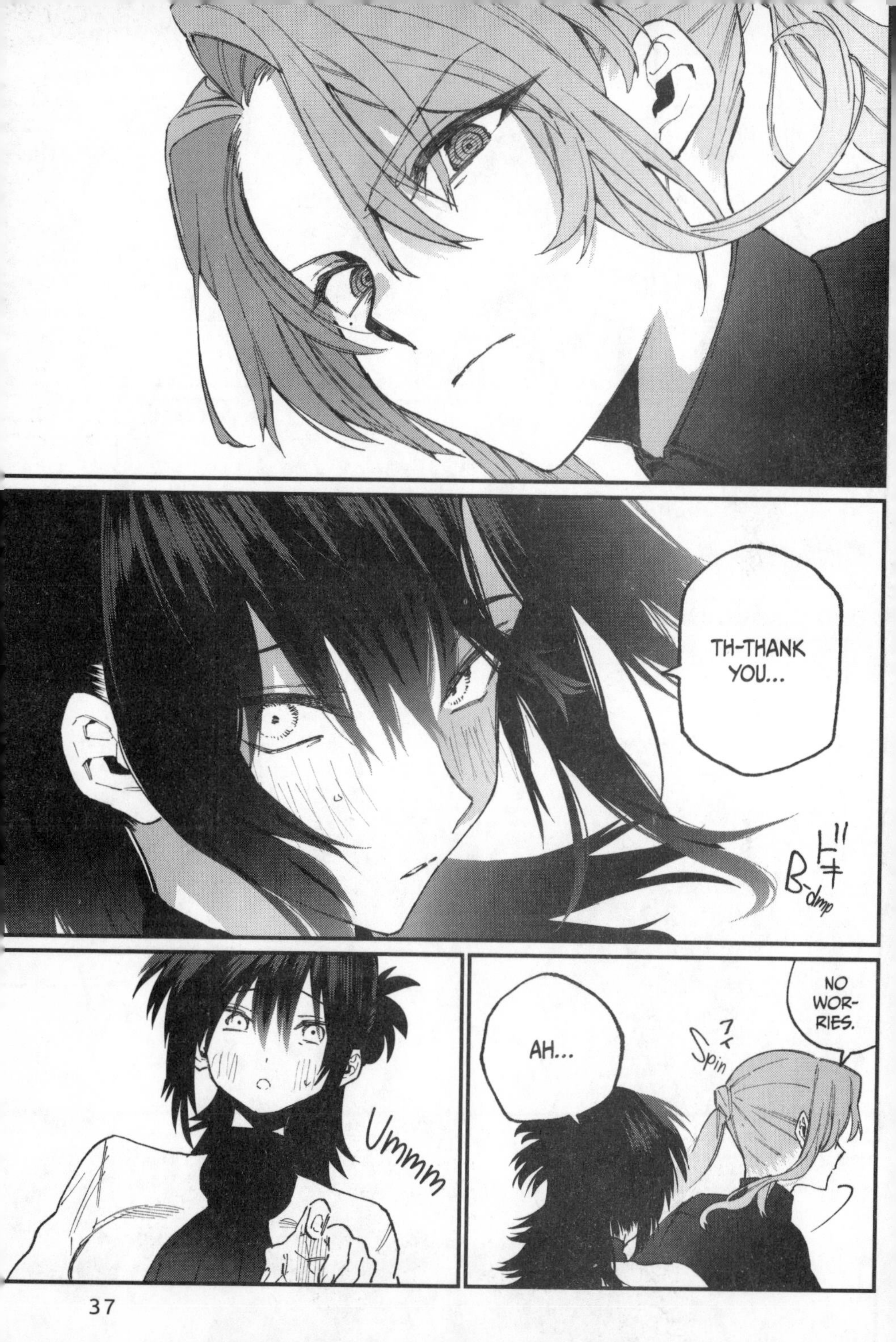
TH-THANK YOU...
ドキ
B-dmp
NO WOR-RIES.
フイ
Spin
AH...
Ummm

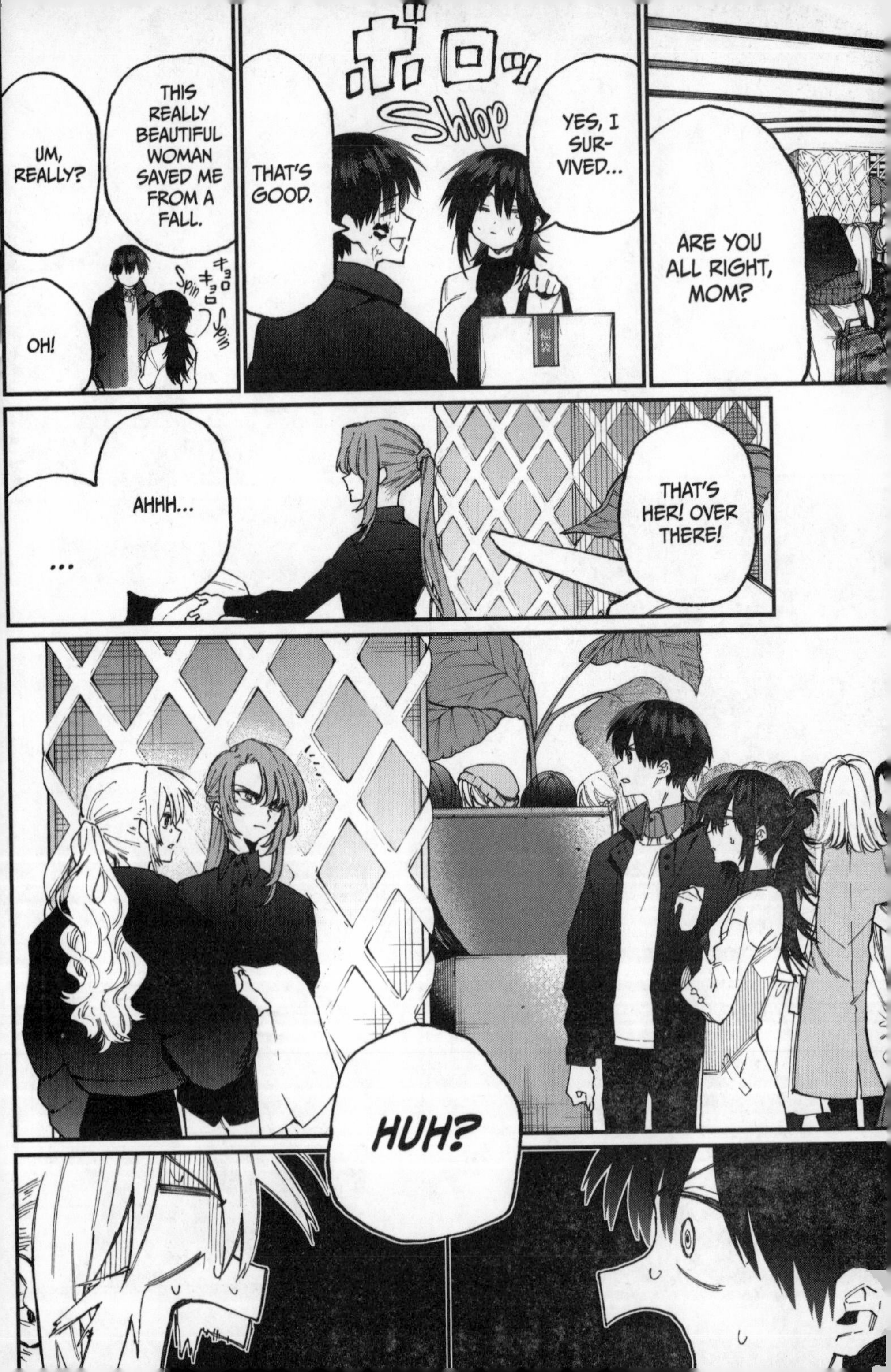
ARE YOU ALL RIGHT, MOM?
ボロッ
Shlop
YES, I SUR-VIVED...
THAT'S GOOD.
THIS REALLY BEAUTIFUL WOMAN SAVED ME FROM A FALL.
UM, REALLY?
キョロキョロ
Spin Spin
OH!
THAT'S HER! OVER THERE!
AHHH...
...
HUH?

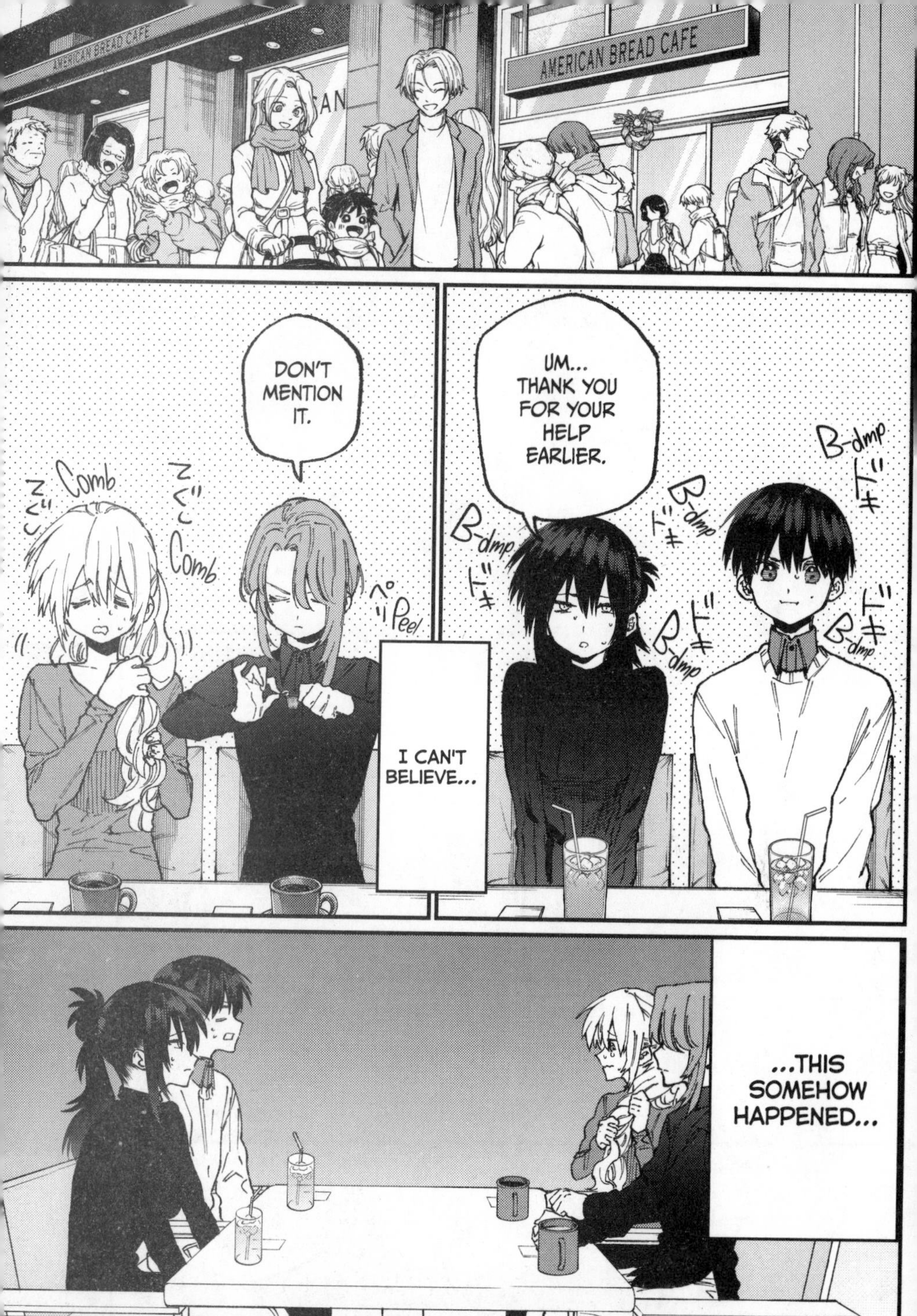
AMERICAN BREAD CAFE
AMERICAN BREAD CAFE
UM... THANK YOU FOR YOUR HELP EARLIER.
B-dmp
B-dmp
B-dmp
B-dmp
B-dmp
DON'T MENTION IT.
Peel
Comb
Comb
I CAN'T BELIEVE...
...THIS SOMEHOW HAPPENED...

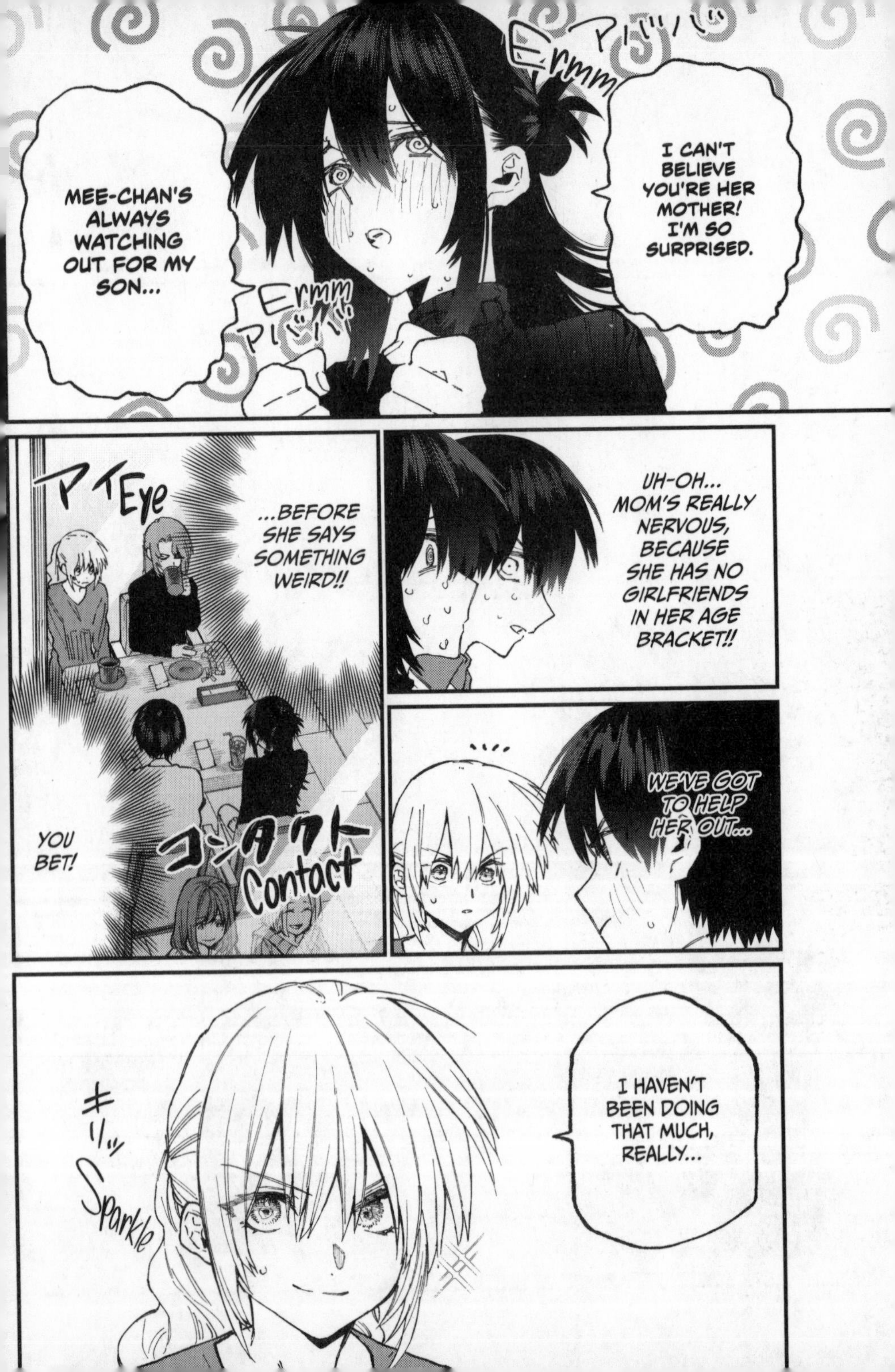
Ermm
I CAN'T BELIEVE YOU'RE HER MOTHER! I'M SO SURPRISED.
Ermm
MEE-CHAN'S ALWAYS WATCHING OUT FOR MY SON...
UH-OH... MOM'S REALLY NERVOUS, BECAUSE SHE HAS NO GIRLFRIENDS IN HER AGE BRACKET!!
WE'VE GOT TO HELP HER OUT...
...BEFORE SHE SAYS SOMETHING WEIRD!!
Eye
YOU BET!
Contact
I HAVEN'T BEEN DOING THAT MUCH, REALLY...
Sparkle

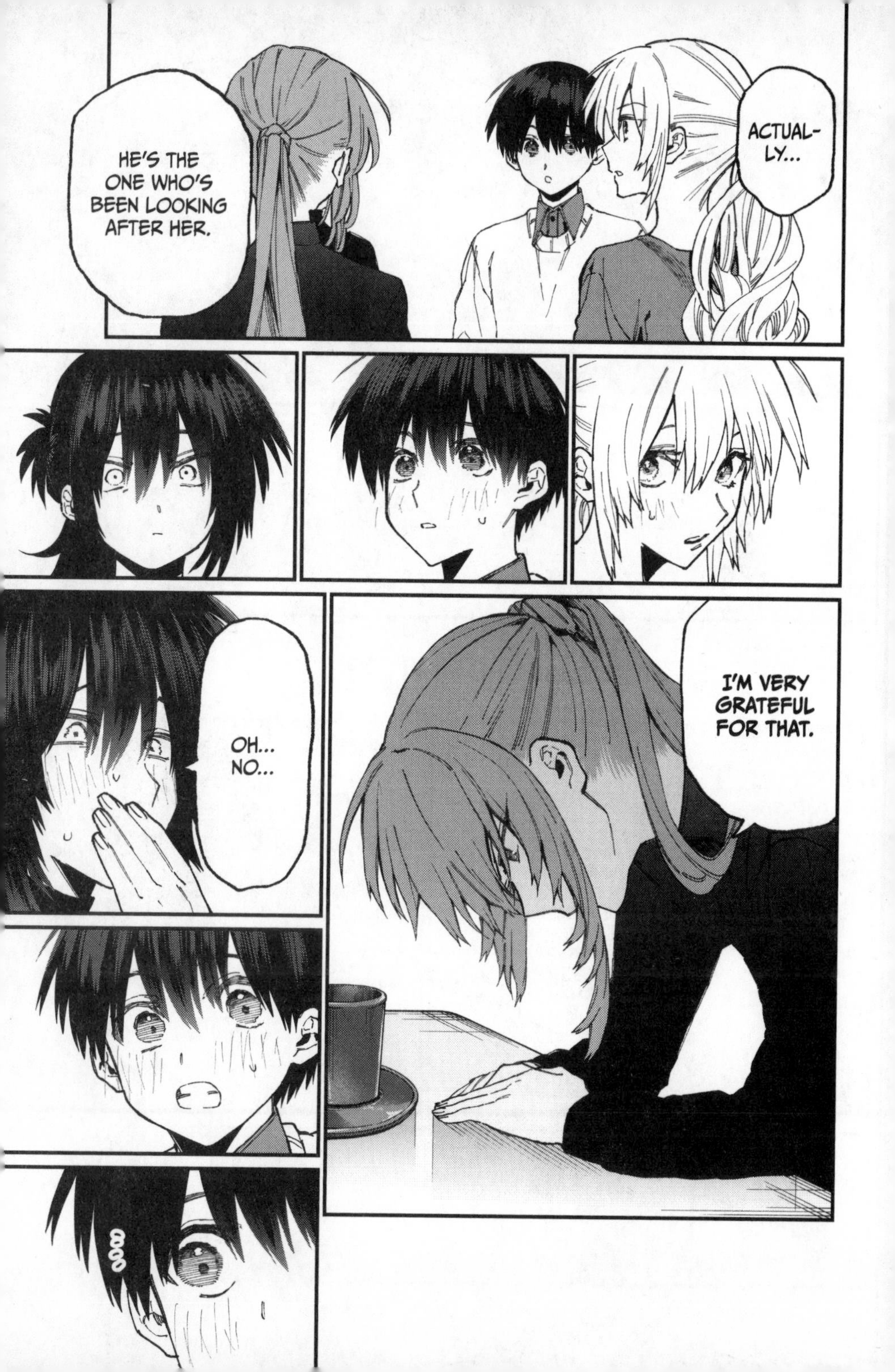
ACTUAL-
LY...
HE'S THE ONE WHO'S BEEN LOOKING AFTER HER.
I'M VERY GRATEFUL FOR THAT.
OH... NO...

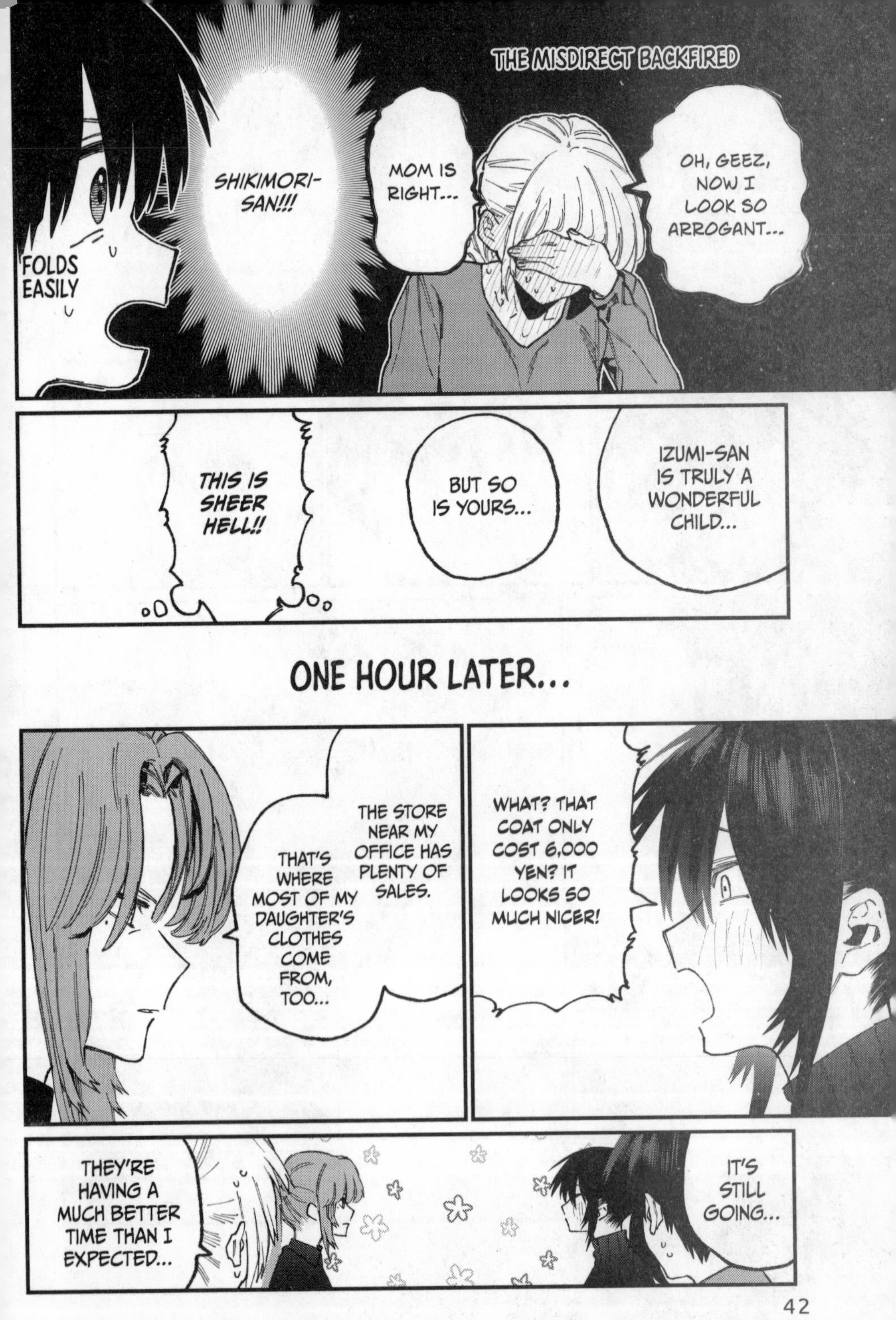
THE MISDIRECT BACKFIRED
OH, GEEZ, NOW I LOOK SO ARROGANT...
MOM IS RIGHT...
SHIKIMORI-SAN!!!
FOLDS EASILY
IZUMI-SAN IS TRULY A WONDERFUL CHILD...
BUT SO IS YOURS...
THIS IS SHEER HELL!!
ONE HOUR LATER...
WHAT? THAT COAT ONLY COST 6,000 YEN? IT LOOKS SO MUCH NICER!
THE STORE NEAR MY OFFICE HAS PLENTY OF SALES.
THAT'S WHERE MOST OF MY DAUGHTER'S CLOTHES COME FROM, TOO...
IT'S STILL GOING...
THEY'RE HAVING A MUCH BETTER TIME THAN I EXPECTED...

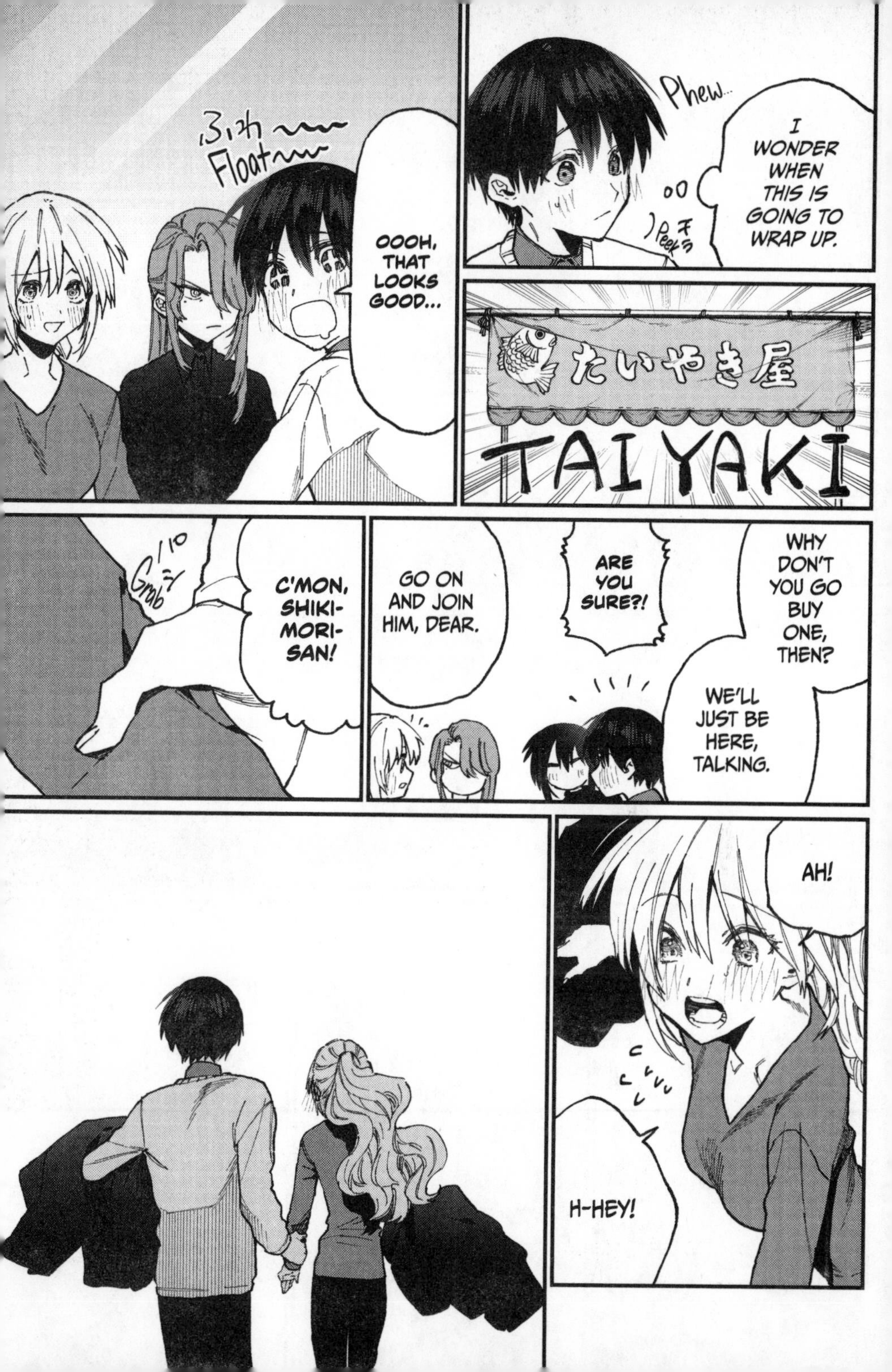

Phew...
I WONDER WHEN THIS IS GOING TO WRAP UP.
Peek
たいやき屋
TAIYAKI
ふわ〜〜
Float〜〜
OOOH, THAT LOOKS GOOD...
WHY DON'T YOU GO BUY ONE, THEN?
ARE YOU SURE?!
GO ON AND JOIN HIM, DEAR.
WE'LL JUST BE HERE, TALKING.
Grab
C'MON, SHIKI-MORI-SAN!
AH!
H-HEY!

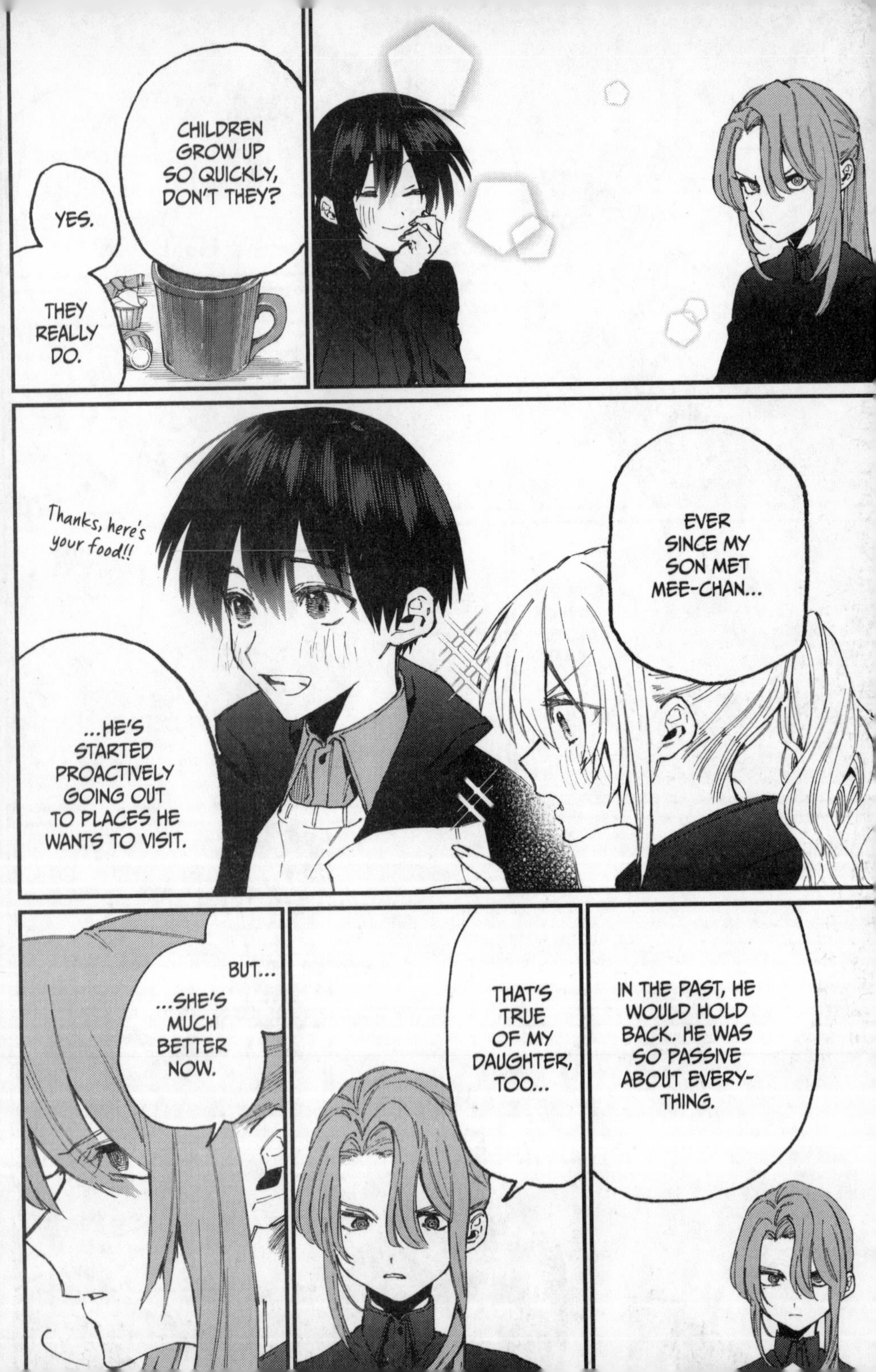
CHILDREN GROW UP SO QUICKLY, DON'T THEY?
YES.
THEY REALLY DO.
EVER SINCE MY SON MET MEE-CHAN...
Thanks, here's your food!!
...HE'S STARTED PROACTIVELY GOING OUT TO PLACES HE WANTS TO VISIT.
IN THE PAST, HE WOULD HOLD BACK. HE WAS SO PASSIVE ABOUT EVERY-THING.
THAT'S TRUE OF MY DAUGHTER, TOO...
BUT...
...SHE'S MUCH BETTER NOW.

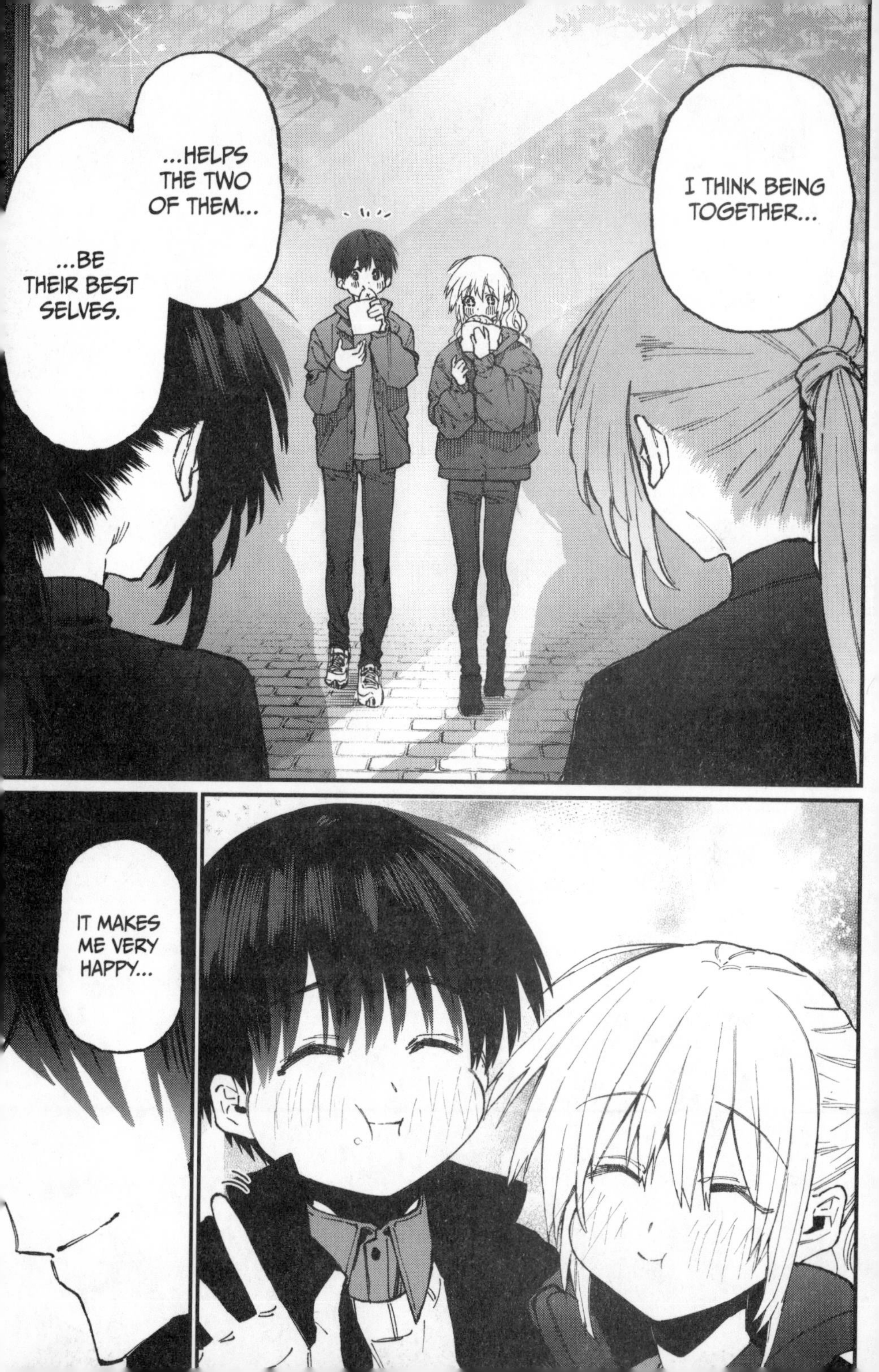
I THINK BEING TOGETHER...
...HELPS THE TWO OF THEM...
...BE THEIR BEST SELVES.
IT MAKES ME VERY HAPPY...

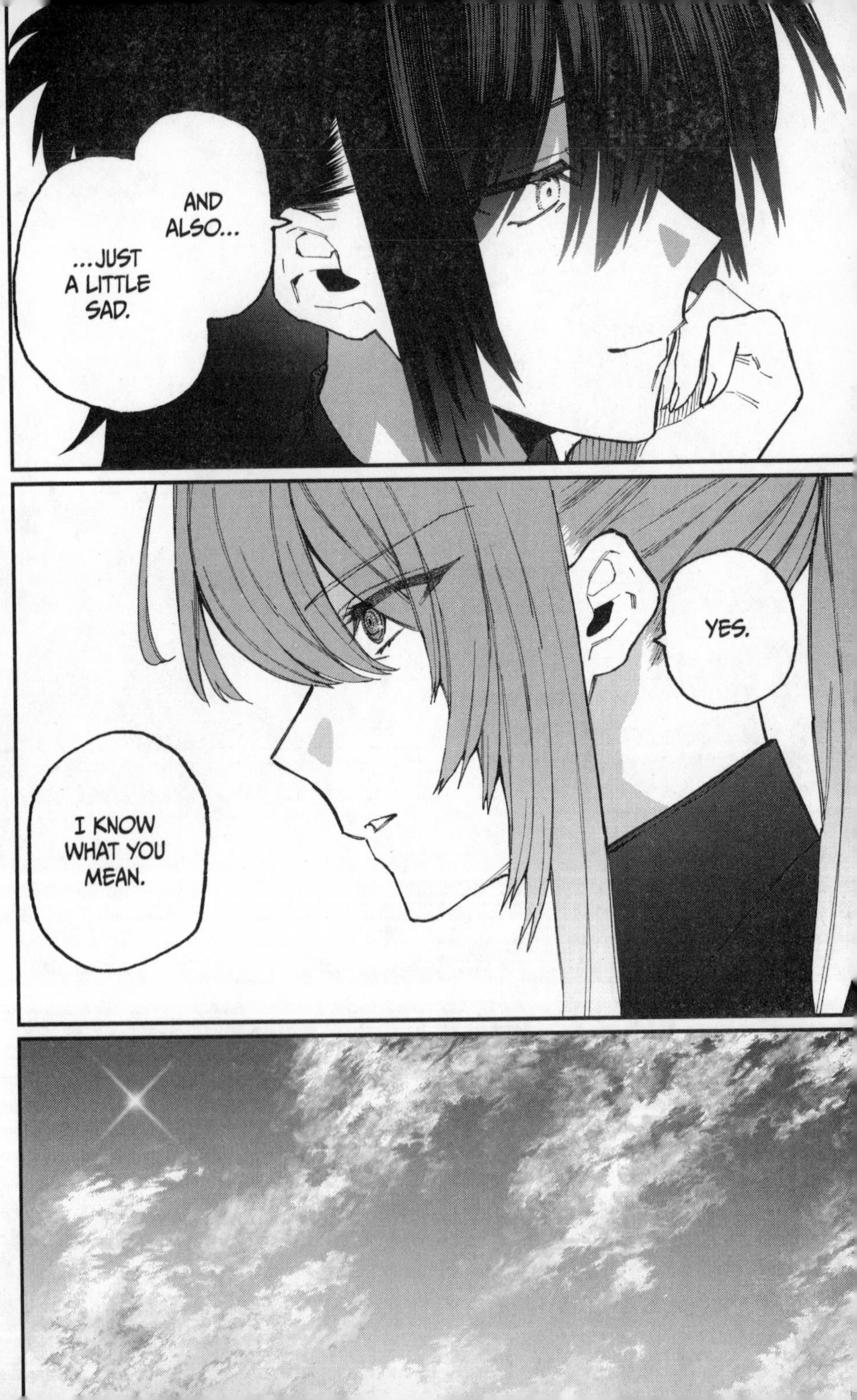
AND ALSO... ...JUST A LITTLE SAD.
YES.
I KNOW WHAT YOU MEAN.

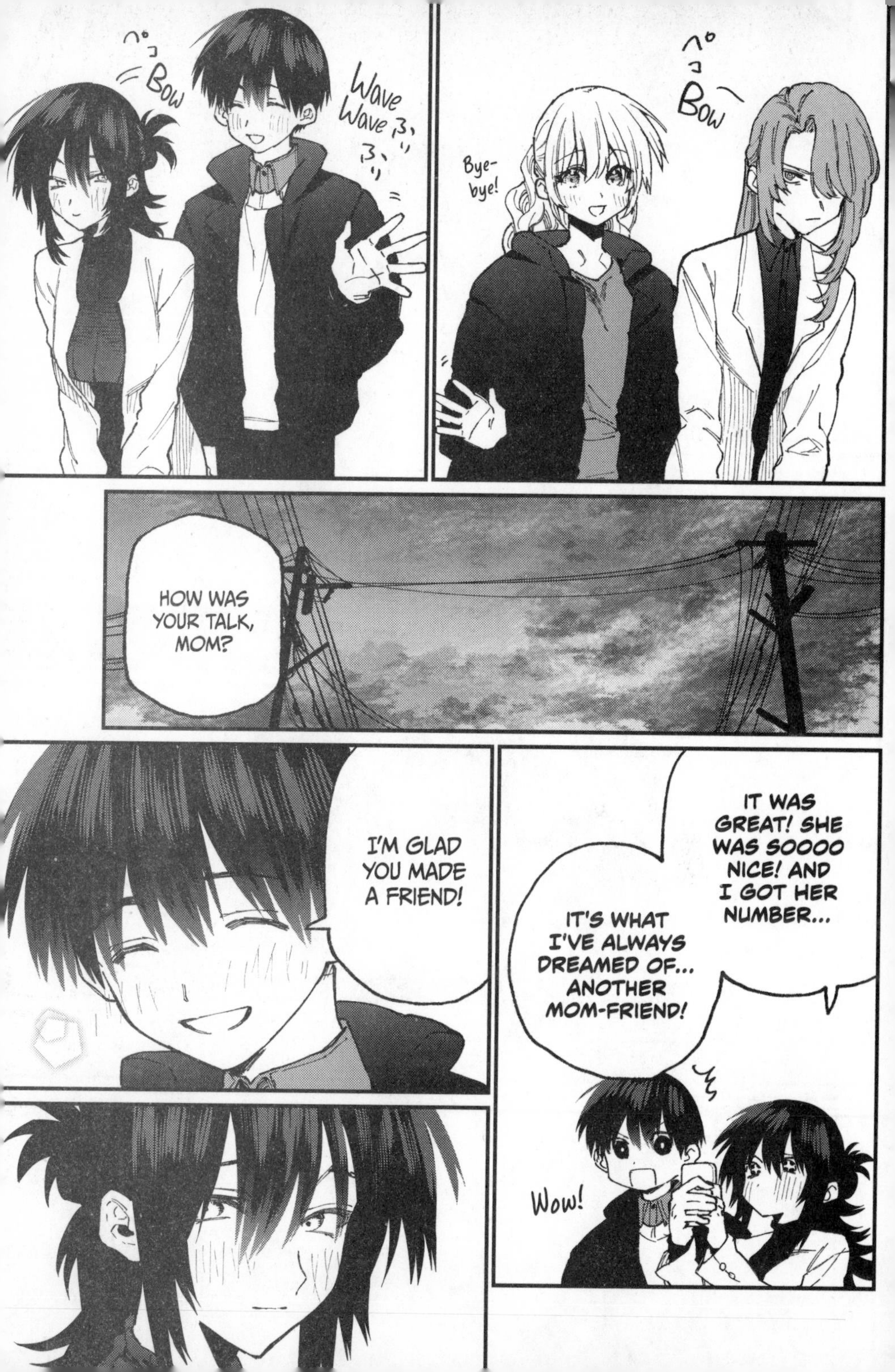
ペコ
Bow
Bye-bye!
ペコ
Bow
Wave Wave
ふり ふり
HOW WAS YOUR TALK, MOM?
IT WAS GREAT! SHE WAS SOOOO NICE! AND I GOT HER NUMBER...
IT'S WHAT I'VE ALWAYS DREAMED OF... ANOTHER MOM-FRIEND!
Wow!
I'M GLAD YOU MADE A FRIEND!

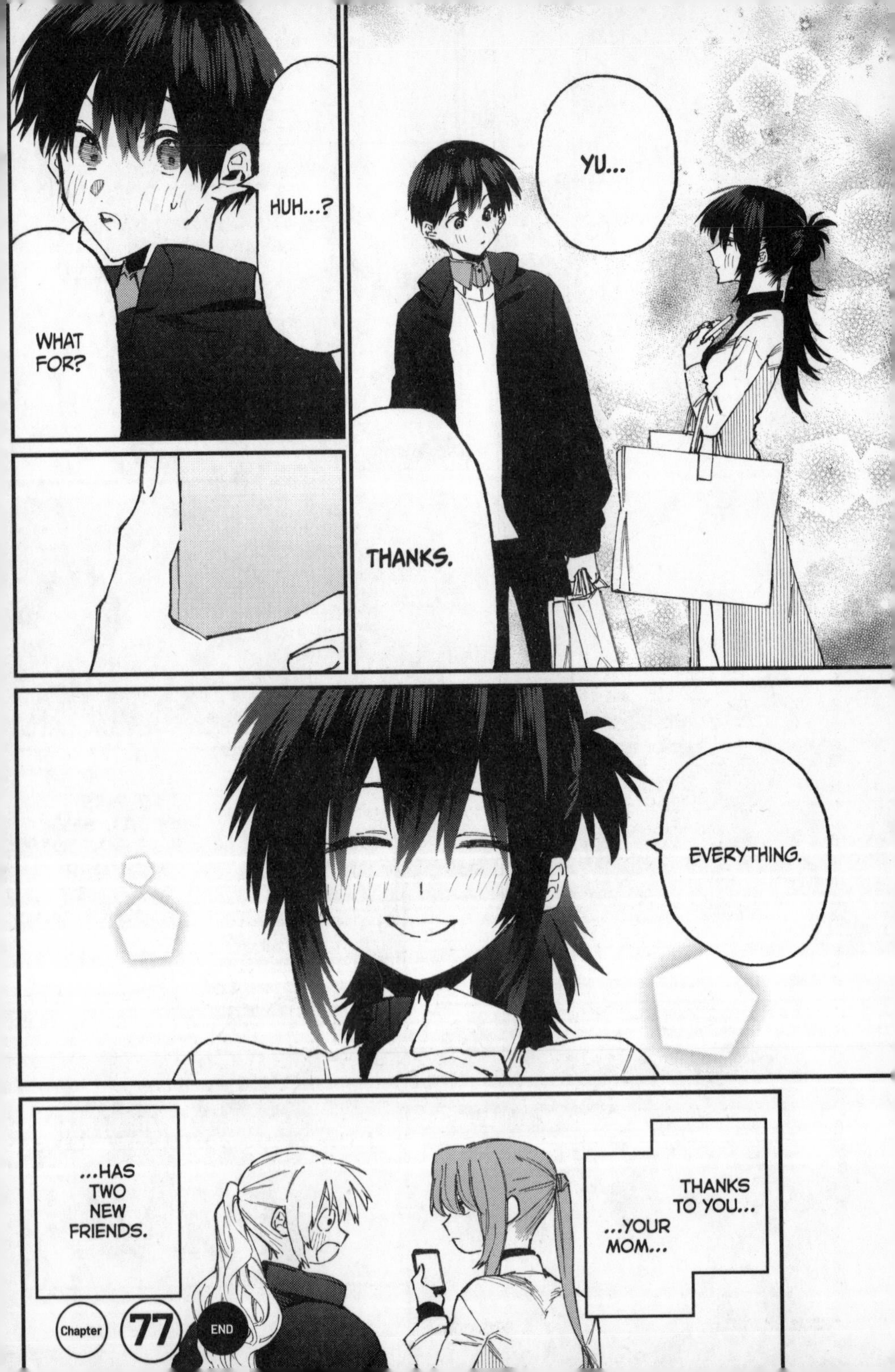
YU...
THANKS.
HUH...?
WHAT FOR?
EVERYTHING.
THANKS TO YOU...
...YOUR MOM...
...HAS TWO NEW FRIENDS.
Chapter 77 END

SHIKIMORI'S not just a cutie

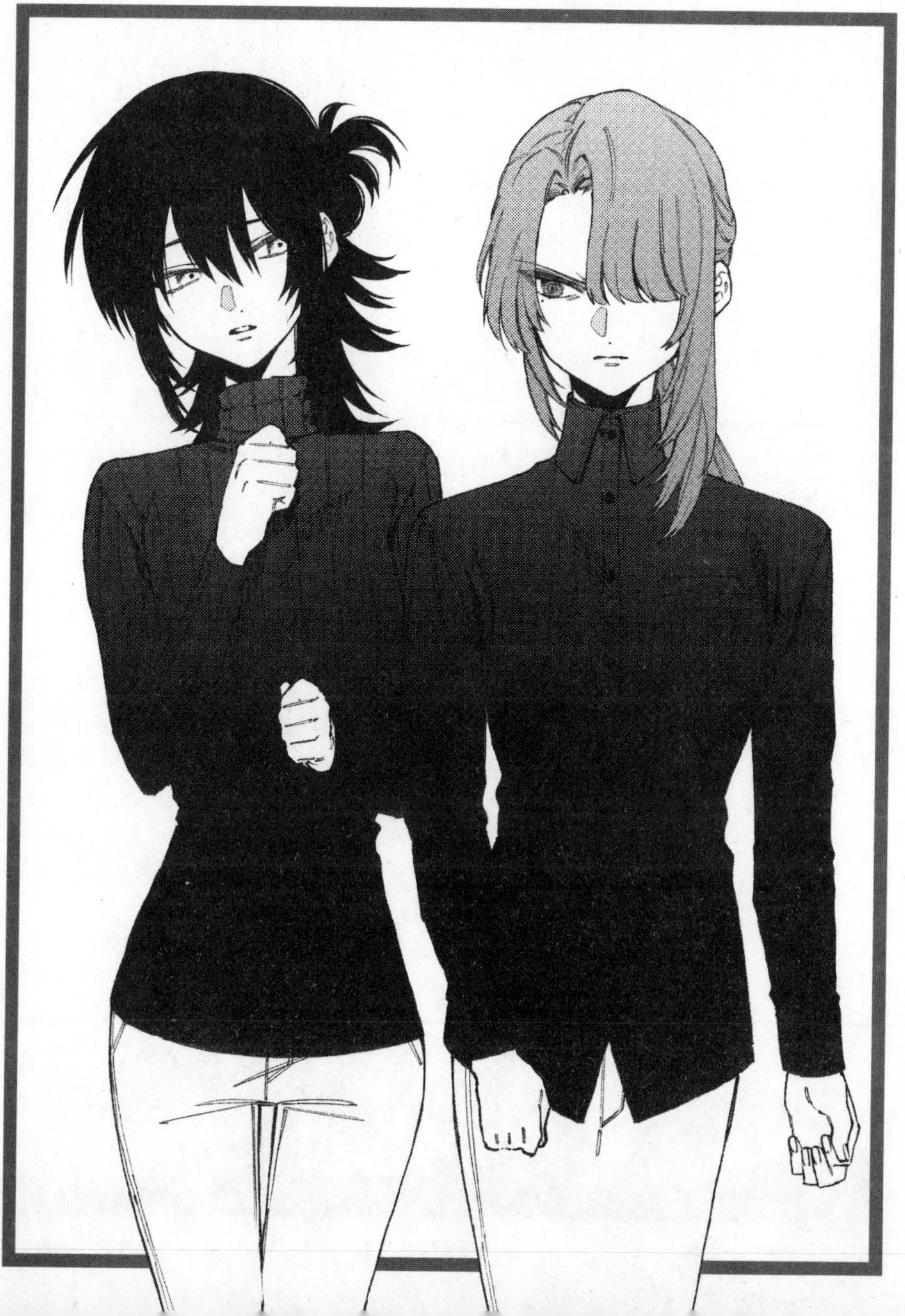

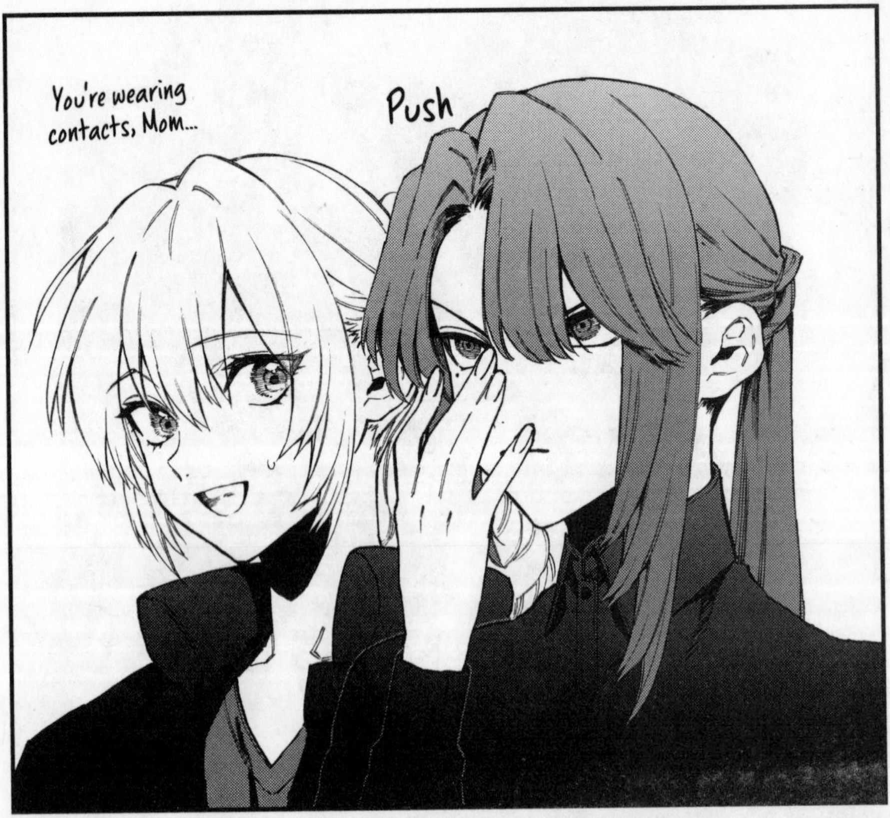
You're wearing contacts, Mom...
Push

SHIKIMORI'S not just a cutie

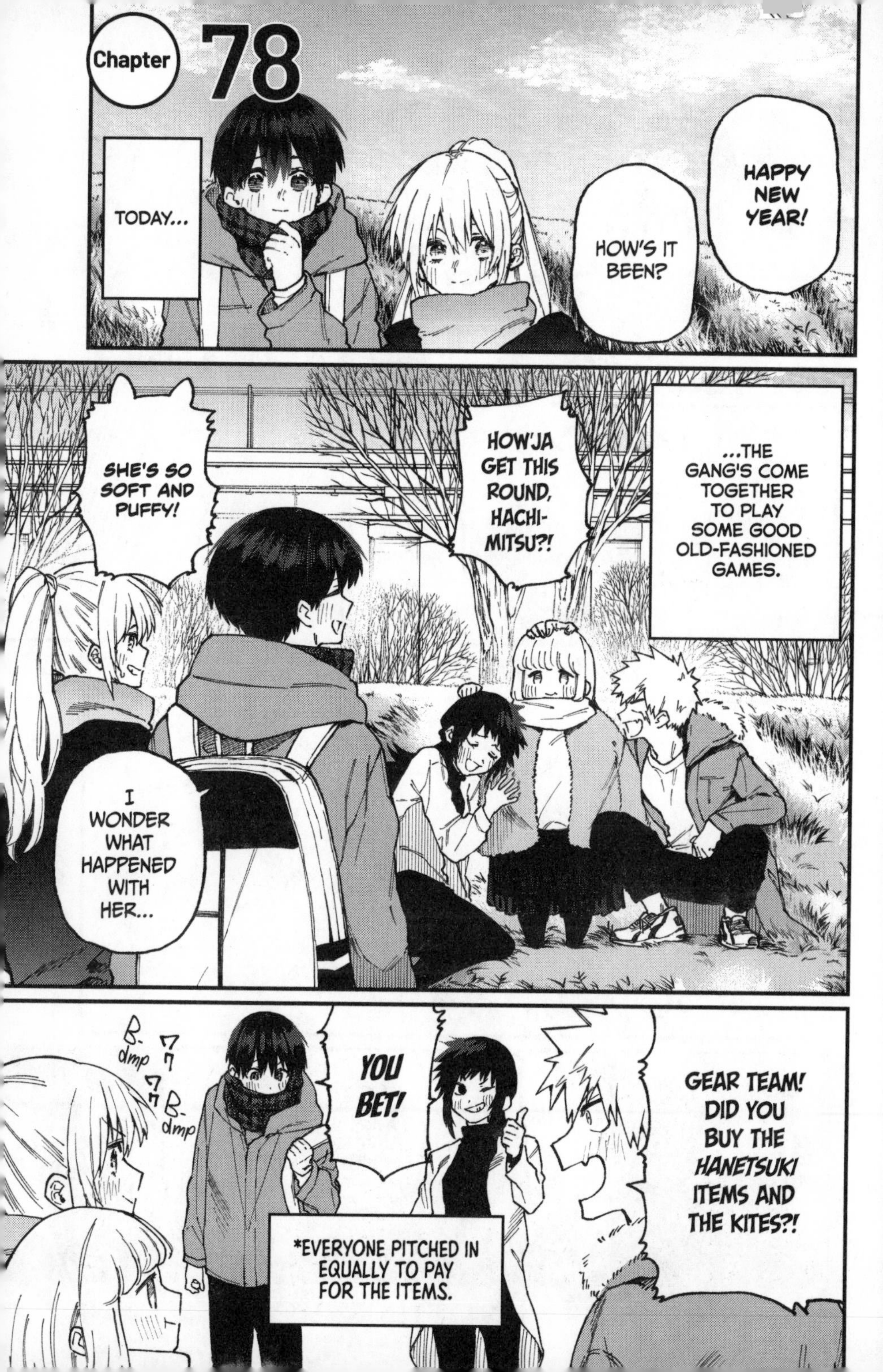
Chapter 78
HAPPY NEW YEAR!
HOW'S IT BEEN?
TODAY...
...THE GANG'S COME TOGETHER TO PLAY SOME GOOD OLD-FASHIONED GAMES.
HOW'JA GET THIS ROUND, HACHIMITSU?!
SHE'S SO SOFT AND PUFFY!
I WONDER WHAT HAPPENED WITH HER...
GEAR TEAM! DID YOU BUY THE *HANETSUKI* ITEMS AND THE KITES?!
YOU BET!
B-dmp
B-dmp
*EVERYONE PITCHED IN EQUALLY TO PAY FOR THE ITEMS.

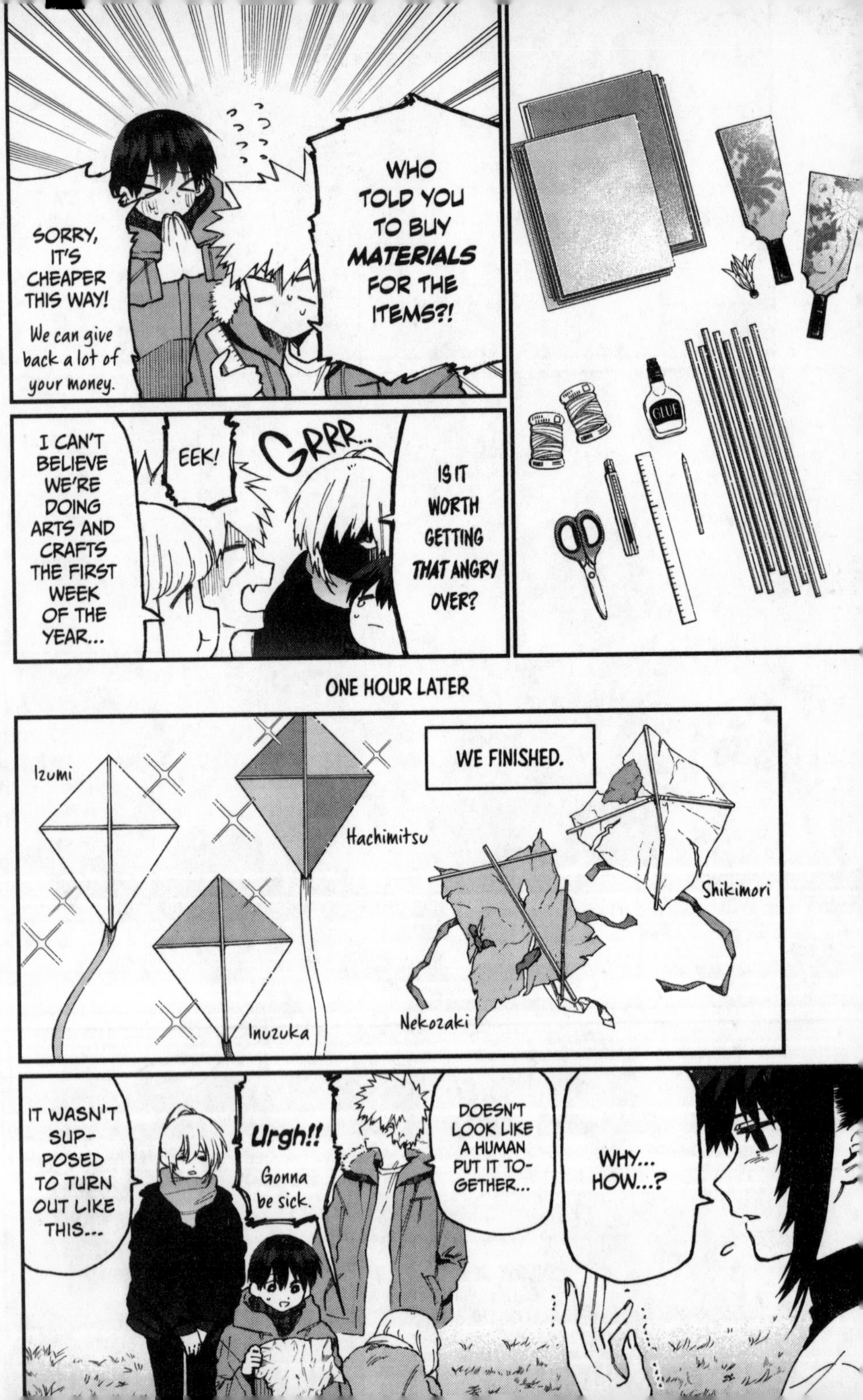
WHO TOLD YOU TO BUY MATERIALS FOR THE ITEMS?!
SORRY, IT'S CHEAPER THIS WAY!
We can give back a lot of your money.
GLUE
IS IT WORTH GETTING THAT ANGRY OVER?
GRRR...
EEK!
I CAN'T BELIEVE WE'RE DOING ARTS AND CRAFTS THE FIRST WEEK OF THE YEAR...
ONE HOUR LATER
WE FINISHED.
Shikimori
Nekozaki
Hachimitsu
Inuzuka
Izumi
WHY... HOW...?
DOESN'T LOOK LIKE A HUMAN PUT IT TOGETHER...
Urgh!!
Gonna be sick.
IT WASN'T SUPPOSED TO TURN OUT LIKE THIS...

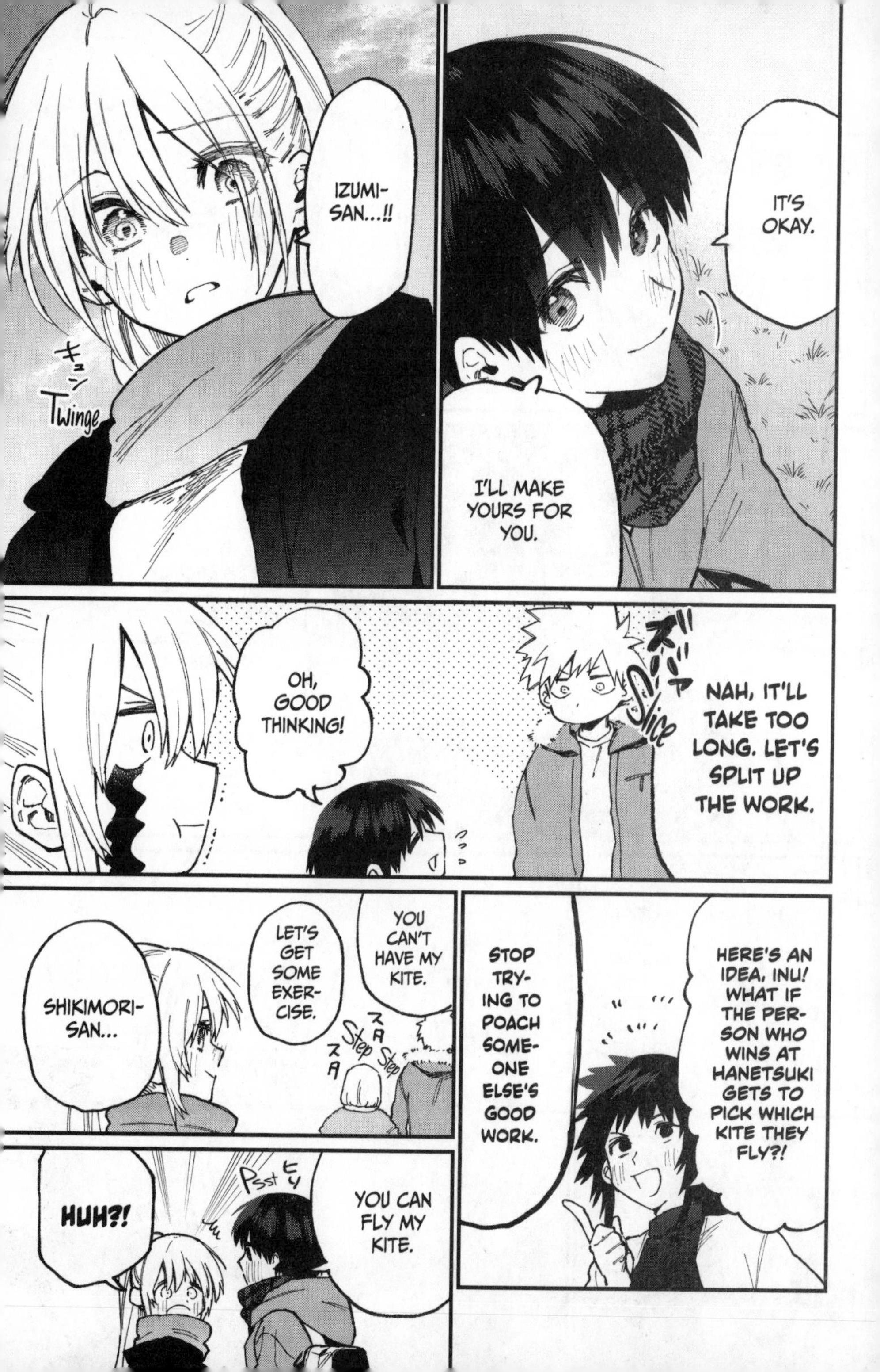
IT'S OKAY.
I'LL MAKE YOURS FOR YOU.
IZUMI-SAN...!!
キュン
Twinge
NAH, IT'LL TAKE TOO LONG. LET'S SPLIT UP THE WORK.
ズバァ
Slice
OH, GOOD THINKING!
HERE'S AN IDEA, INU! WHAT IF THE PERSON WHO WINS AT HANETSUKI GETS TO PICK WHICH KITE THEY FLY?!
STOP TRYING TO POACH SOMEONE ELSE'S GOOD WORK.
YOU CAN'T HAVE MY KITE.
LET'S GET SOME EXERCISE.
スタ
Step
スタ
Step
SHIKIMORI-SAN...
YOU CAN FLY MY KITE.
ピッ
Psst
HUH?!

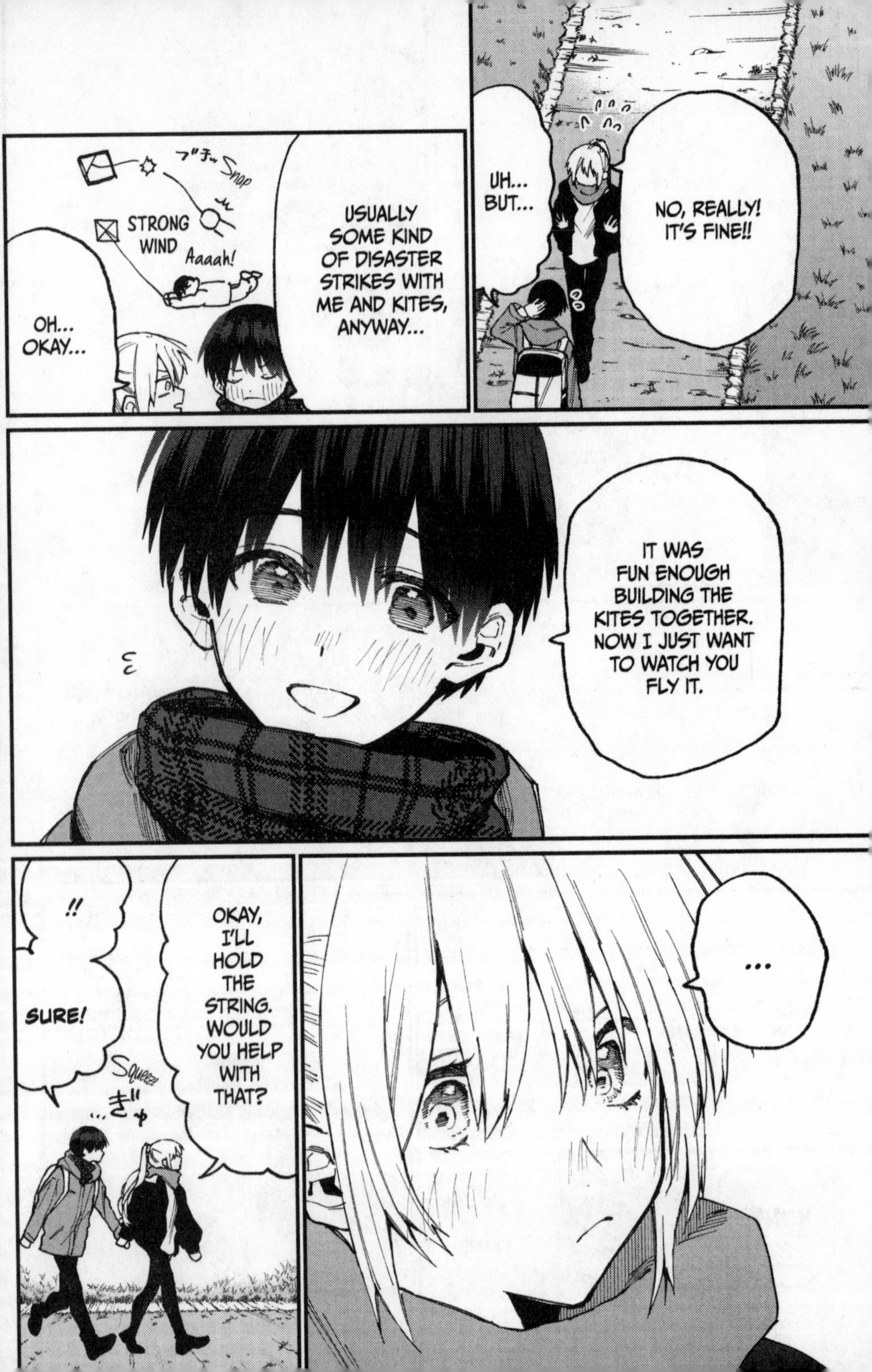
NO, REALLY! IT'S FINE!!
UH... BUT...
USUALLY SOME KIND OF DISASTER STRIKES WITH ME AND KITES, ANYWAY...
Snap
STRONG WIND
Aaaah!
OH... OKAY...
IT WAS FUN ENOUGH BUILDING THE KITES TOGETHER. NOW I JUST WANT TO WATCH YOU FLY IT.
...
OKAY, I'LL HOLD THE STRING. WOULD YOU HELP WITH THAT?
!!
SURE!
Squeeze
ぎゅ
...

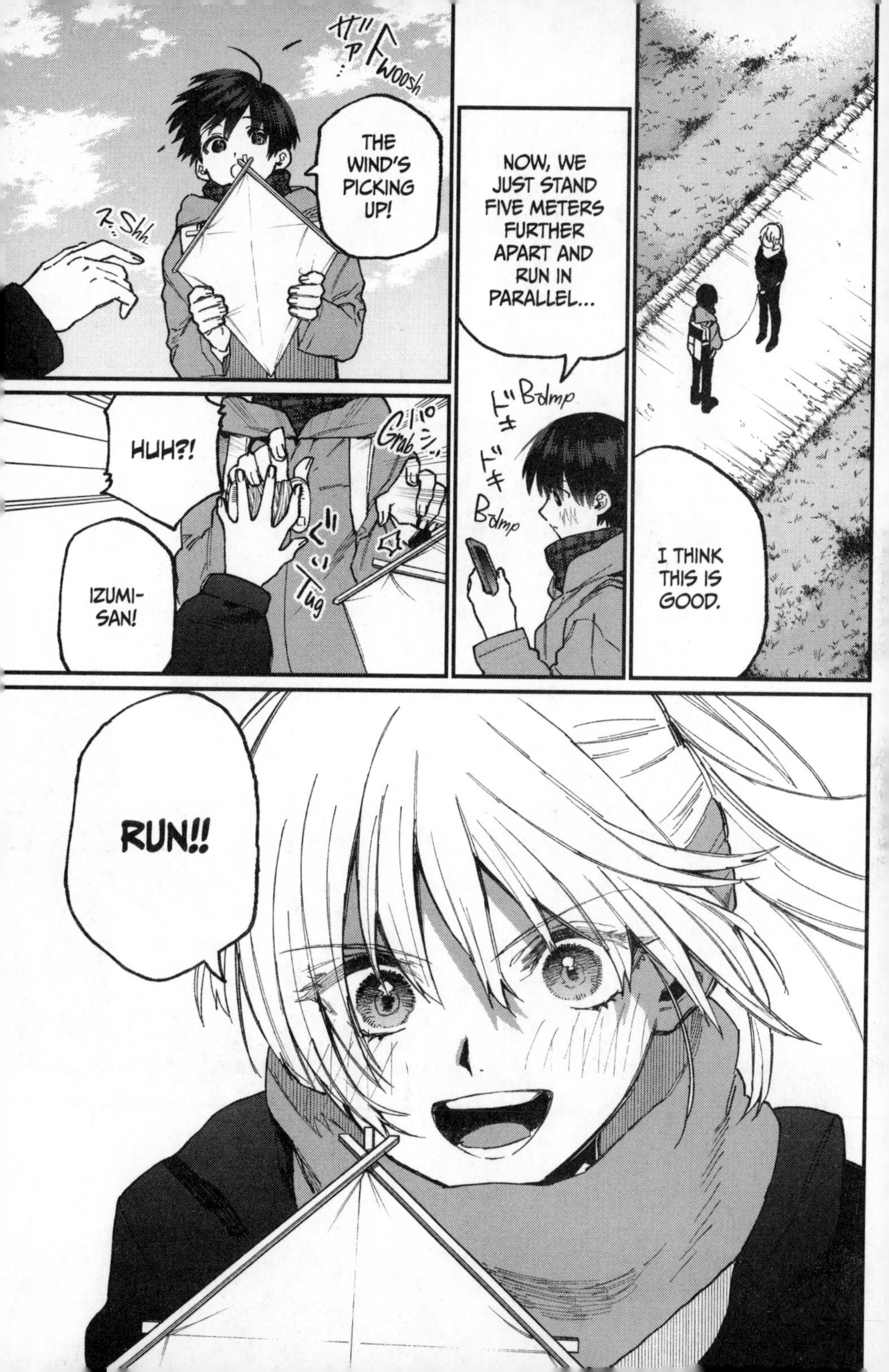
I THINK THIS IS GOOD.
NOW, WE JUST STAND FIVE METERS FURTHER APART AND RUN IN PARALLEL...
Bdmp
Bdmp
Woosh
THE WIND'S PICKING UP!
Shh
Grab
Tug
HUH?!
IZUMI-SAN!
RUN!!

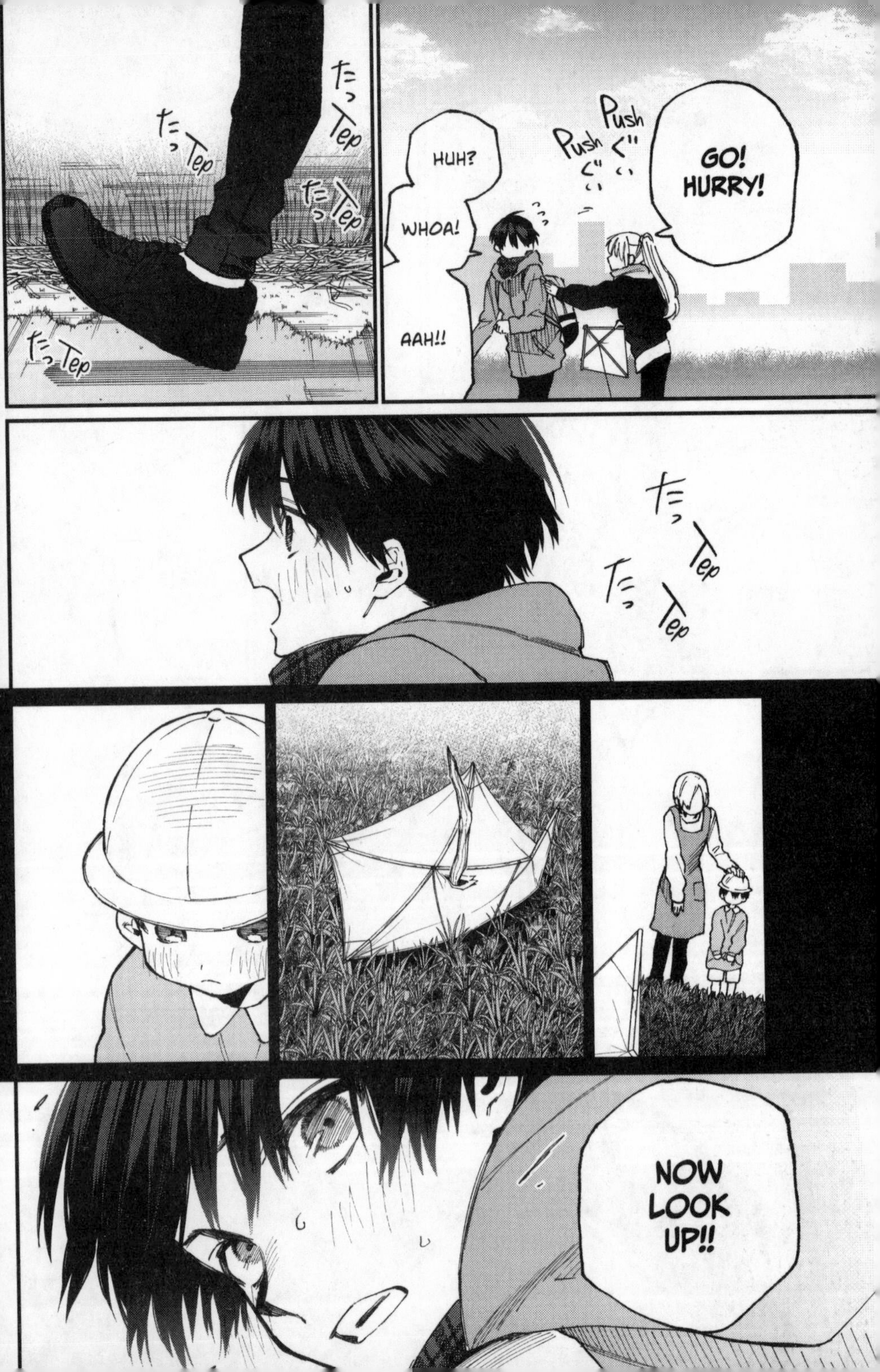
GO! HURRY!
Push ぐい
Push ぐい
HUH?
WHOA!
AAH!!
たっ Tep
たっ Tep
たっ Tep
たっ Tep
たっ Tep
たっ Tep
NOW LOOK UP!!

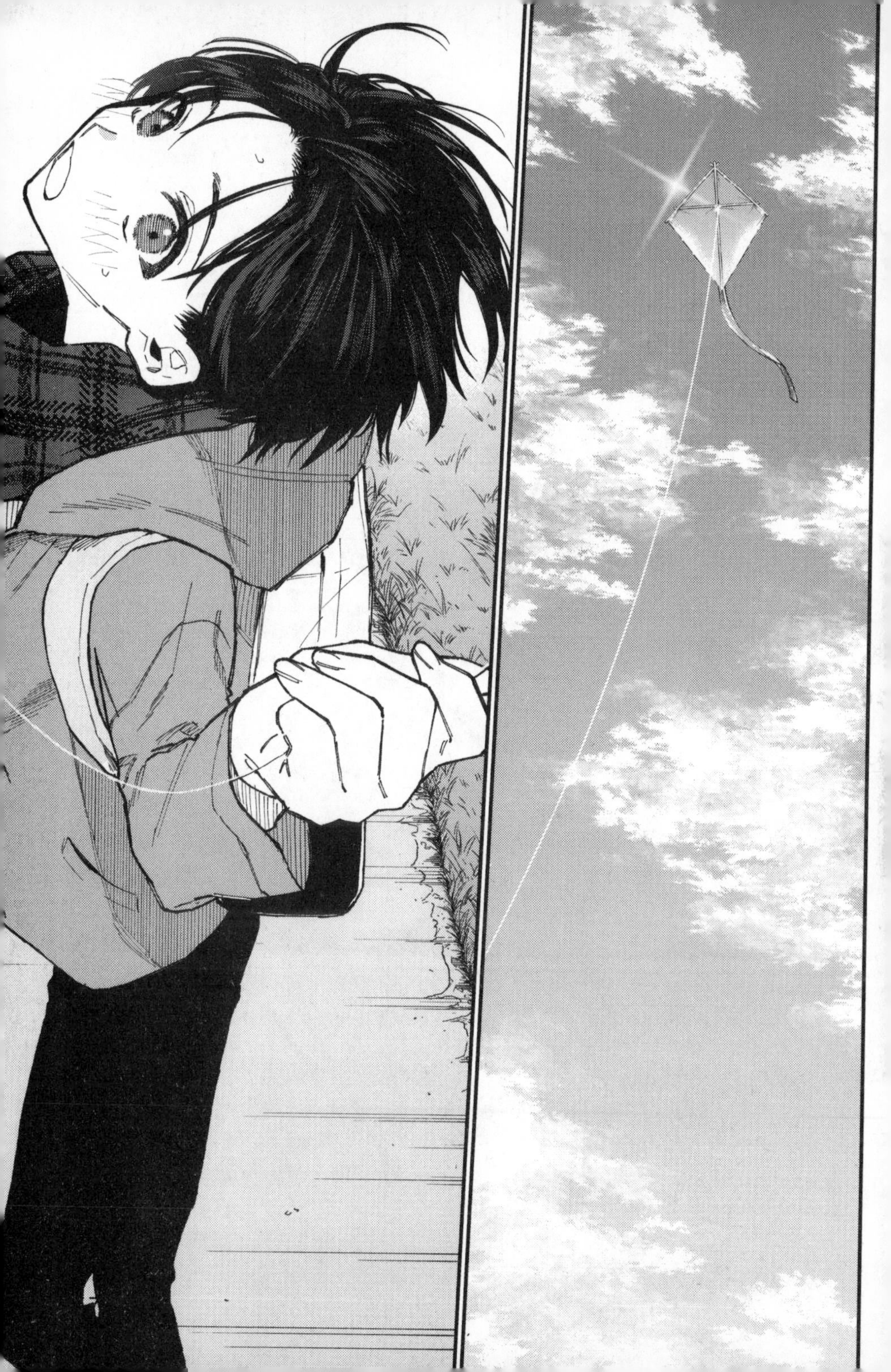

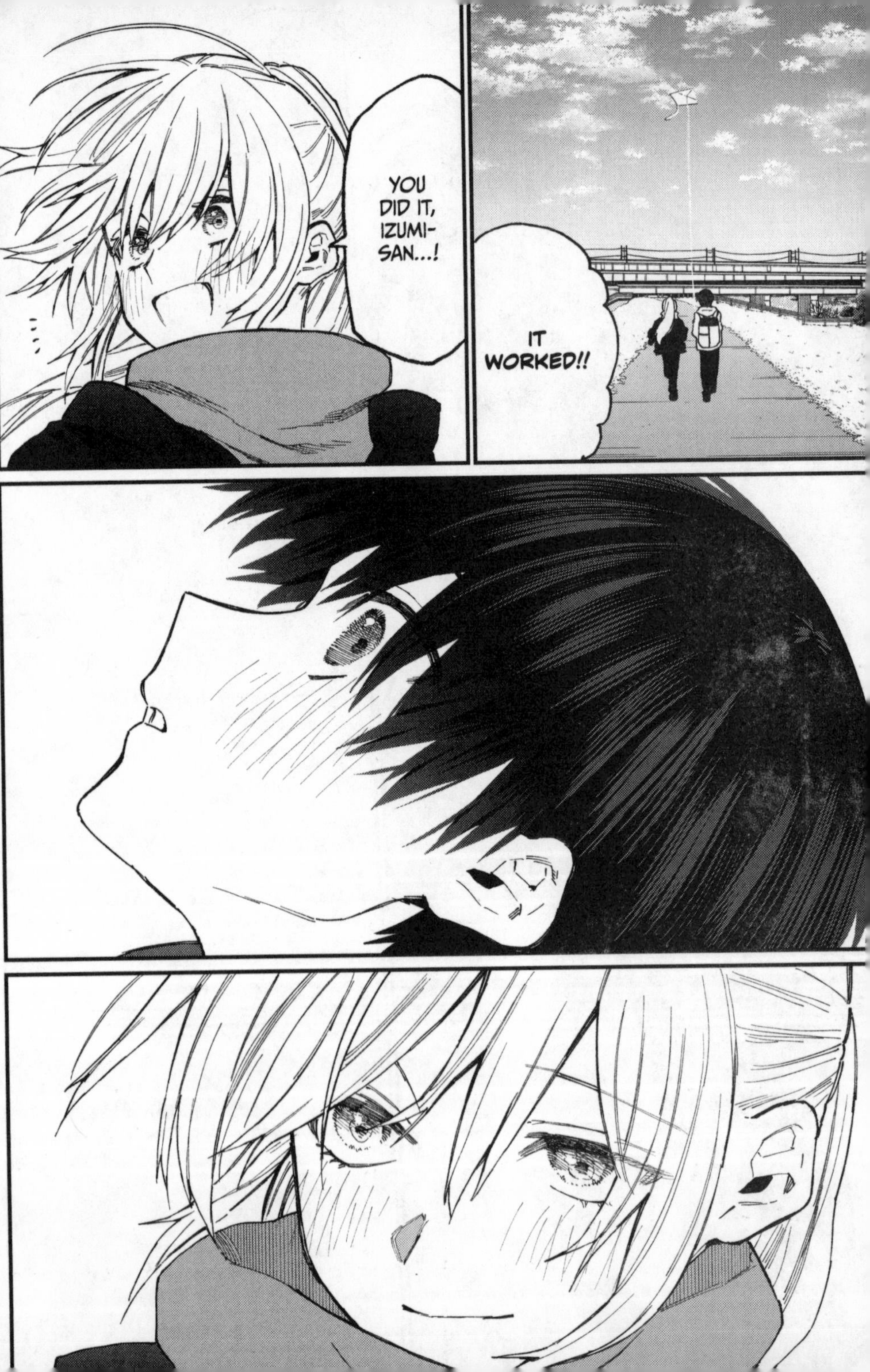
IT WORKED!!
YOU DID IT, IZUMI-SAN...!

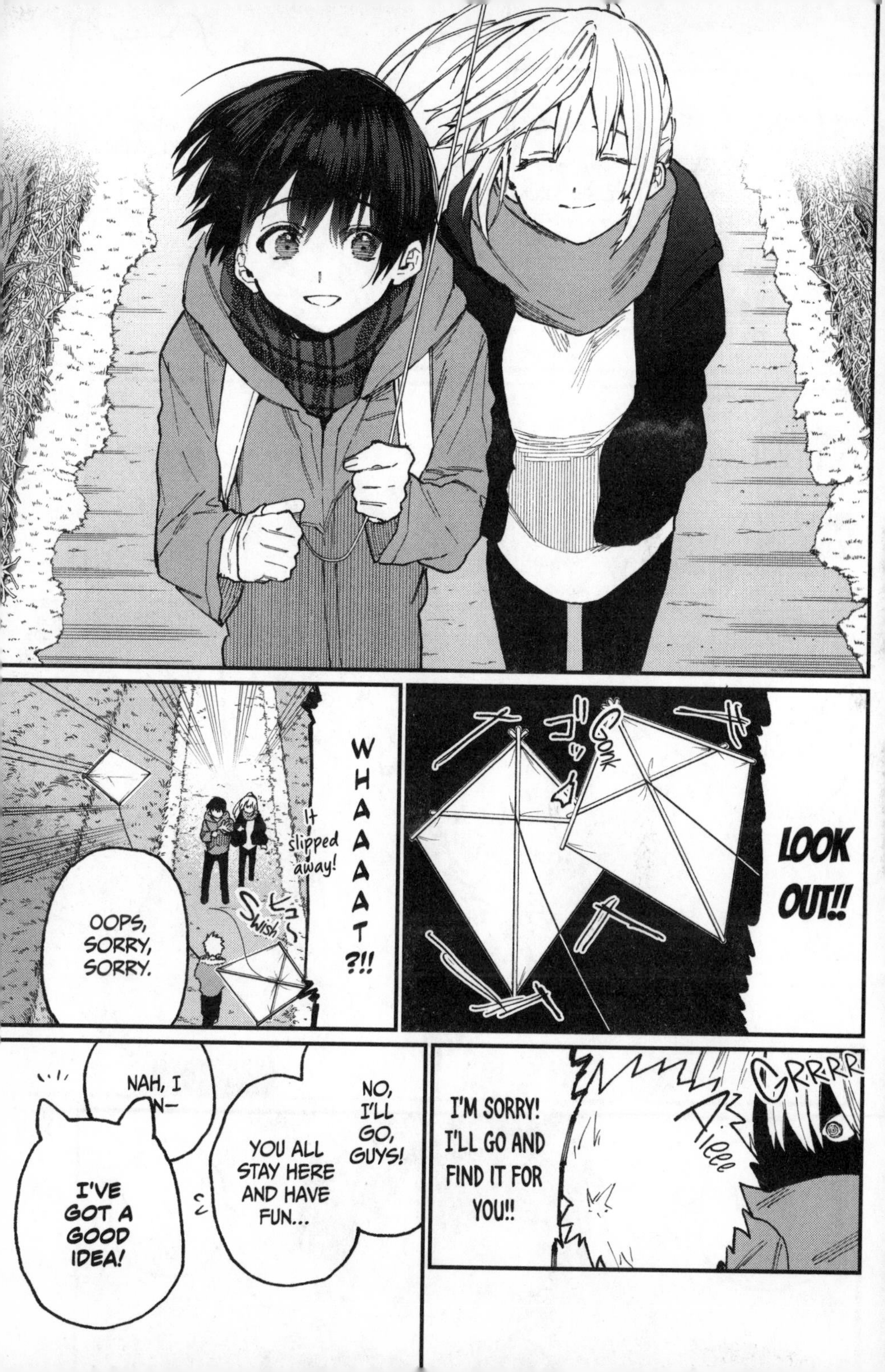
LOOK OUT!!
Gonk
WHAAAAAT?!!
It slipped away!
Swish
OOPS, SORRY, SORRY.
GRRRR
Aieee
I'M SORRY! I'LL GO AND FIND IT FOR YOU!!
NO, I'LL GO, GUYS!
YOU ALL STAY HERE AND HAVE FUN...
NAH, I CAN—
I'VE GOT A GOOD IDEA!

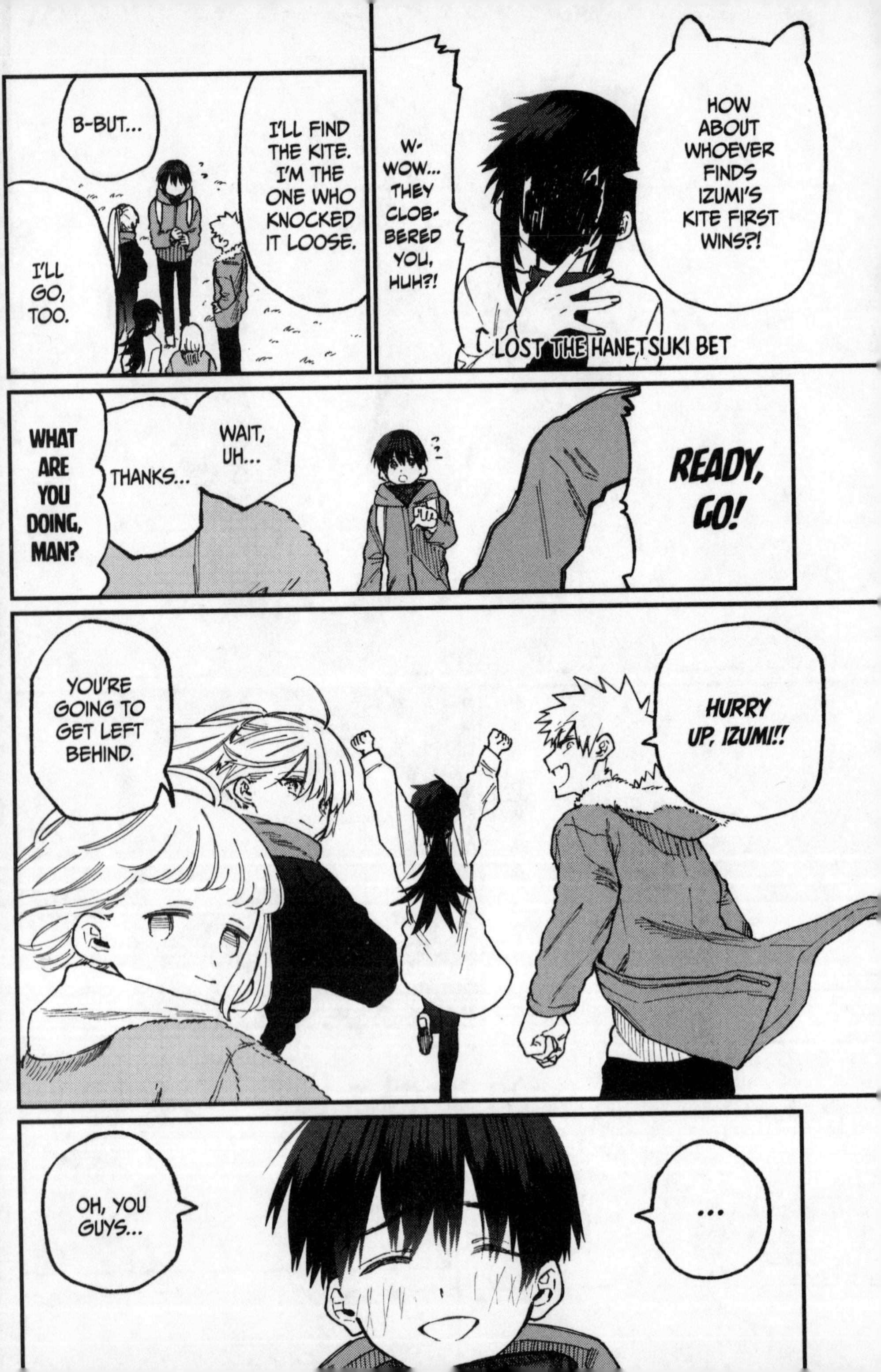
HOW ABOUT WHOEVER FINDS IZUMI'S KITE FIRST WINS?!
W-WOW... THEY CLOBBERED YOU, HUH?!
LOST THE HANETSUKI BET
I'LL FIND THE KITE. I'M THE ONE WHO KNOCKED IT LOOSE.
B-BUT...
I'LL GO, TOO.
READY, GO!
WAIT, UH...
THANKS...
WHAT ARE YOU DOING, MAN?
HURRY UP, IZUMI!!
YOU'RE GOING TO GET LEFT BEHIND.
...
OH, YOU GUYS...

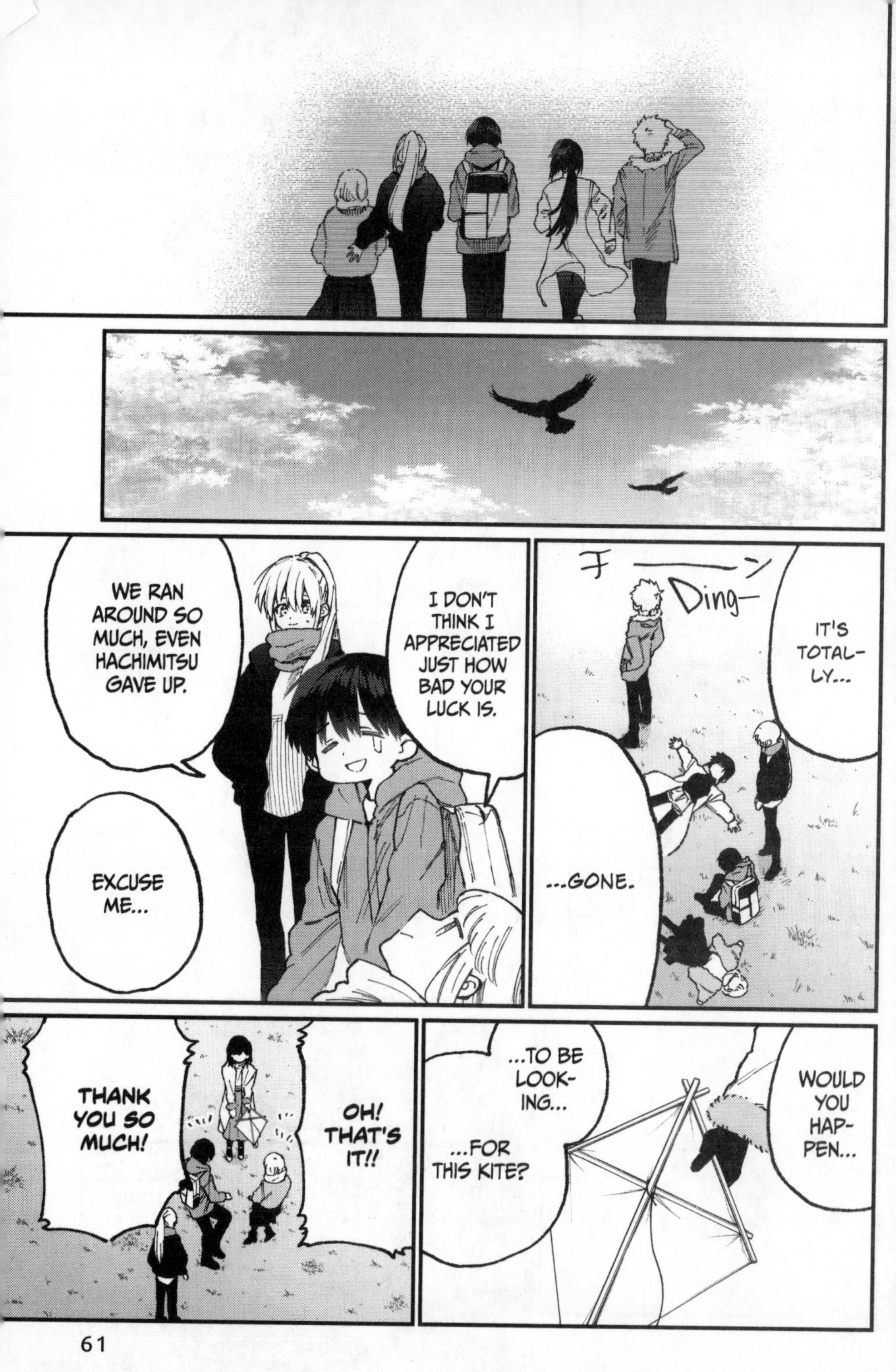
チーーン
Ding—
IT'S TOTAL-LY...
...GONE.
I DON'T THINK I APPRECIATED JUST HOW BAD YOUR LUCK IS.
WE RAN AROUND SO MUCH, EVEN HACHIMITSU GAVE UP.
EXCUSE ME...
WOULD YOU HAP-PEN...
...TO BE LOOK-ING...
...FOR THIS KITE?
OH! THAT'S IT!!
THANK YOU SO MUCH!

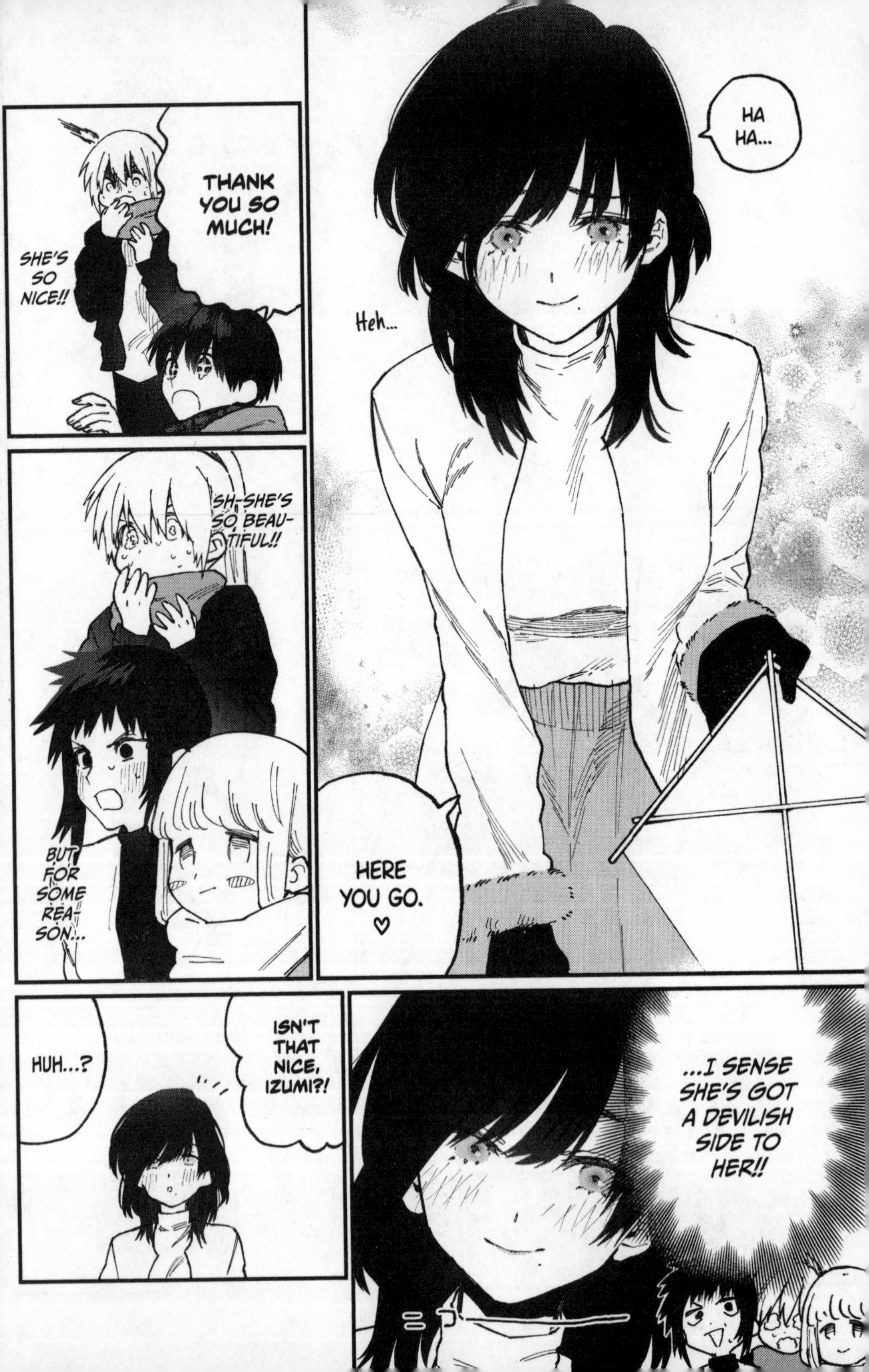

HA HA...
Heh...
HERE YOU GO. ♥
THANK YOU SO MUCH!
SHE'S SO NICE!!
SH-SHE'S SO BEAU-TIFUL!!
BUT FOR SOME REA-SON...
...I SENSE SHE'S GOT A DEVILISH SIDE TO HER!!
ISN'T THAT NICE, IZUMI?!
HUH...?

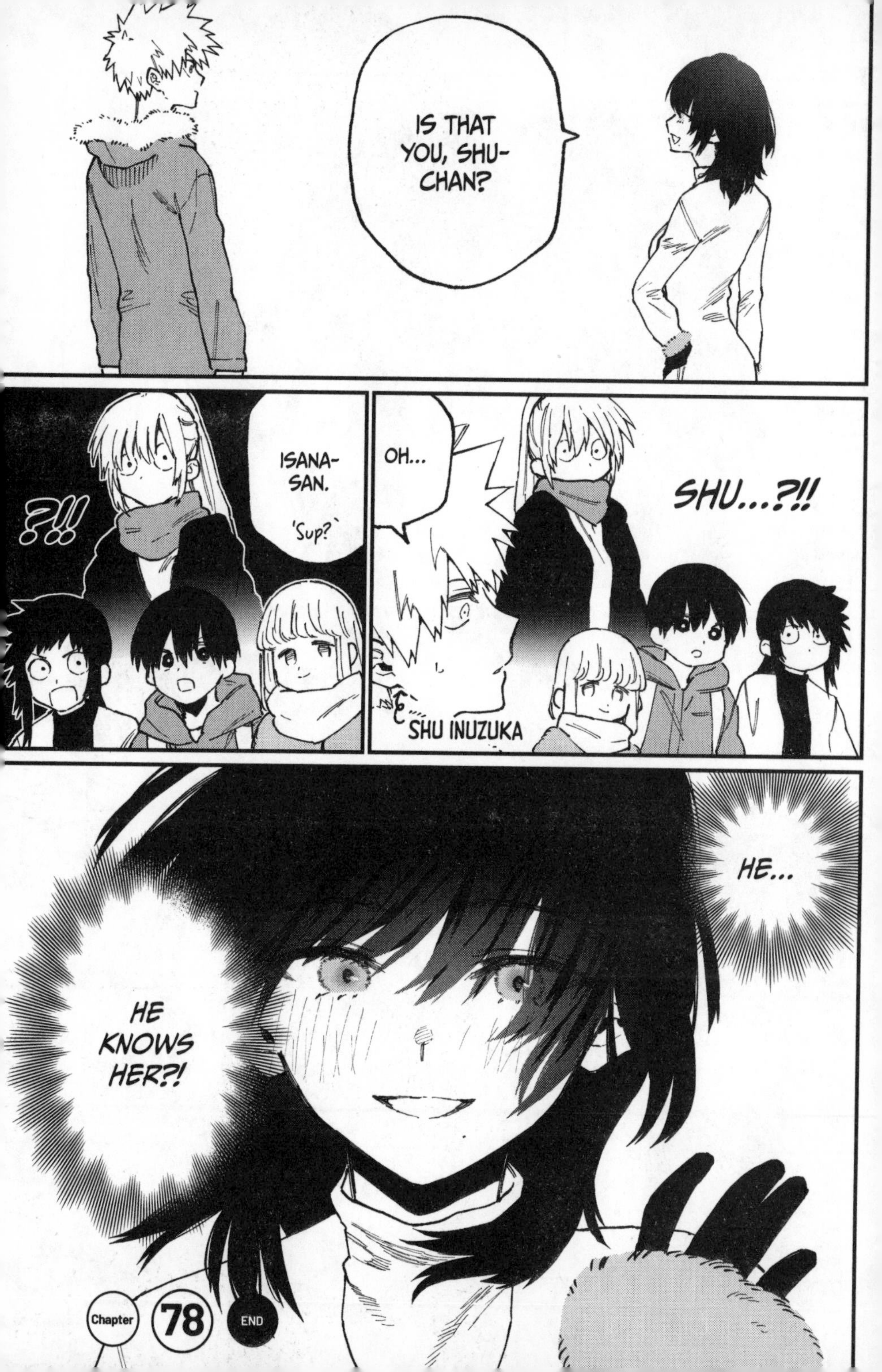
IS THAT YOU, SHU-CHAN?
SHU...?!!
OH...
SHU INUZUKA
ISANA-SAN.
'Sup?'
?!!
HE...
HE KNOWS HER?!
Chapter 78 END

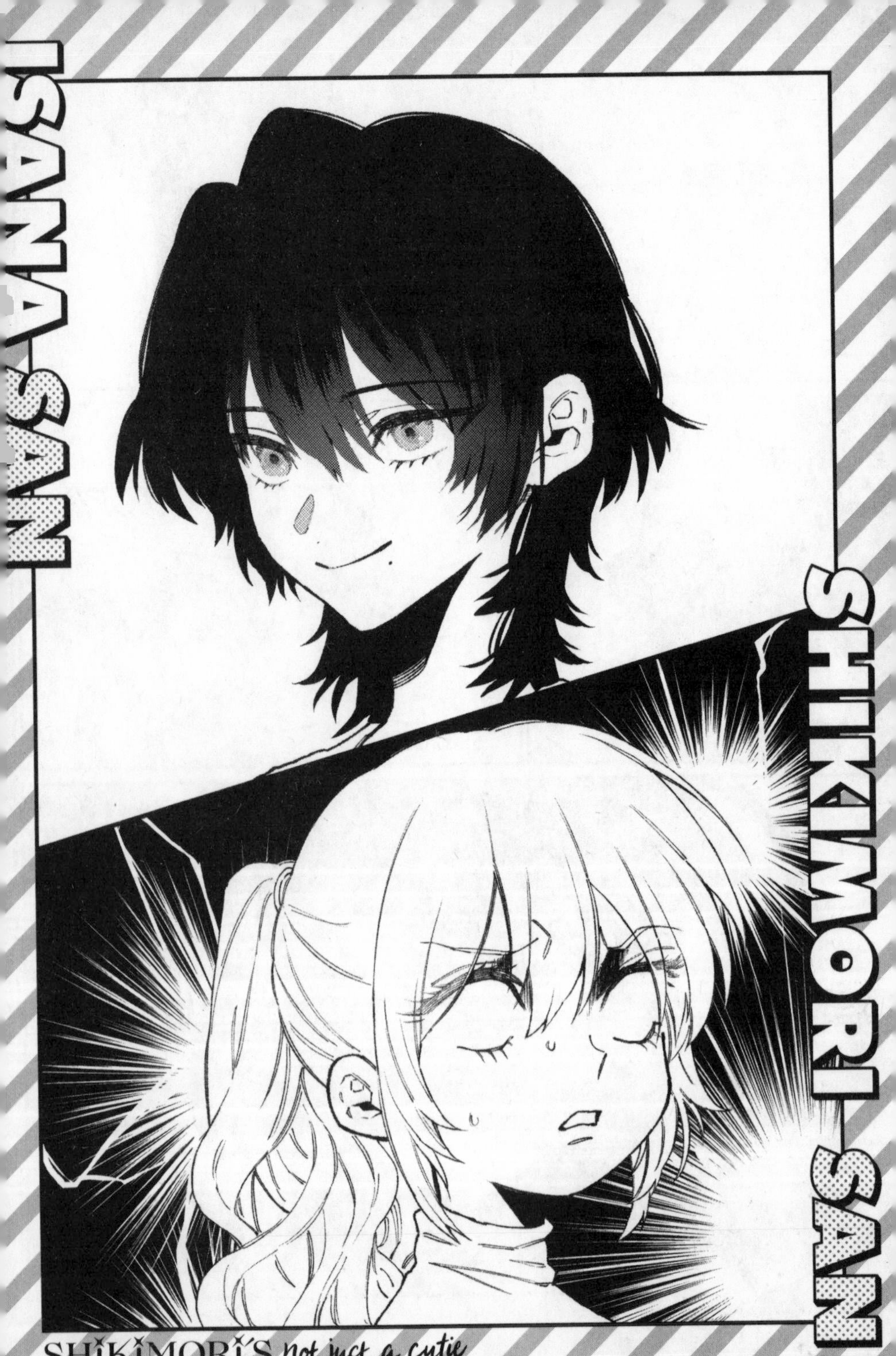
SHIKIMORI-SAN
ISANA-SAN

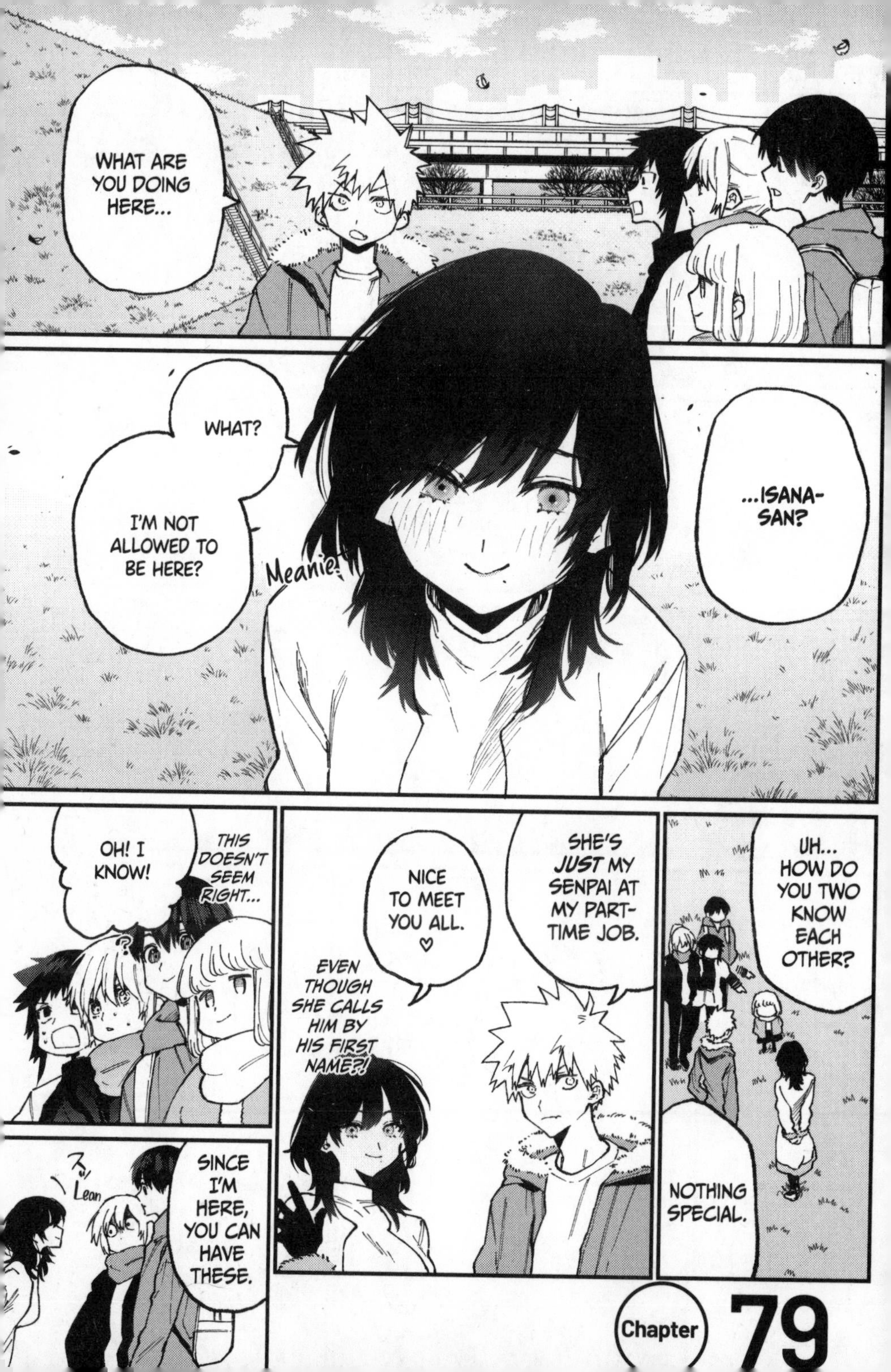
WHAT ARE YOU DOING HERE...
...ISANA-SAN?
WHAT?
I'M NOT ALLOWED TO BE HERE?
Meanie
UH... HOW DO YOU TWO KNOW EACH OTHER?
NOTHING SPECIAL.
SHE'S JUST MY SENPAI AT MY PART-TIME JOB.
NICE TO MEET YOU ALL. ♡
EVEN THOUGH SHE CALLS HIM BY HIS FIRST NAME?!
THIS DOESN'T SEEM RIGHT...
OH! I KNOW!
SINCE I'M HERE, YOU CAN HAVE THESE.
Lean
Chapter 79

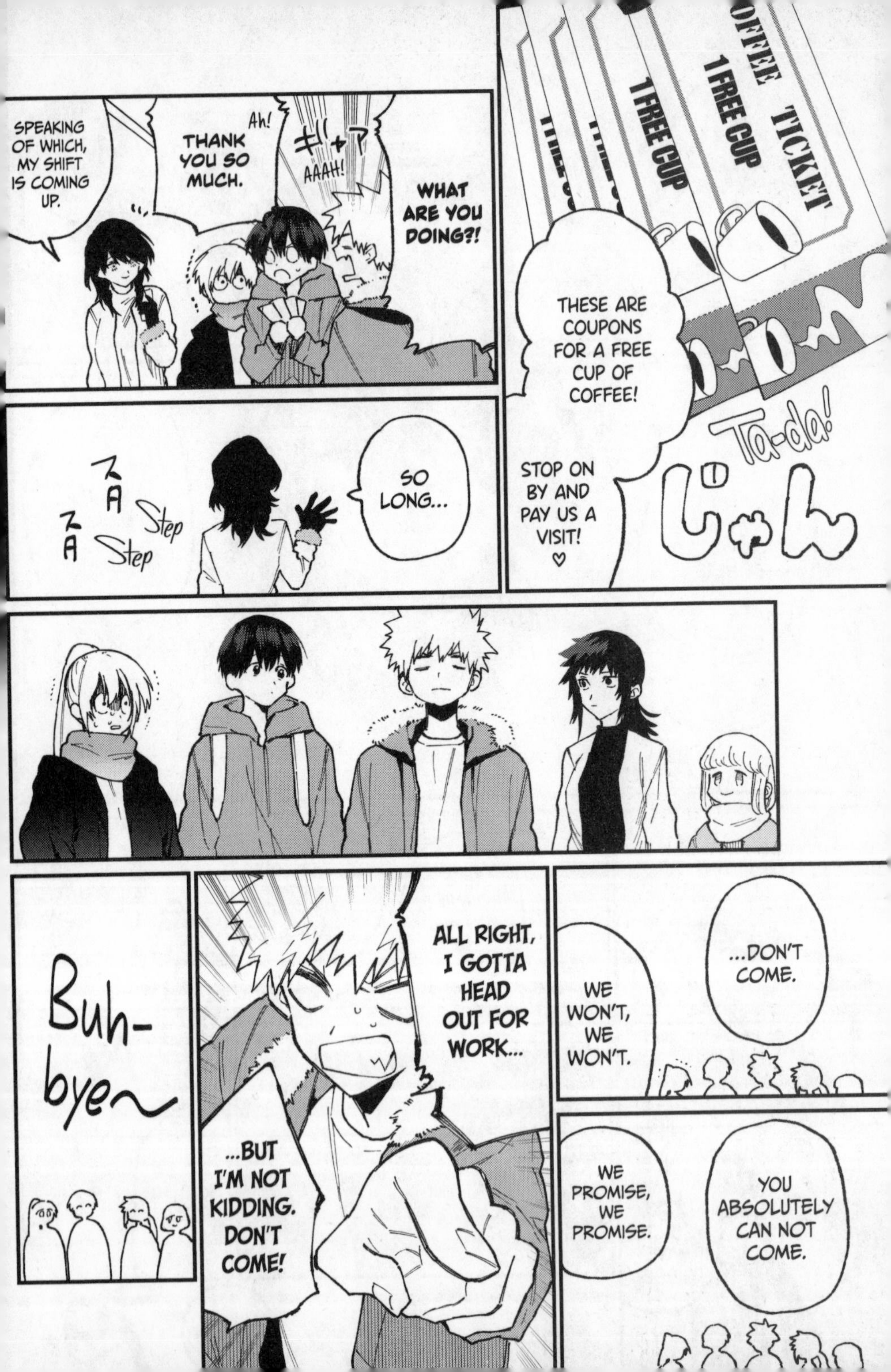
OFFEE TICKET
1 FREE CUP
1 FREE CUP
THESE ARE COUPONS FOR A FREE CUP OF COFFEE!
STOP ON BY AND PAY US A VISIT! ♡
Ta-da!
じゃん
WHAT ARE YOU DOING?!
ギャア
AAAH!
Ah!
THANK YOU SO MUCH.
SPEAKING OF WHICH, MY SHIFT IS COMING UP.
SO LONG...
スタ Step
スタ Step
...DON'T COME.
WE WON'T, WE WON'T.
YOU ABSOLUTELY CAN NOT COME.
WE PROMISE, WE PROMISE.
ALL RIGHT, I GOTTA HEAD OUT FOR WORK...
...BUT I'M NOT KIDDING. DON'T COME!
Buh-bye~

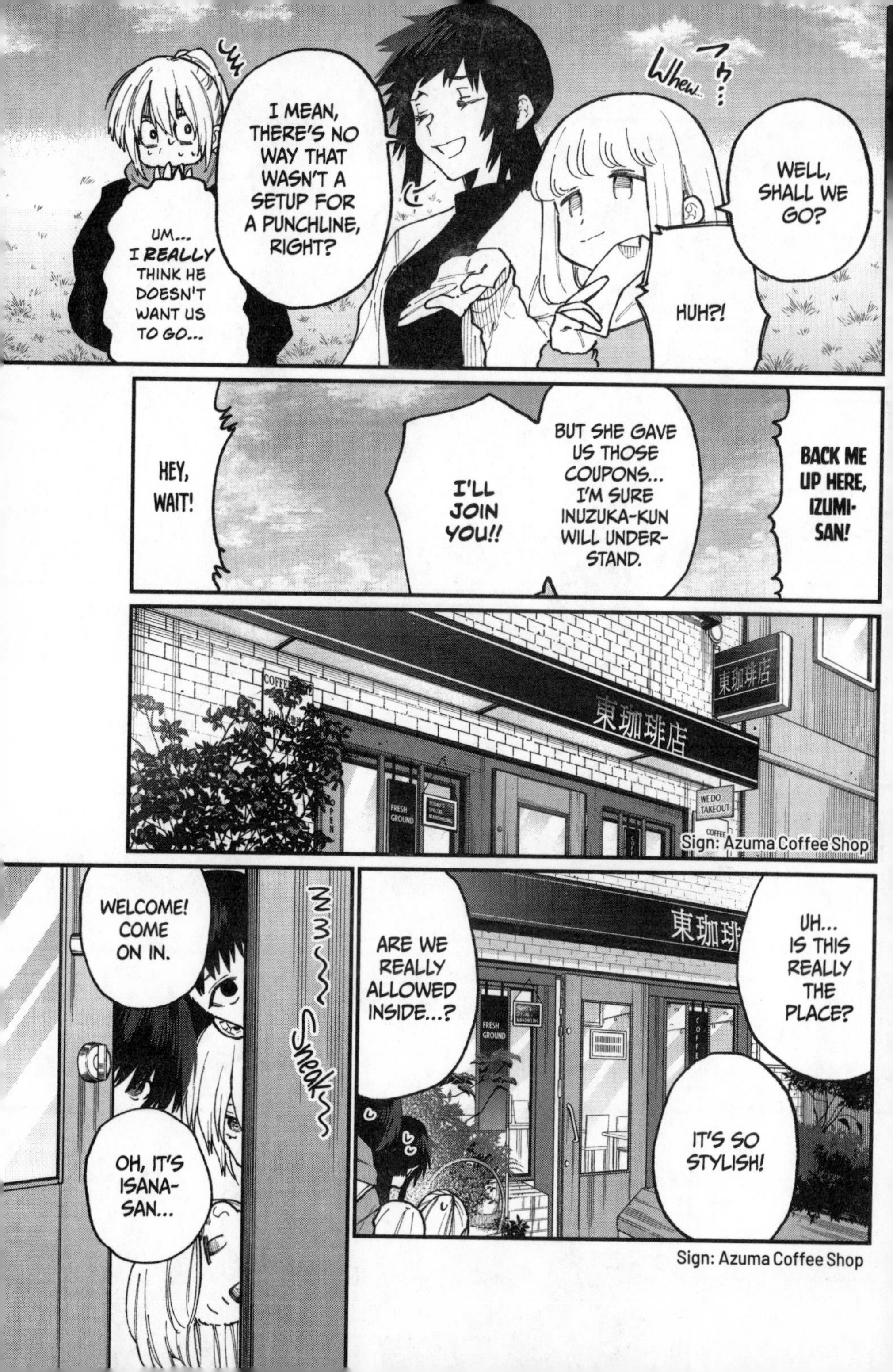
Whew...
WELL, SHALL WE GO?
HUH?!
I MEAN, THERE'S NO WAY THAT WASN'T A SETUP FOR A PUNCHLINE, RIGHT?
UM... I REALLY THINK HE DOESN'T WANT US TO GO...
BACK ME UP HERE, IZUMI-SAN!
BUT SHE GAVE US THOSE COUPONS... I'M SURE INUZUKA-KUN WILL UNDERSTAND.
I'LL JOIN YOU!!
HEY, WAIT!
東珈琲店
東珈琲店
WE DO TAKEOUT
FRESH GROUND
Sign: Azuma Coffee Shop
UH... IS THIS REALLY THE PLACE?
IT'S SO STYLISH!
ARE WE REALLY ALLOWED INSIDE...?
Sign: Azuma Coffee Shop
Sneak~
WELCOME! COME ON IN.
OH, IT'S ISANA-SAN...

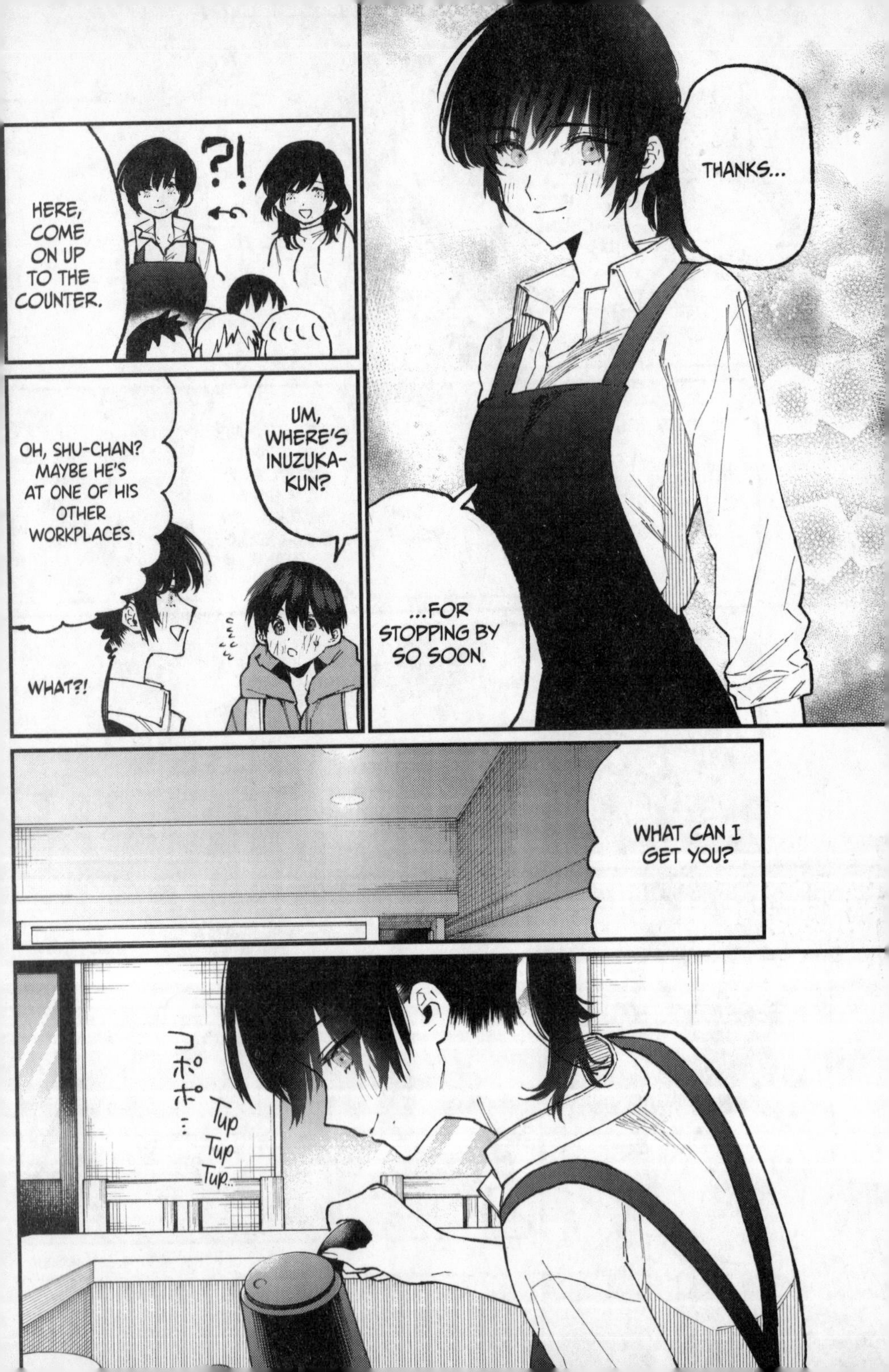
THANKS...
...FOR STOPPING BY SO SOON.
HERE, COME ON UP TO THE COUNTER.
?!
UM, WHERE'S INUZUKA-KUN?
OH, SHU-CHAN? MAYBE HE'S AT ONE OF HIS OTHER WORKPLACES.
WHAT?!
WHAT CAN I GET YOU?
コポポ…
Tup Tup Tup...

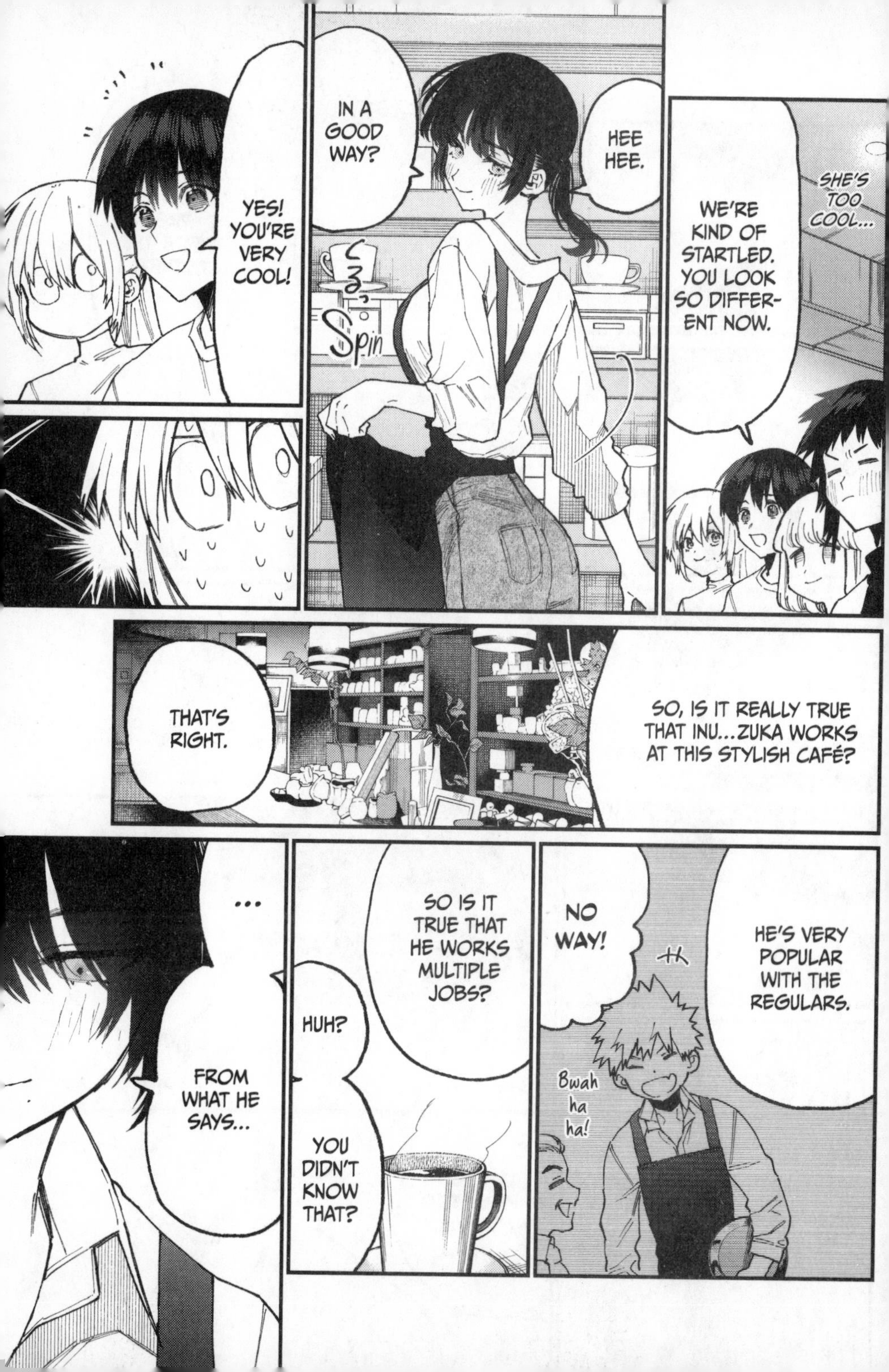
WE'RE KIND OF STARTLED. YOU LOOK SO DIFFER-ENT NOW.
SHE'S TOO COOL...
HEE HEE.
IN A GOOD WAY?
Spin
YES! YOU'RE VERY COOL!
SO, IS IT REALLY TRUE THAT INU...ZUKA WORKS AT THIS STYLISH CAFÉ?
THAT'S RIGHT.
HE'S VERY POPULAR WITH THE REGULARS.
NO WAY!
Bwah ha ha!
SO IS IT TRUE THAT HE WORKS MULTIPLE JOBS?
HUH?
YOU DIDN'T KNOW THAT?
...
FROM WHAT HE SAYS...

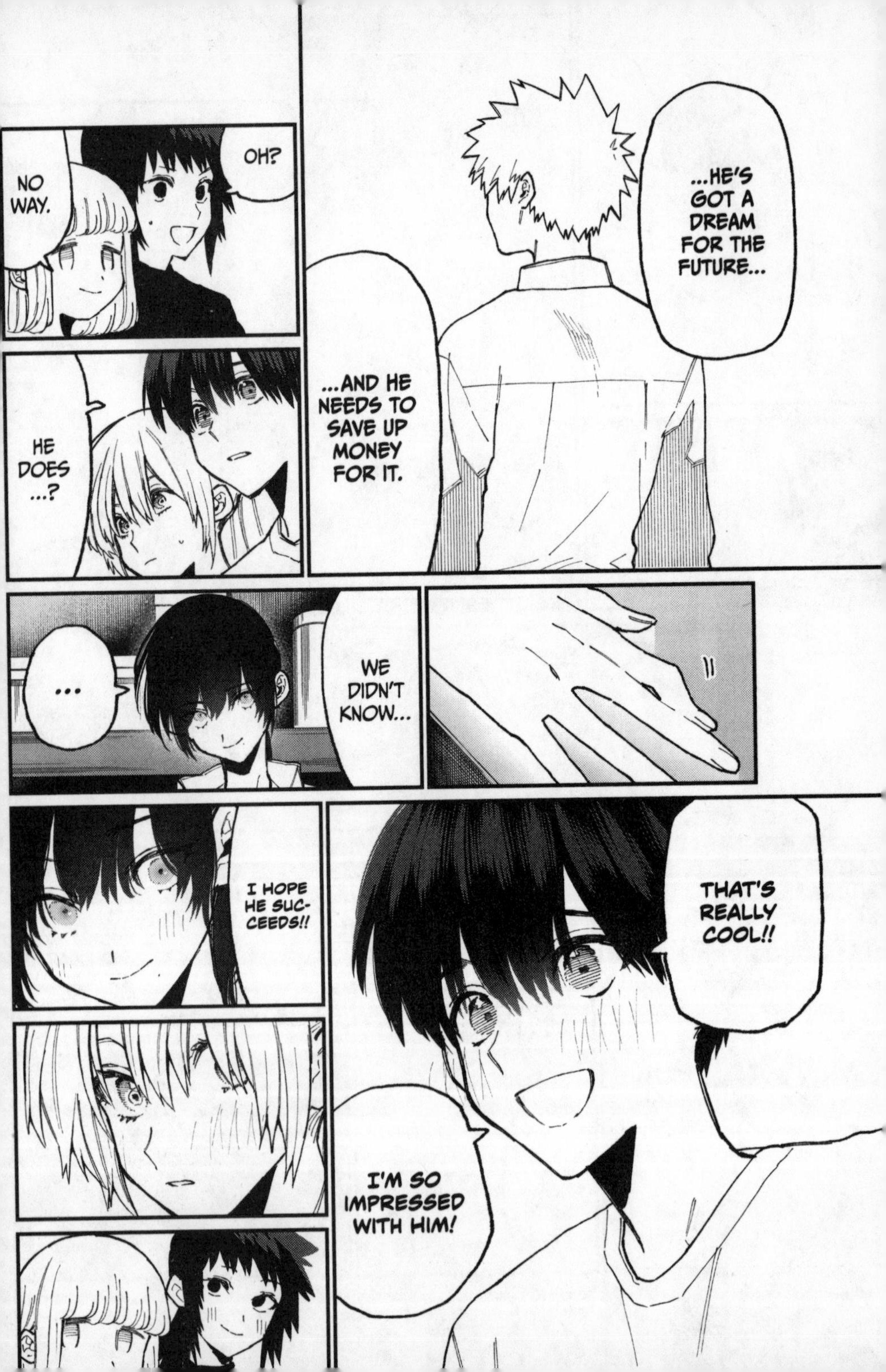
...HE'S GOT A DREAM FOR THE FUTURE...
...AND HE NEEDS TO SAVE UP MONEY FOR IT.
OH?
NO WAY.
HE DOES ...?
!!
WE DIDN'T KNOW...
...
THAT'S REALLY COOL!!
I'M SO IMPRESSED WITH HIM!
I HOPE HE SUC-CEEDS!!

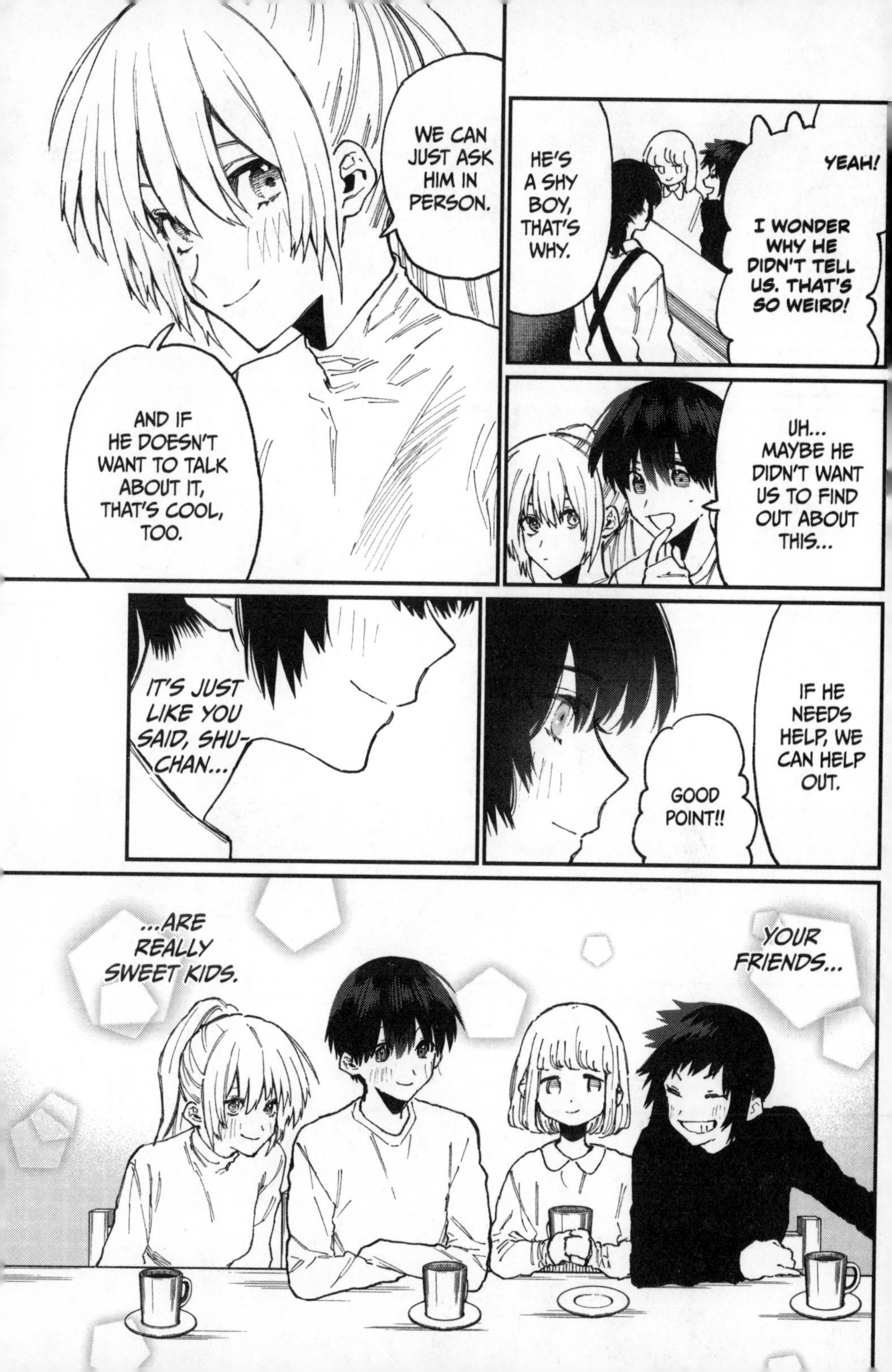
YEAH!
I WONDER WHY HE DIDN'T TELL US. THAT'S SO WEIRD!
HE'S A SHY BOY, THAT'S WHY.
UH... MAYBE HE DIDN'T WANT US TO FIND OUT ABOUT THIS...
WE CAN JUST ASK HIM IN PERSON.
AND IF HE DOESN'T WANT TO TALK ABOUT IT, THAT'S COOL, TOO.
IF HE NEEDS HELP, WE CAN HELP OUT.
GOOD POINT!!
IT'S JUST LIKE YOU SAID, SHU-CHAN...
YOUR FRIENDS...
...ARE REALLY SWEET KIDS.

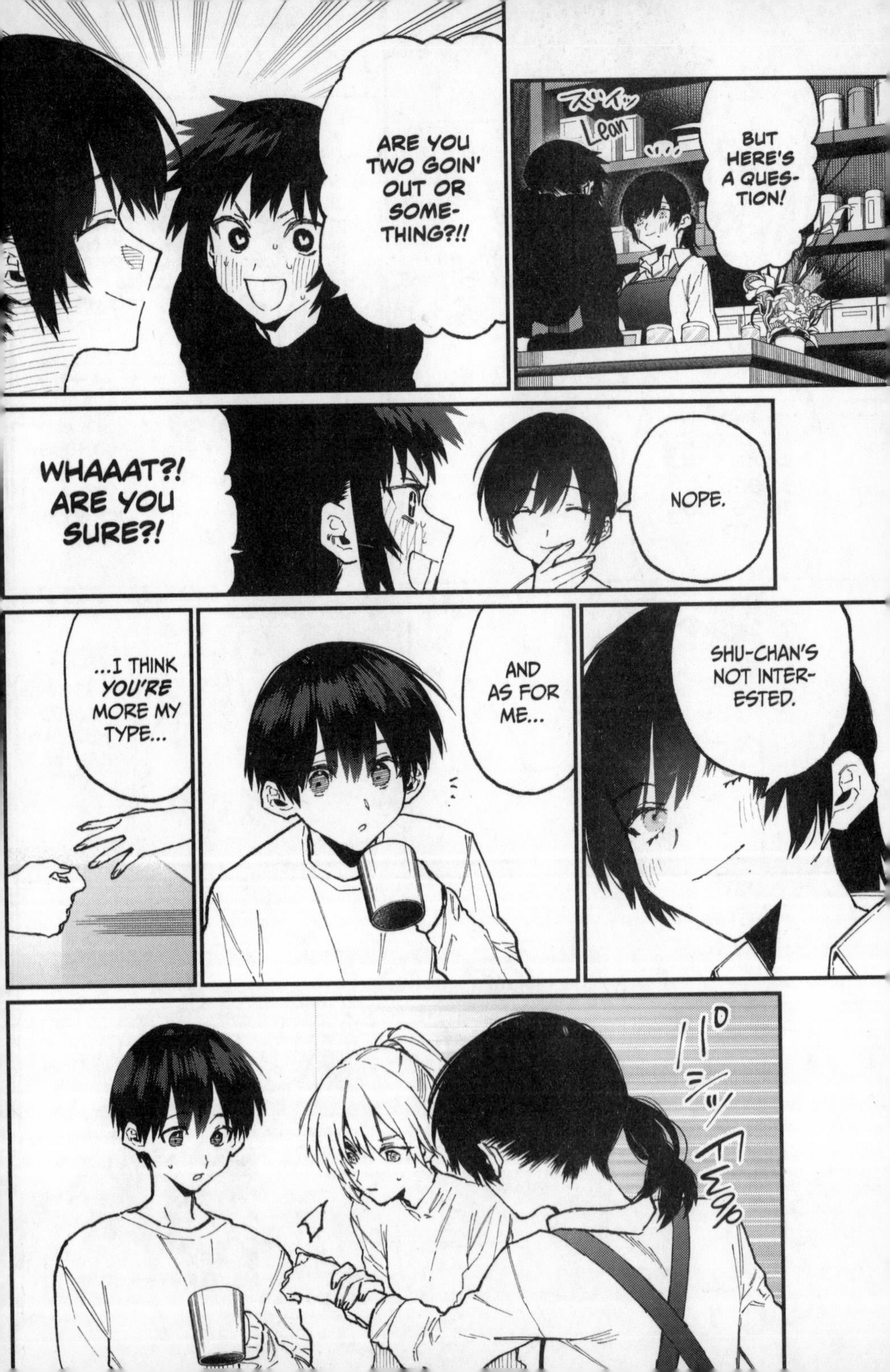
スイッ
Lean
BUT HERE'S A QUESTION!
ARE YOU TWO GOIN' OUT OR SOMETHING?!!
NOPE.
WHAAAT?! ARE YOU SURE?!
SHU-CHAN'S NOT INTERESTED.
AND AS FOR ME...
...I THINK *YOU'RE* MORE MY TYPE...
パシッ
Fwap

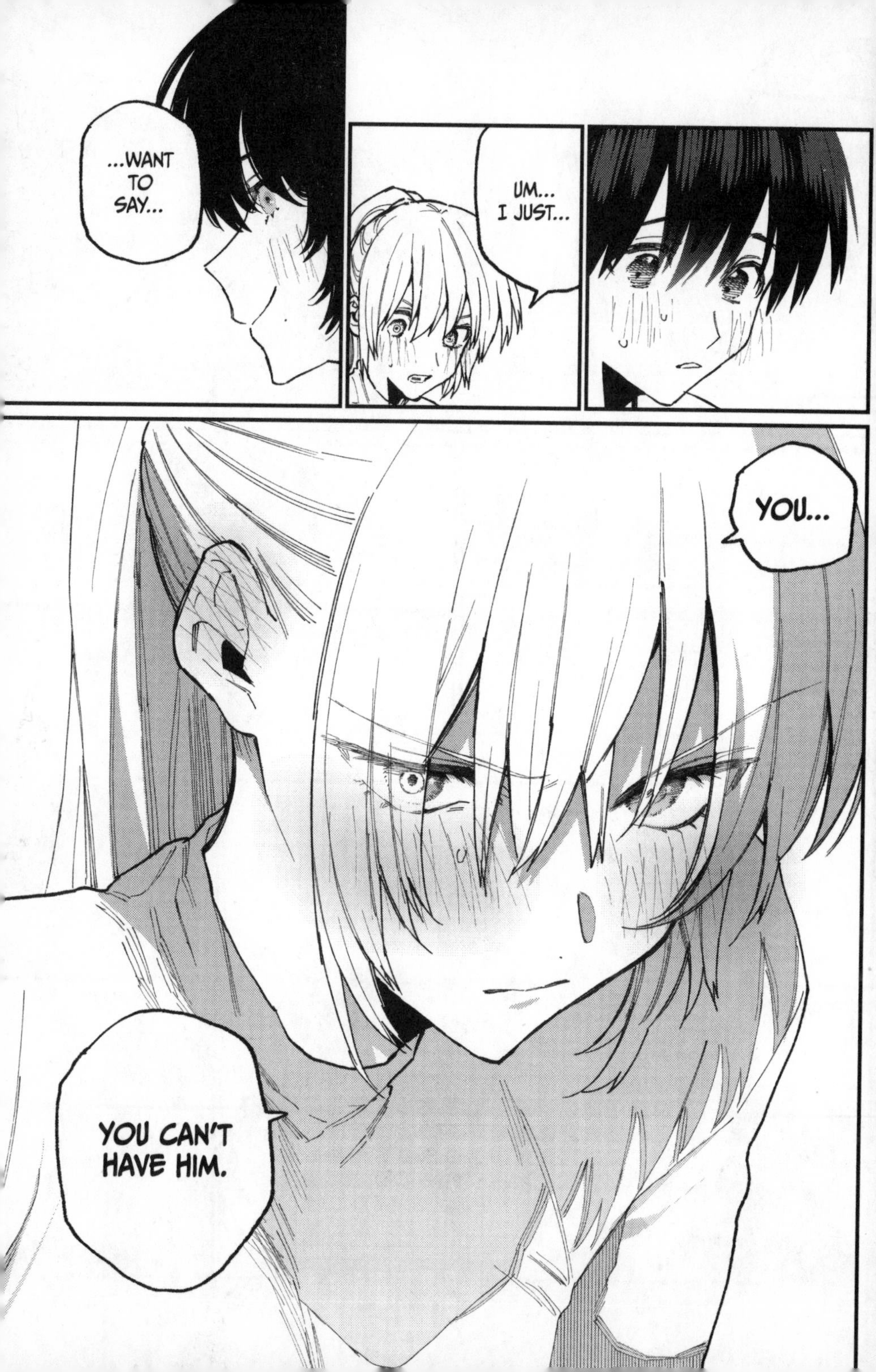
UM... I JUST...
...WANT TO SAY...
YOU...
YOU CAN'T HAVE HIM.

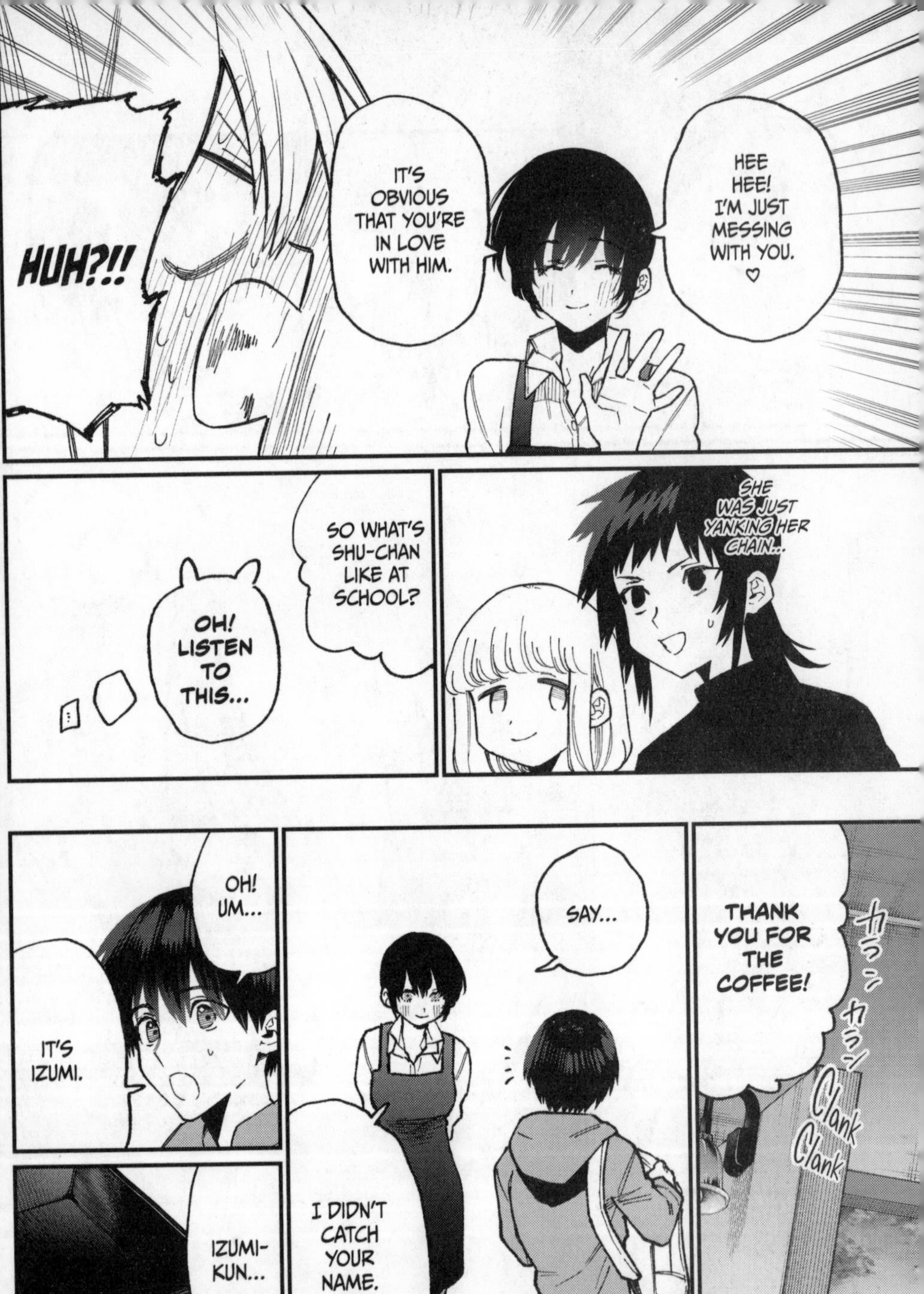
HEE HEE! I'M JUST MESSING WITH YOU. ♡
IT'S OBVIOUS THAT YOU'RE IN LOVE WITH HIM.
HUH?!!
SHE WAS JUST YANKING HER CHAIN...
SO WHAT'S SHU-CHAN LIKE AT SCHOOL?
OH! LISTEN TO THIS...
THANK YOU FOR THE COFFEE!
カランカラン
Clank Clank
SAY...
I DIDN'T CATCH YOUR NAME.
OH! UM...
IT'S IZUMI.
IZUMI-KUN...

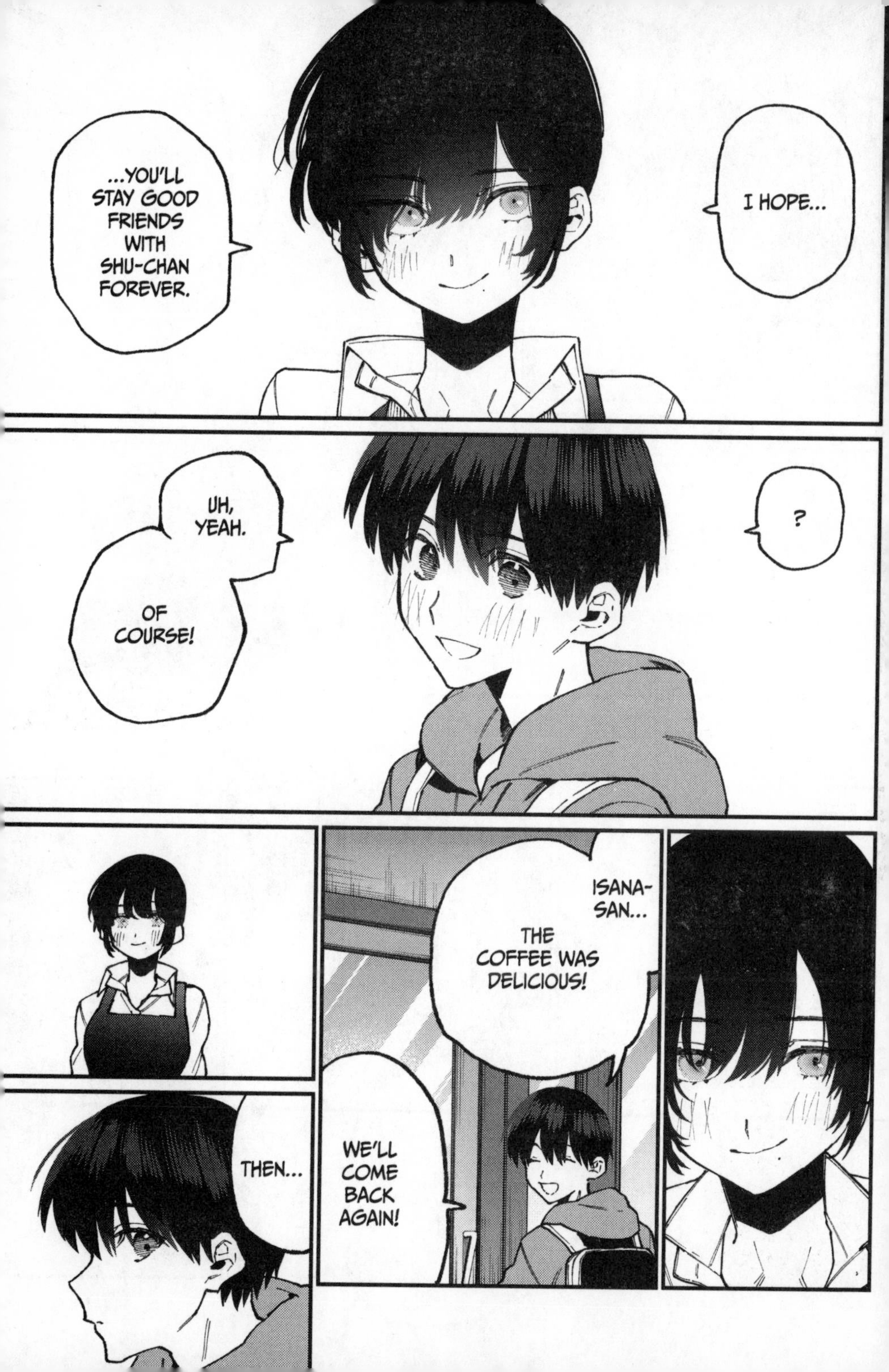
I HOPE...
...YOU'LL STAY GOOD FRIENDS WITH SHU-CHAN FOREVER.
?
UH, YEAH.
OF COURSE!
ISANA-SAN... THE COFFEE WAS DELICIOUS!
WE'LL COME BACK AGAIN!
THEN...

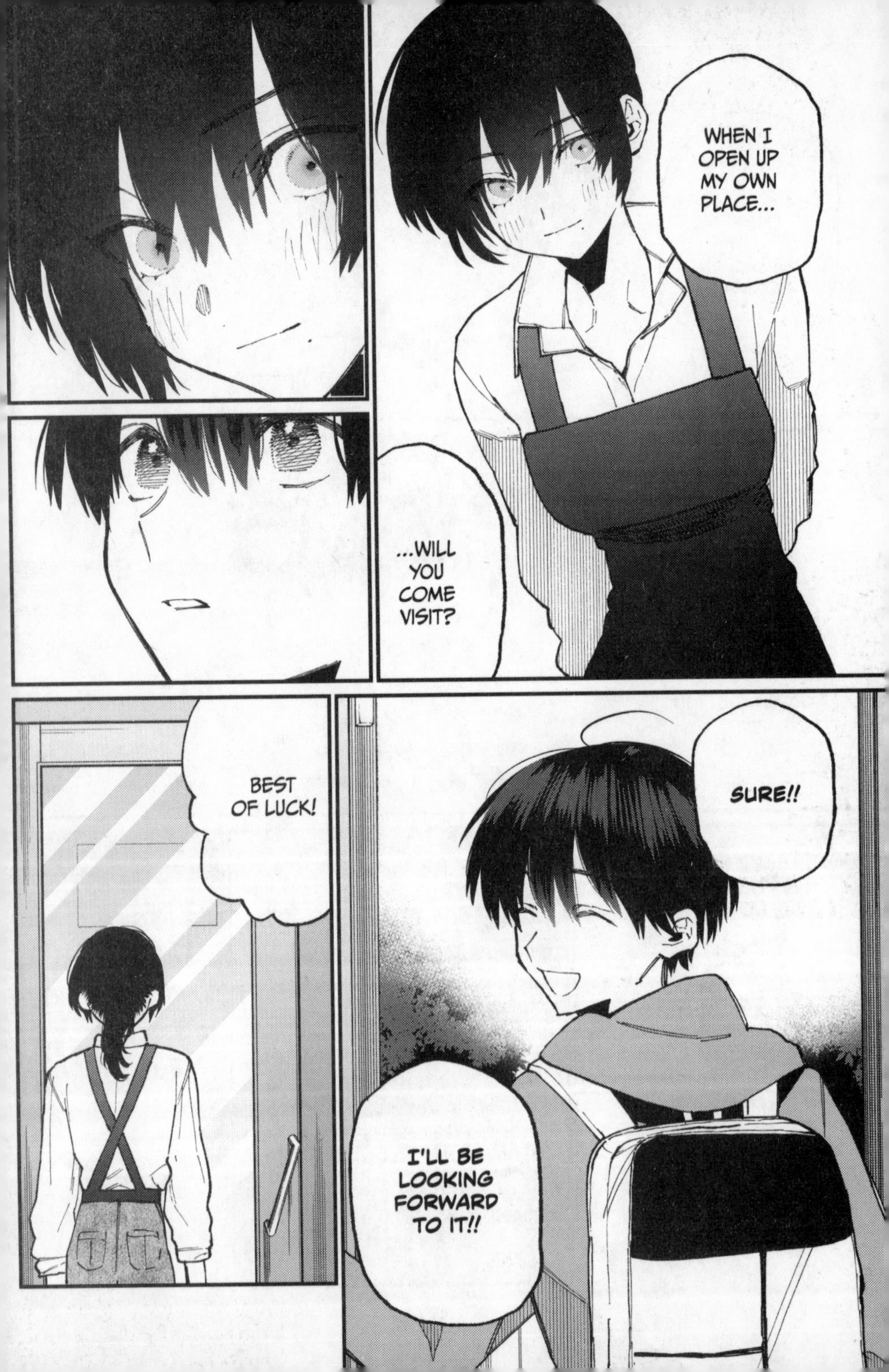
WHEN I OPEN UP MY OWN PLACE...
...WILL YOU COME VISIT?
SURE!!
I'LL BE LOOKING FORWARD TO IT!!
BEST OF LUCK!

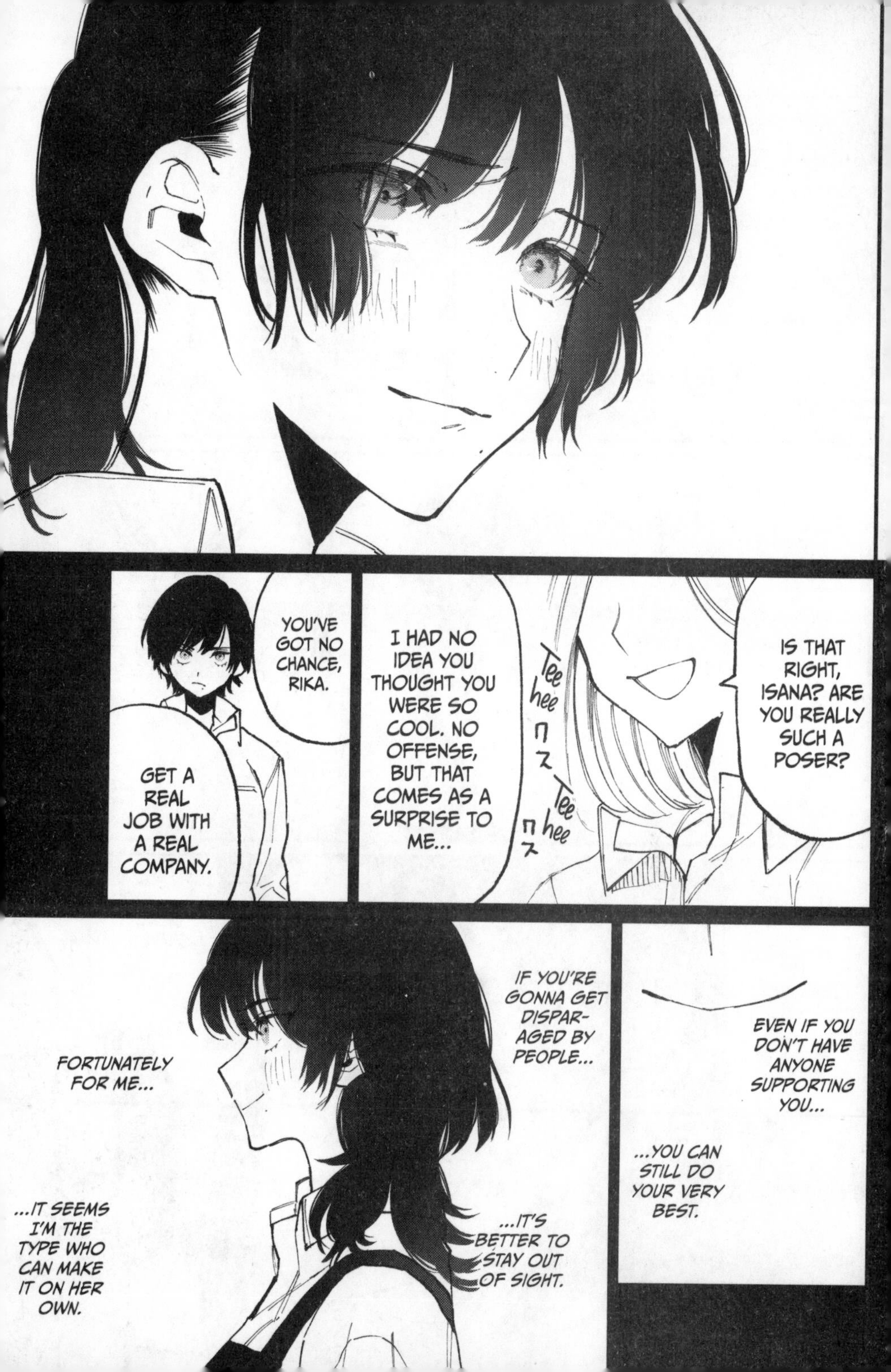
IS THAT RIGHT, ISANA? ARE YOU REALLY SUCH A POSER?
Tee hee
Tee hee
I HAD NO IDEA YOU THOUGHT YOU WERE SO COOL. NO OFFENSE, BUT THAT COMES AS A SURPRISE TO ME...
YOU'VE GOT NO CHANCE, RIKA.
GET A REAL JOB WITH A REAL COMPANY.
EVEN IF YOU DON'T HAVE ANYONE SUPPORTING YOU...
...YOU CAN STILL DO YOUR VERY BEST.
IF YOU'RE GONNA GET DISPAR-AGED BY PEOPLE...
...IT'S BETTER TO STAY OUT OF SIGHT.
FORTUNATELY FOR ME...
...IT SEEMS I'M THE TYPE WHO CAN MAKE IT ON HER OWN.

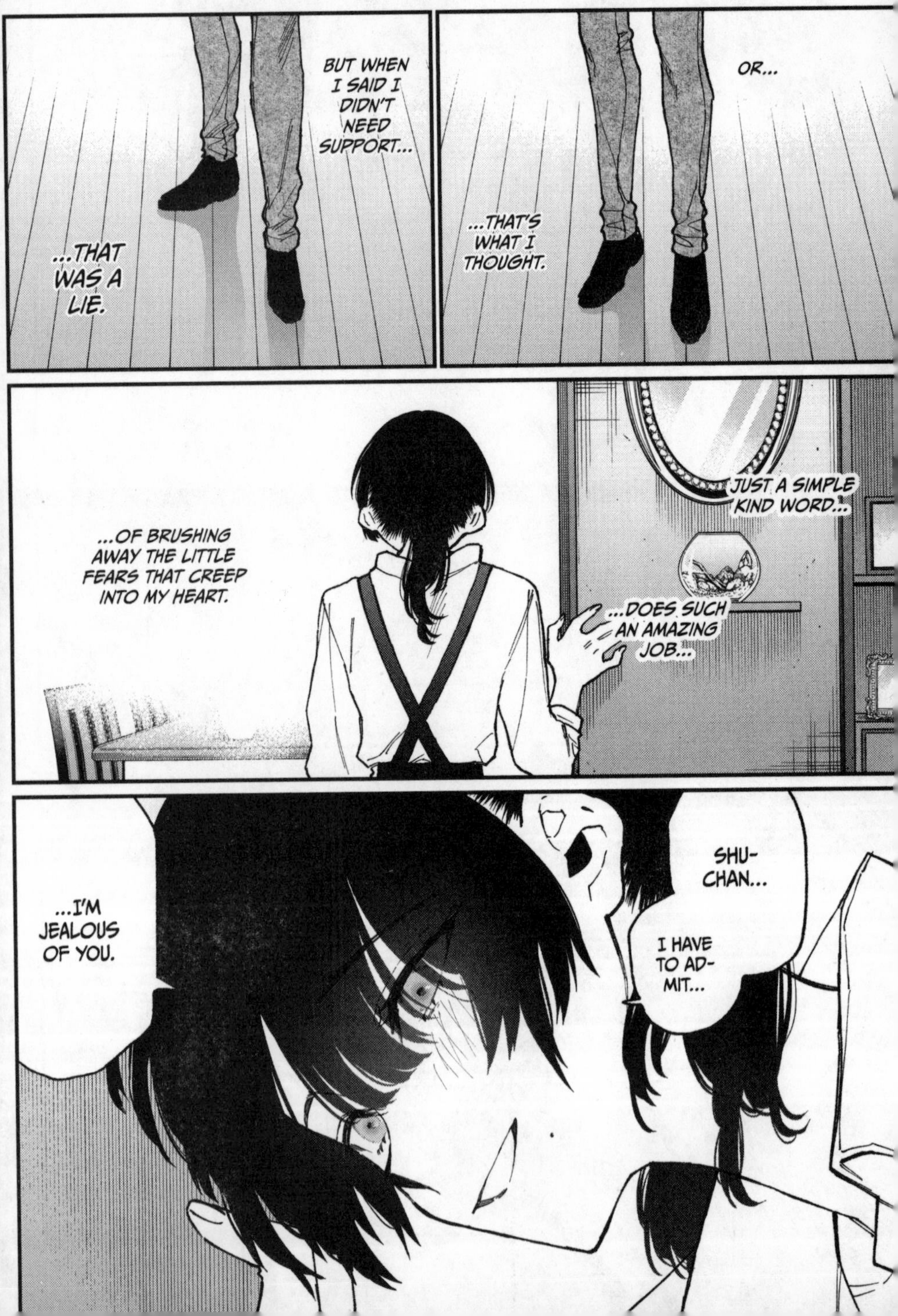
OR...
...THAT'S WHAT I THOUGHT.
BUT WHEN I SAID I DIDN'T NEED SUPPORT...
...THAT WAS A LIE.
JUST A SIMPLE KIND WORD...
...DOES SUCH AN AMAZING JOB...
...OF BRUSHING AWAY THE LITTLE FEARS THAT CREEP INTO MY HEART.
SHU-CHAN...
I HAVE TO AD-MIT...
...I'M JEALOUS OF YOU.

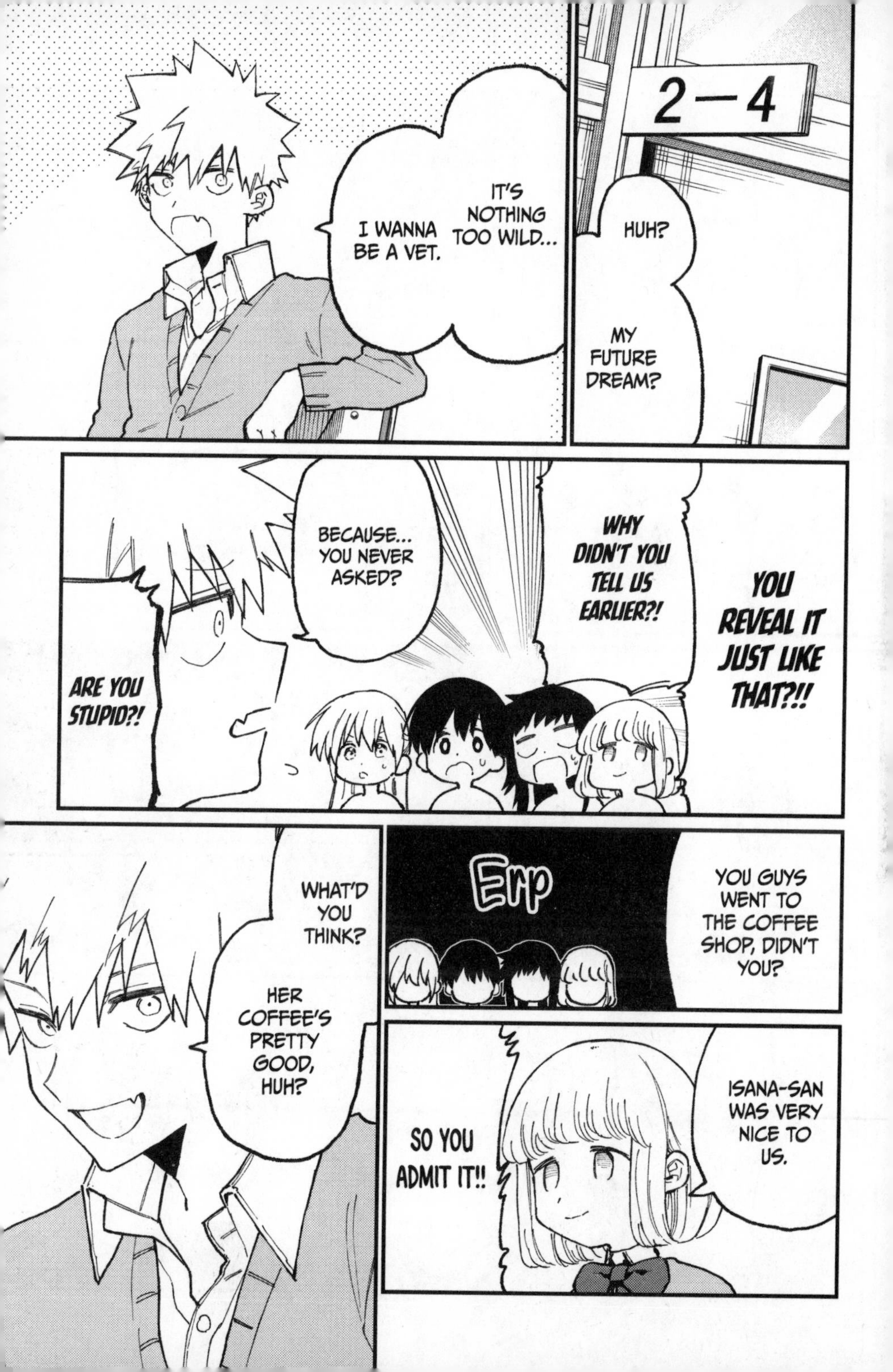
2—4
HUH?
MY FUTURE DREAM?
IT'S NOTHING TOO WILD...
I WANNA BE A VET.
YOU REVEAL IT JUST LIKE THAT?!!
WHY DIDN'T YOU TELL US EARLIER?!
BECAUSE... YOU NEVER ASKED?
ARE YOU STUPID?!
YOU GUYS WENT TO THE COFFEE SHOP, DIDN'T YOU?
Erp
ISANA-SAN WAS VERY NICE TO US.
SO YOU ADMIT IT!!
WHAT'D YOU THINK?
HER COFFEE'S PRETTY GOOD, HUH?

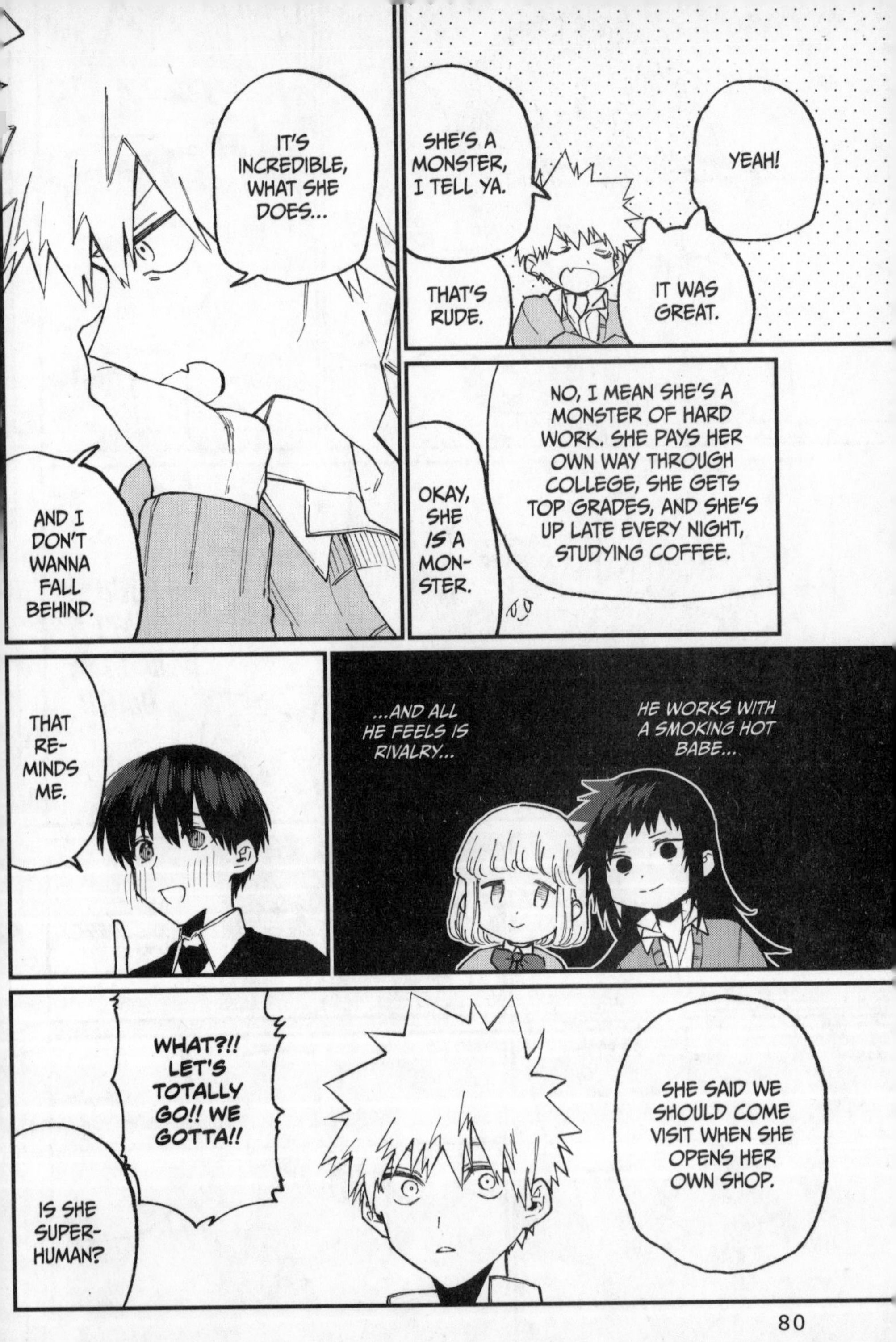
YEAH!
SHE'S A MONSTER, I TELL YA.
IT WAS GREAT.
THAT'S RUDE.
NO, I MEAN SHE'S A MONSTER OF HARD WORK. SHE PAYS HER OWN WAY THROUGH COLLEGE, SHE GETS TOP GRADES, AND SHE'S UP LATE EVERY NIGHT, STUDYING COFFEE.
OKAY, SHE *IS* A MONSTER.
IT'S INCREDIBLE, WHAT SHE DOES...
AND I DON'T WANNA FALL BEHIND.
HE WORKS WITH A SMOKING HOT BABE...
...AND ALL HE FEELS IS RIVALRY...
THAT REMINDS ME.
SHE SAID WE SHOULD COME VISIT WHEN SHE OPENS HER OWN SHOP.
WHAT?!! LET'S TOTALLY GO!! WE GOTTA!!
IS SHE SUPERHUMAN?

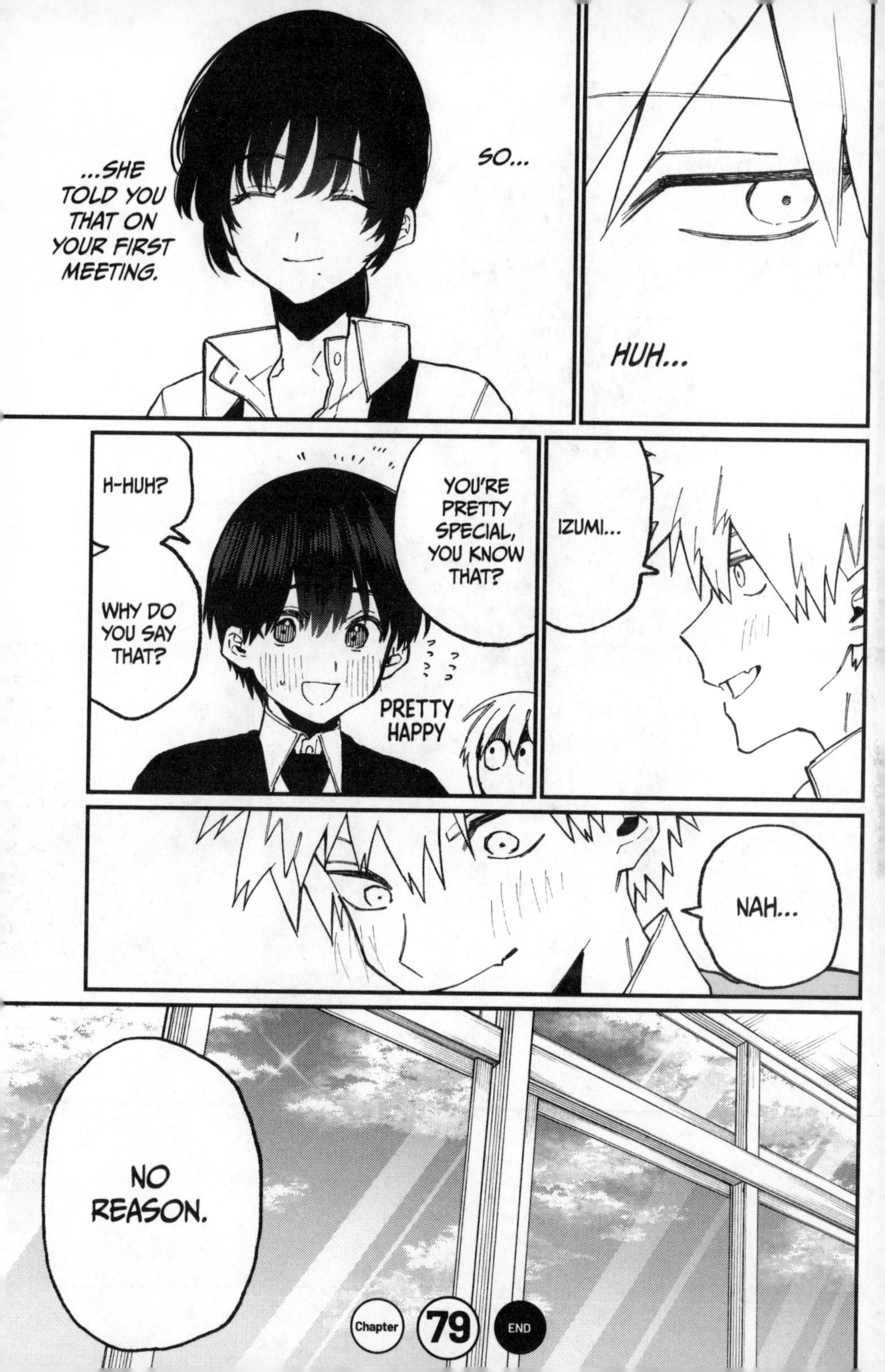
HUH...
SO...
...SHE TOLD YOU THAT ON YOUR FIRST MEETING.
IZUMI...
YOU'RE PRETTY SPECIAL, YOU KNOW THAT?
H-HUH?
WHY DO YOU SAY THAT?
PRETTY HAPPY
NAH...
NO REASON.
Chapter 79 END

CHARACTERS

Loves hard workers. Not very interested in romance. Tends to intimidate people.

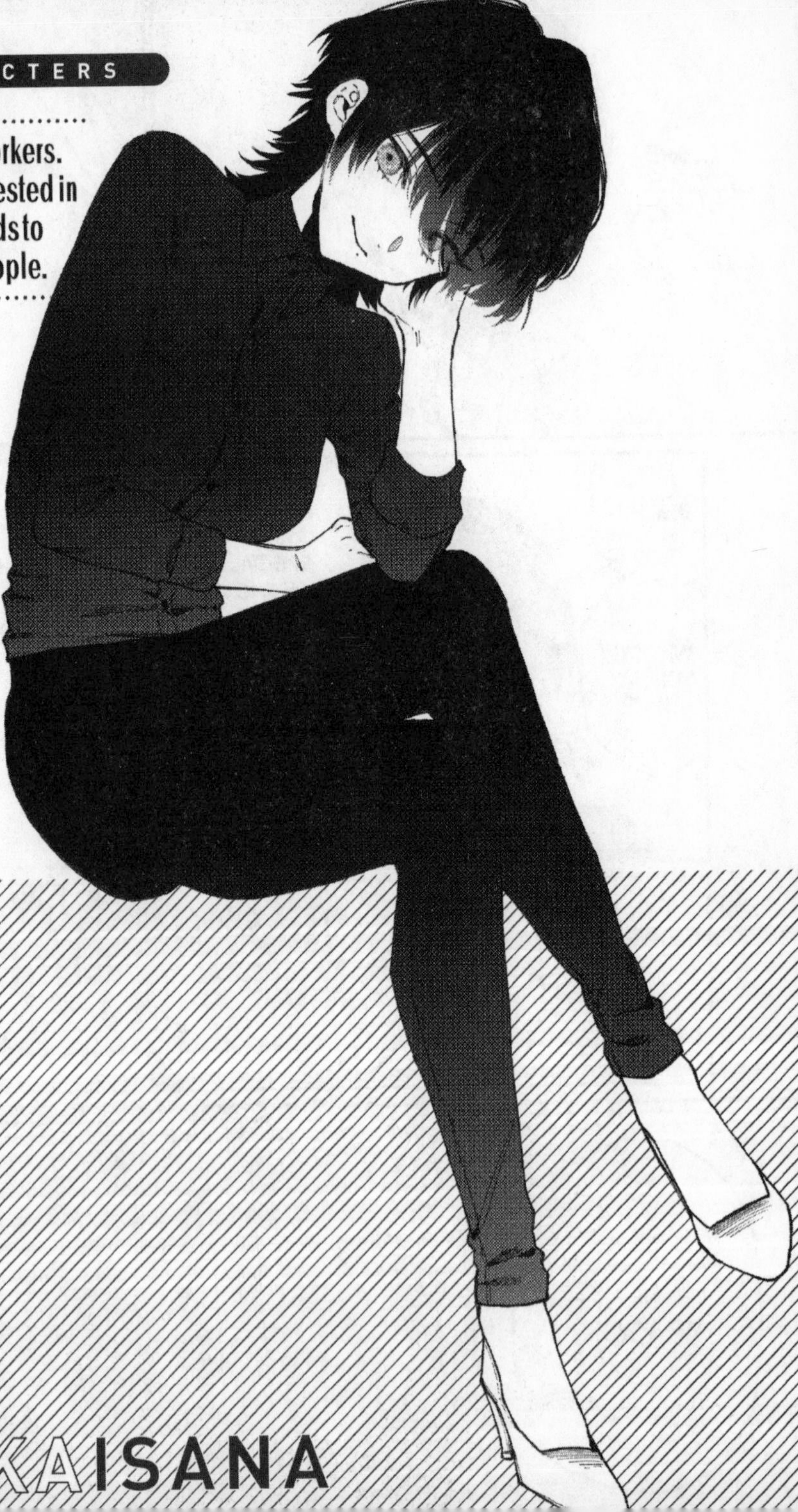

RIKA ISANA

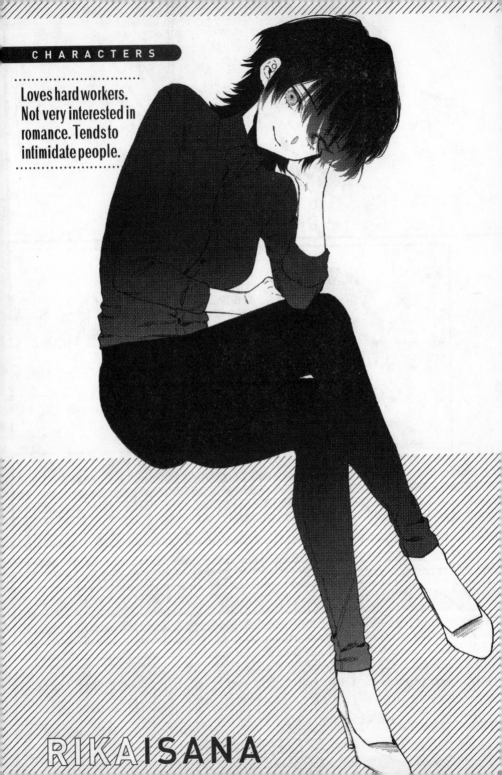

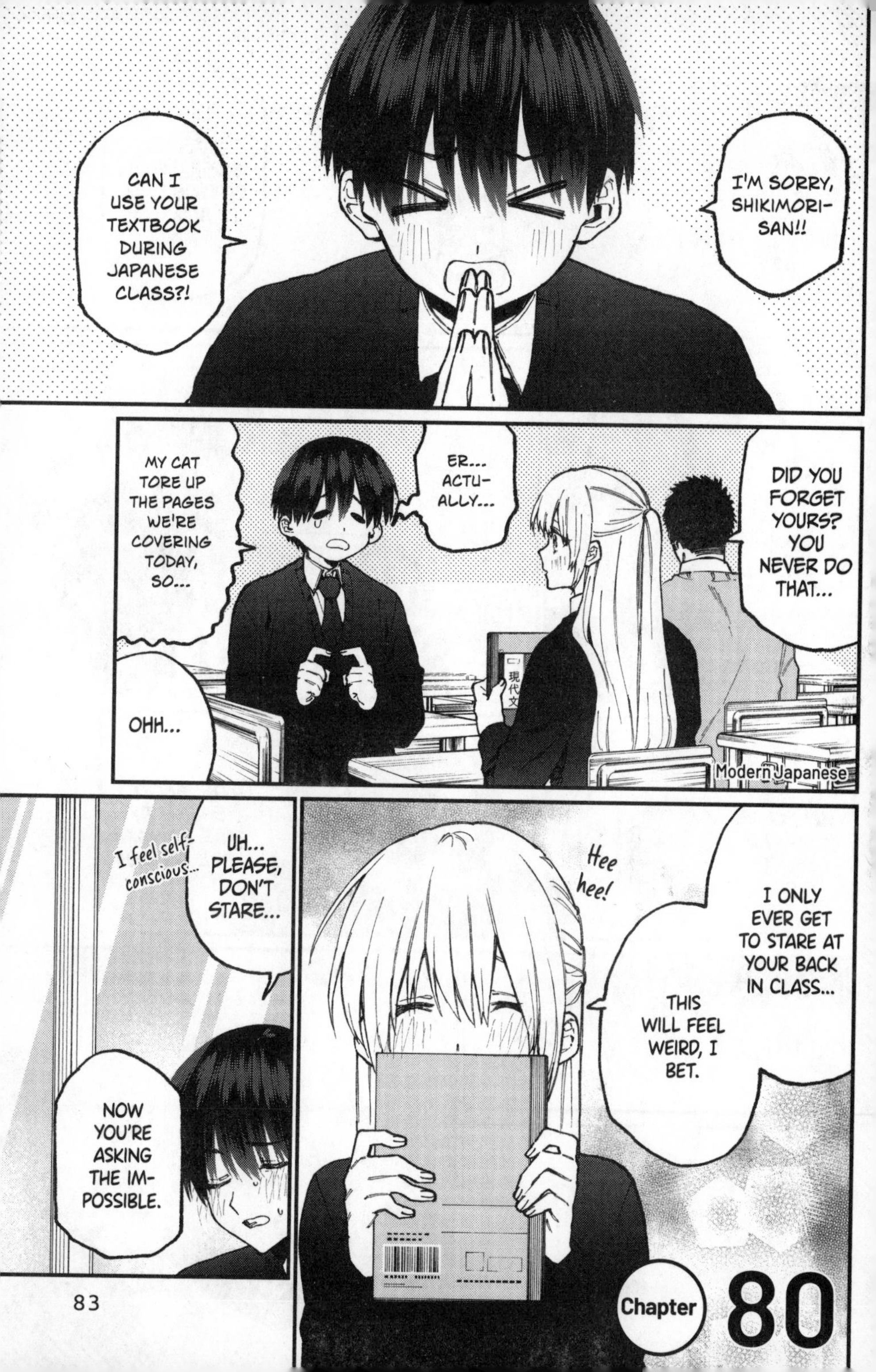

I'M SORRY, SHIKIMORI-SAN!!
CAN I USE YOUR TEXTBOOK DURING JAPANESE CLASS?!
DID YOU FORGET YOURS? YOU NEVER DO THAT...
ER... ACTU-ALLY...
MY CAT TORE UP THE PAGES WE'RE COVERING TODAY, SO...
OHH...
現代文
Modern Japanese
Hee hee!
I ONLY EVER GET TO STARE AT YOUR BACK IN CLASS...
THIS WILL FEEL WEIRD, I BET.
Chapter 80
UH... PLEASE, DON'T STARE...
I feel self-conscious...
NOW YOU'RE ASKING THE IM-POSSIBLE.

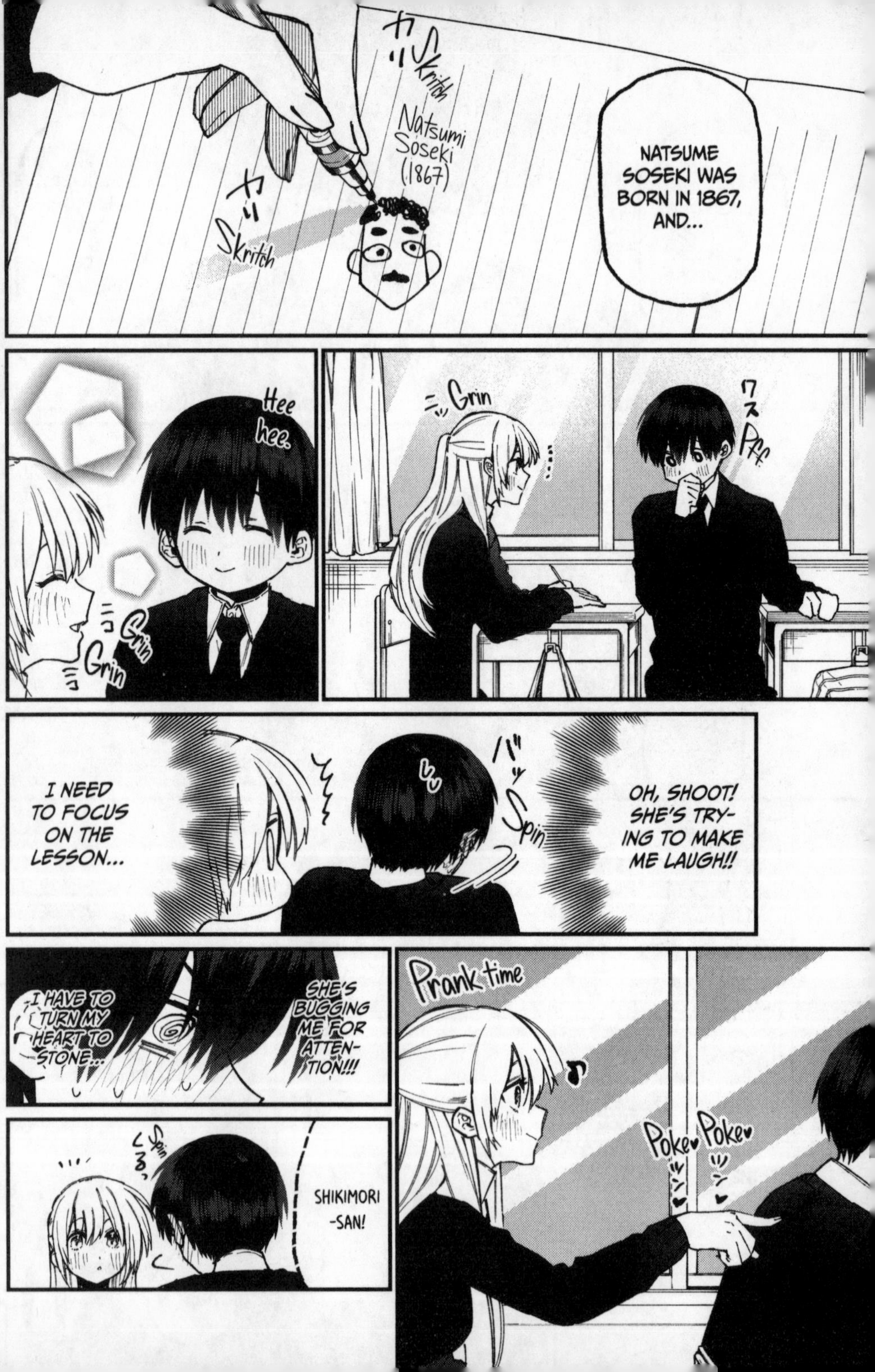

NATSUME SOSEKI WAS BORN IN 1867, AND...
Skritch
Natsumi Soseki (1867)
Skritch
Grin
Pff
Hee hee.
Grin
Grin
OH, SHOOT! SHE'S TRYING TO MAKE ME LAUGH!!
Spin
I NEED TO FOCUS ON THE LESSON...
Prank time
Poke♥ Poke♥
SHE'S BUGGING ME FOR ATTENTION!!!
I HAVE TO TURN MY HEART TO STONE...
SHIKIMORI-SAN!
Spin

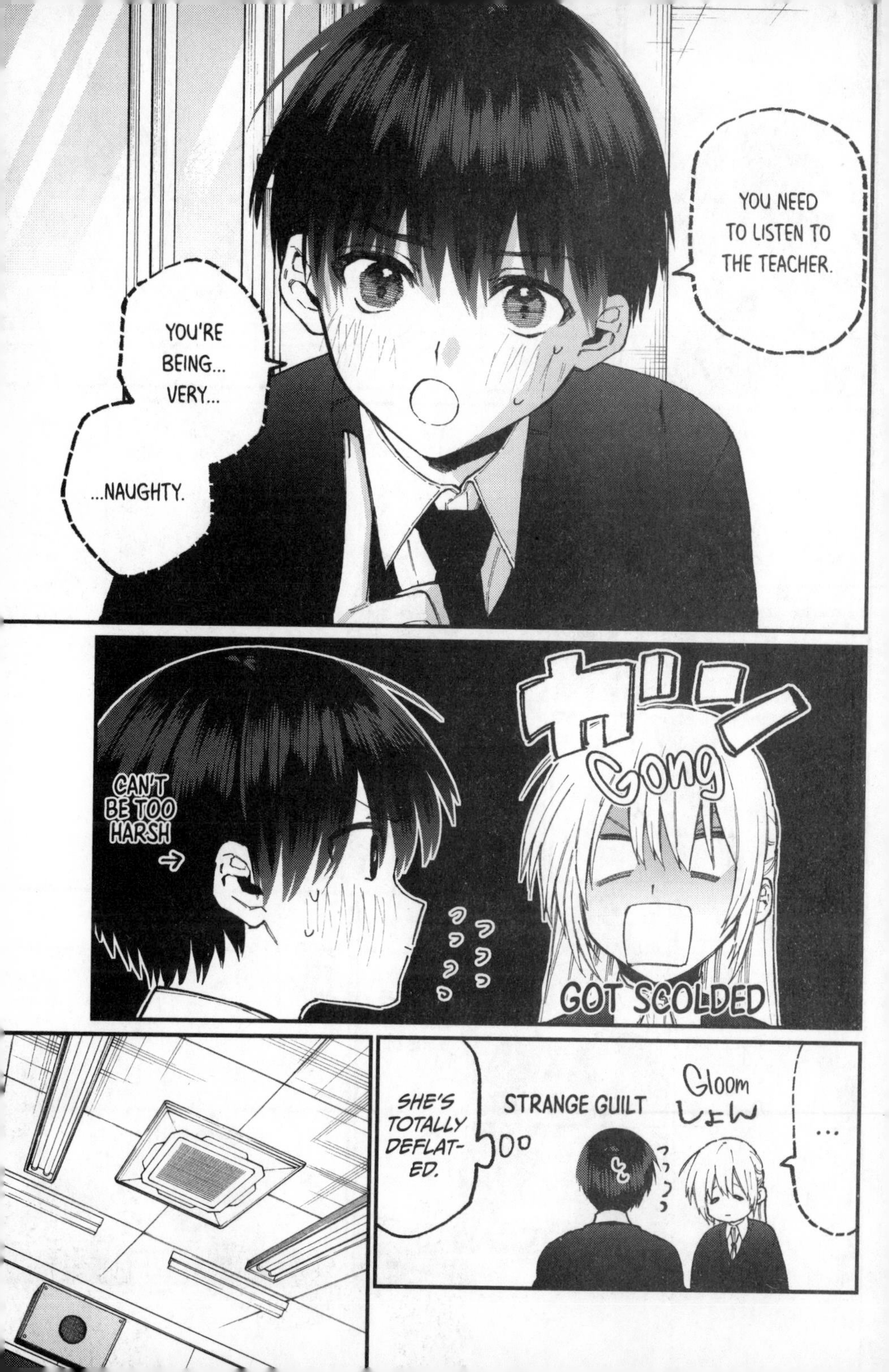
YOU NEED TO LISTEN TO THE TEACHER.
YOU'RE BEING... VERY...
...NAUGHTY.
ガーン
Gong
GOT SCOLDED
CAN'T BE TOO HARSH
...
Gloom
しょん
STRANGE GUILT
SHE'S TOTALLY DEFLATED.

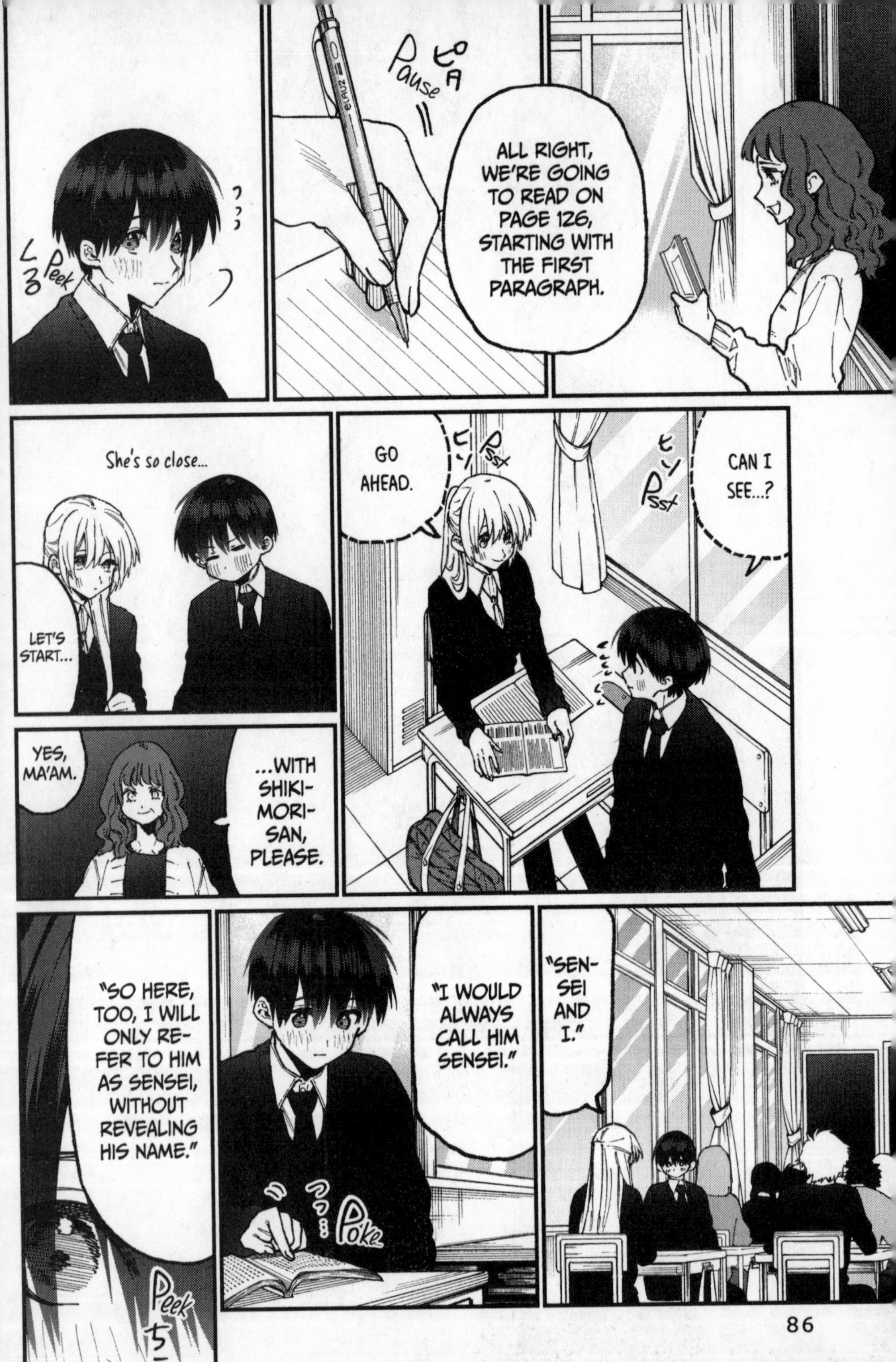
ALL RIGHT, WE'RE GOING TO READ ON PAGE 126, STARTING WITH THE FIRST PARAGRAPH.
Pause
Peek
CAN I SEE...?
Pssst
GO AHEAD.
Pssst
She's so close...
LET'S START...
...WITH SHIKI-MORI-SAN, PLEASE.
YES, MA'AM.
"SEN-SEI AND I."
"I WOULD ALWAYS CALL HIM SENSEI."
Poke
"SO HERE, TOO, I WILL ONLY RE-FER TO HIM AS SENSEI, WITHOUT REVEALING HIS NAME."
Peek

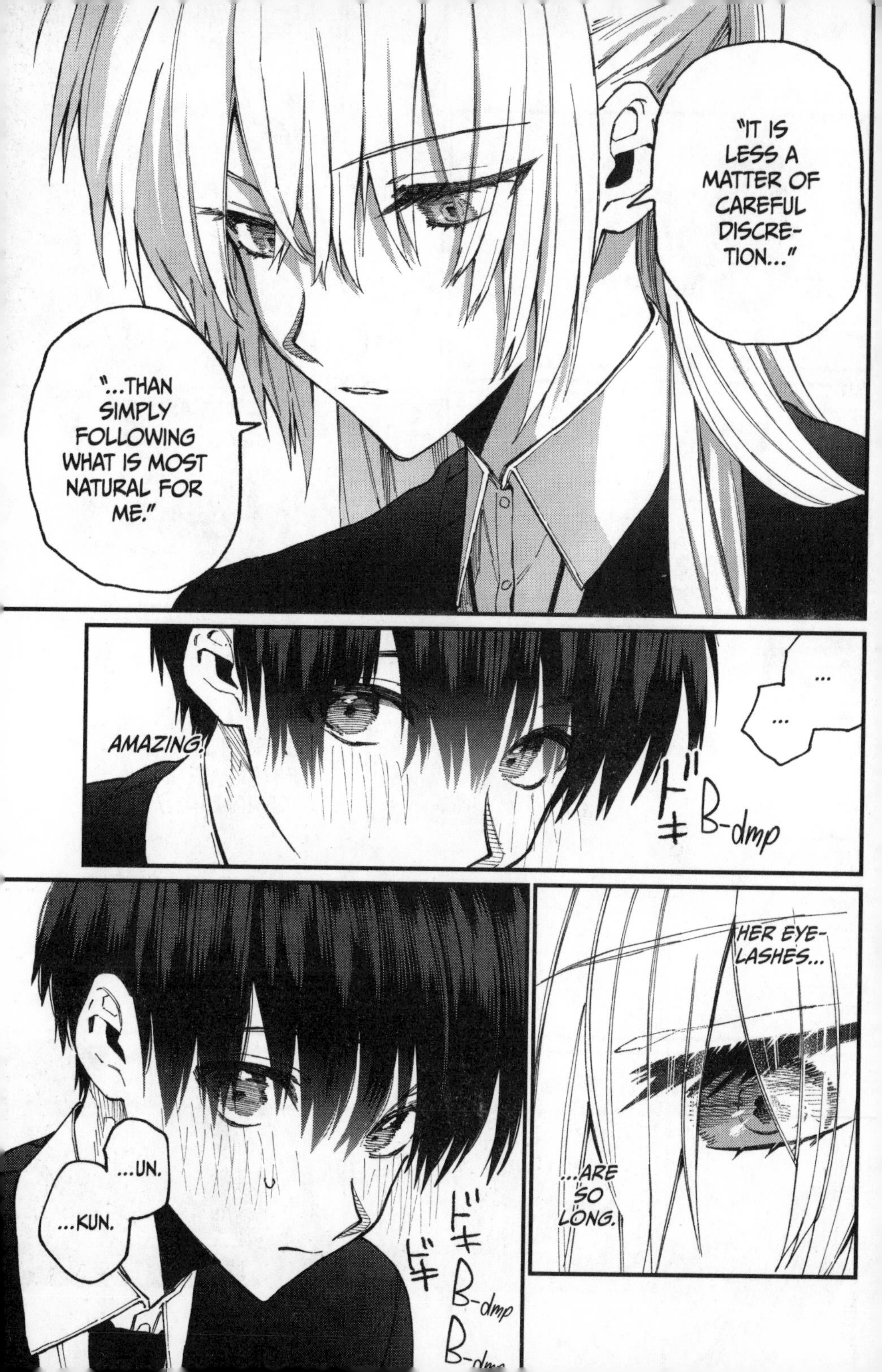
"IT IS LESS A MATTER OF CAREFUL DISCRETION..."
"...THAN SIMPLY FOLLOWING WHAT IS MOST NATURAL FOR ME."
... ...
AMAZING.
ドキ
B-dmp
HER EYELASHES...
...ARE SO LONG.
...UN.
...KUN.
ドキ ドキ
B-dmp

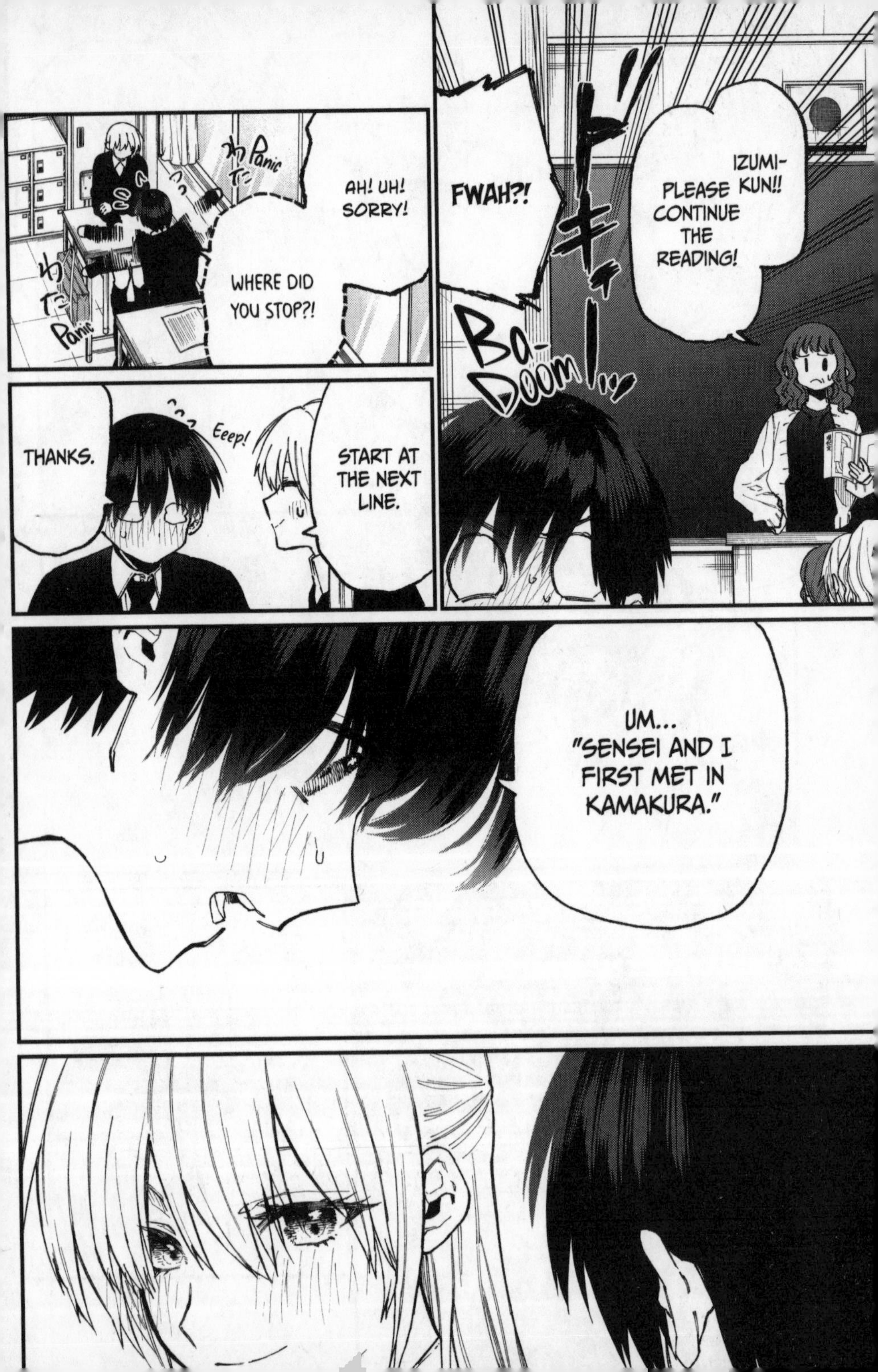
IZUMI-KUN!! PLEASE CONTINUE THE READING!
FWAH?!
Ba-Doom!!
AH! UH! SORRY!
WHERE DID YOU STOP?!
Panic
Panic
START AT THE NEXT LINE.
Eeep!
THANKS.
UM... "SENSEI AND I FIRST MET IN KAMAKURA."

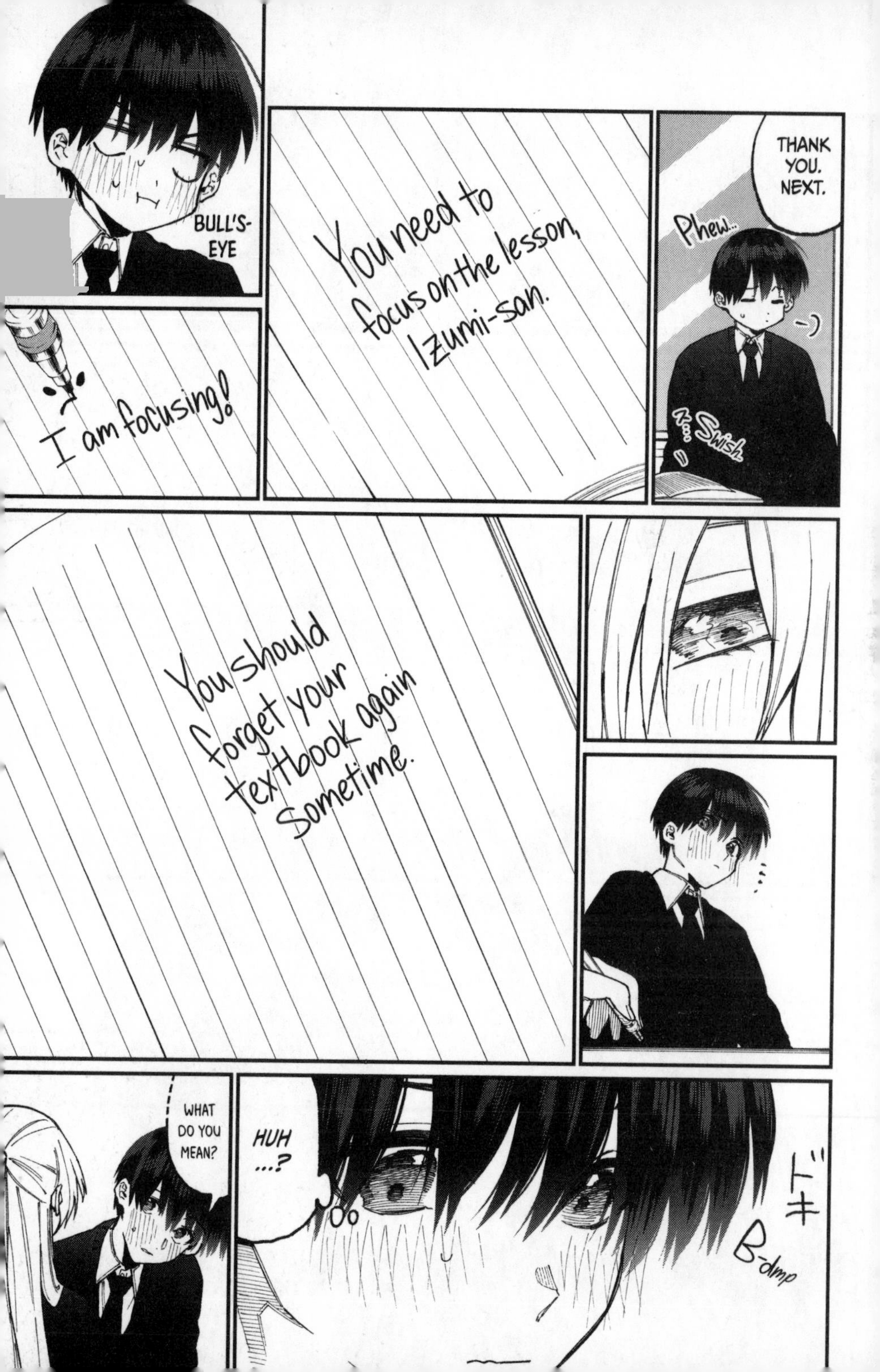
THANK YOU. NEXT.
Phew...
Swish
You need to focus on the lesson, Izumi-san.
BULL'S-EYE
I am focusing!
You should forget your textbook again Sometime.
HUH ...?
ドキ
B-dmp
WHAT DO YOU MEAN?

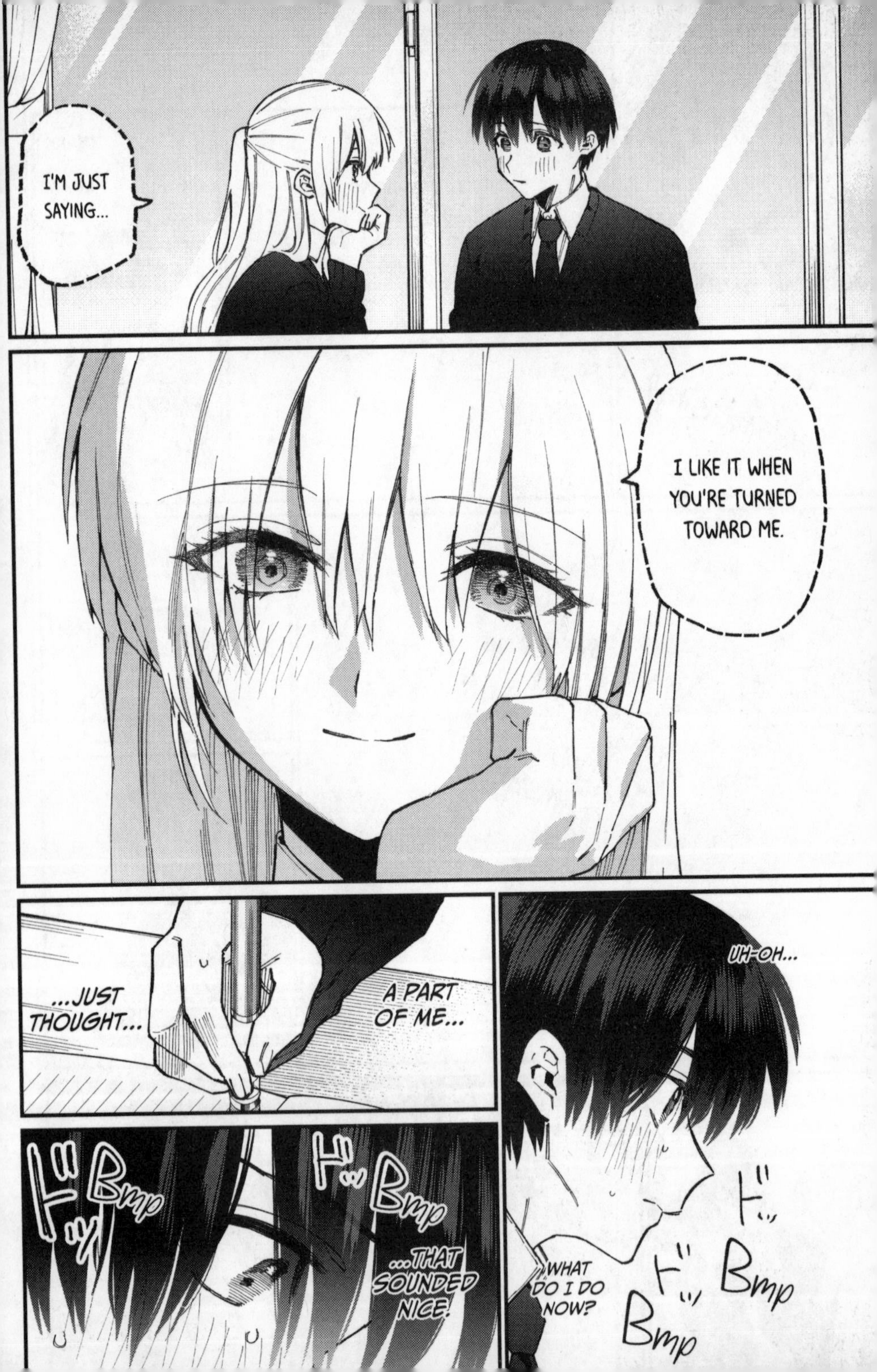
I'M JUST SAYING...
I LIKE IT WHEN YOU'RE TURNED TOWARD ME.
UH-OH...
WHAT DO I DO NOW?
ドッ Bmp
ドッ Bmp
A PART OF ME...
...JUST THOUGHT...
ドッ Bmp
ドッ Bmp
...THAT SOUNDED NICE!

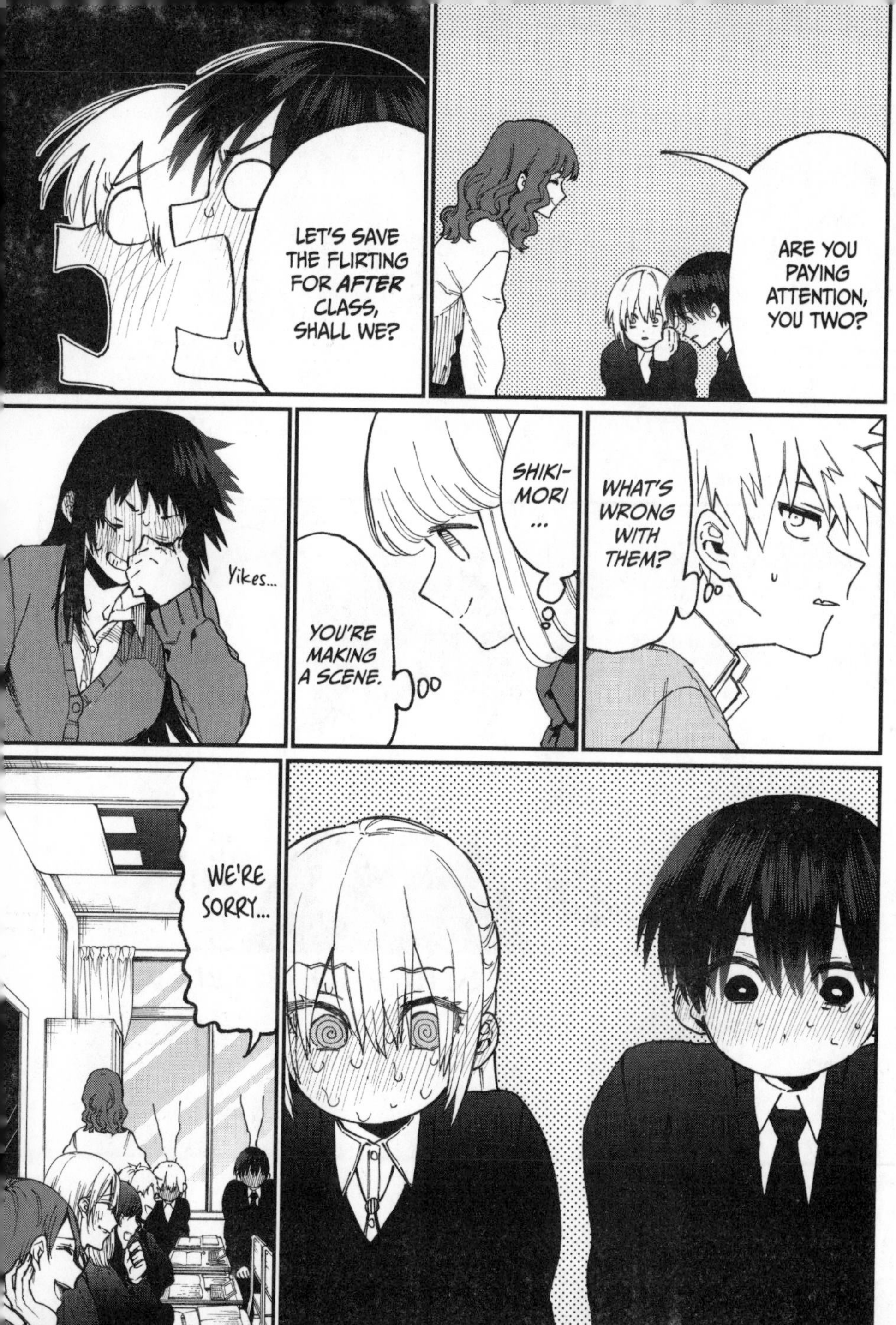
ARE YOU PAYING ATTENTION, YOU TWO?
LET'S SAVE THE FLIRTING FOR AFTER CLASS, SHALL WE?
WHAT'S WRONG WITH THEM?
SHIKI-MORI ...
YOU'RE MAKING A SCENE.
Yikes...
WE'RE SORRY...

Chapter 80 END

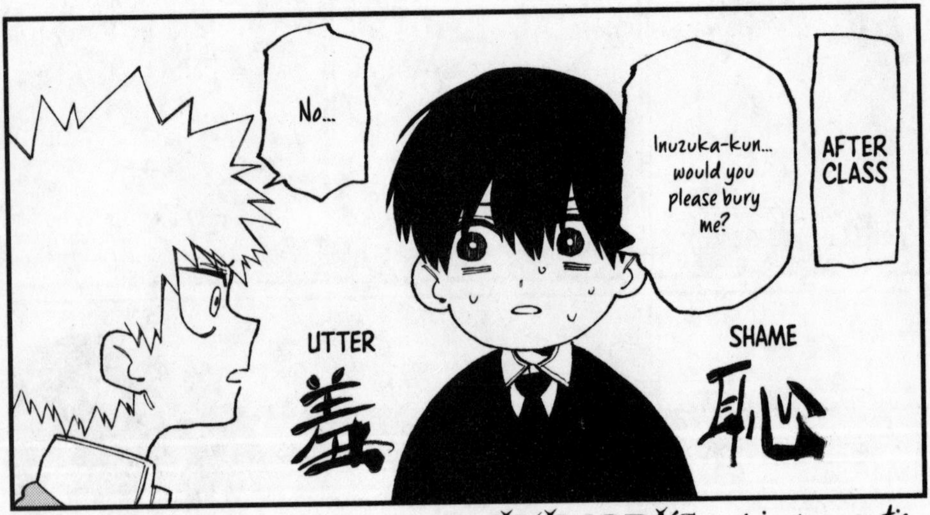
AFTER CLASS
Inuzuka-kun... would you please bury me?
No...
SHAME
恥
UTTER
羞

SHIKIMORI'S not just a cutie

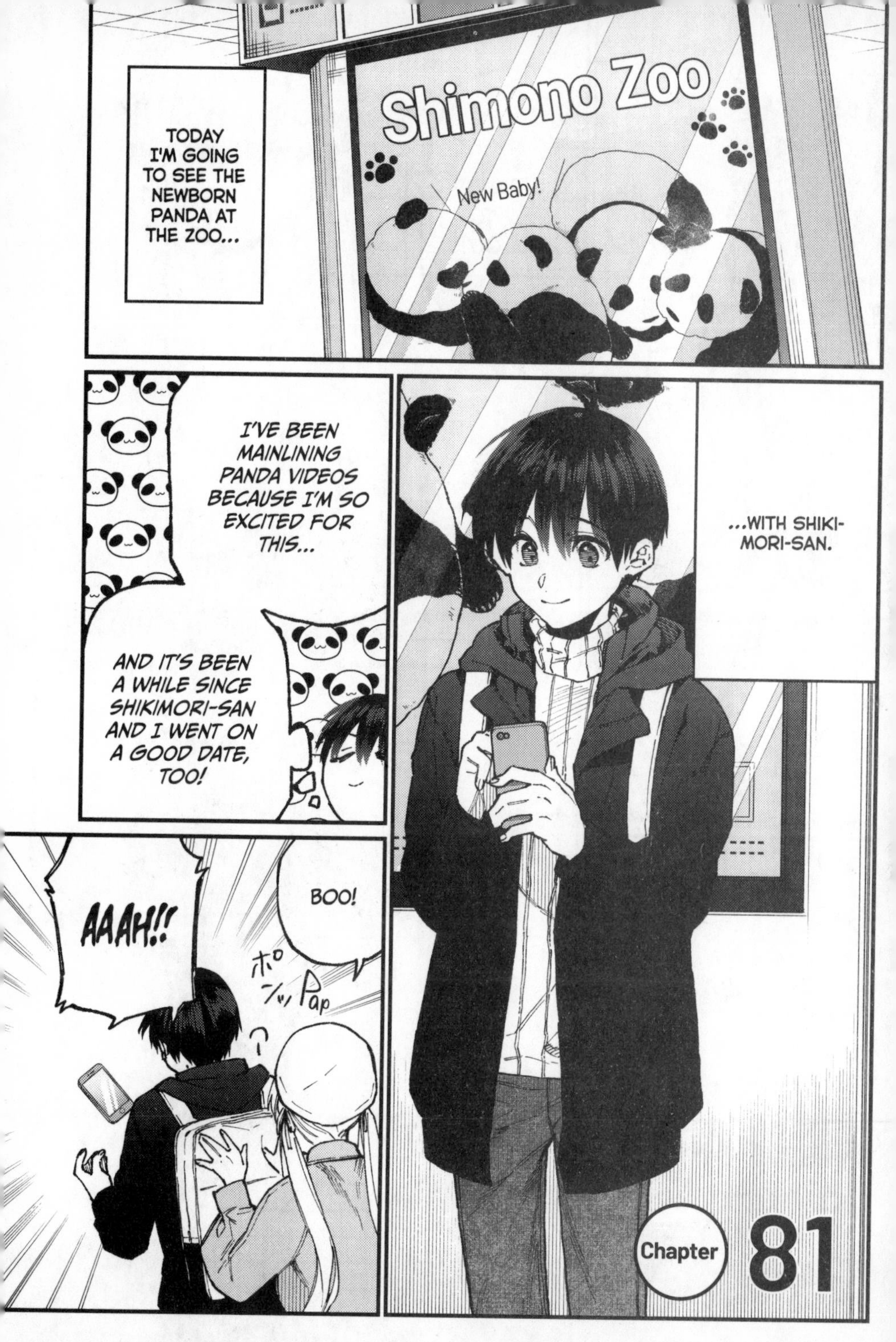
Shimono Zoo
New Baby!
TODAY I'M GOING TO SEE THE NEWBORN PANDA AT THE ZOO...
...WITH SHIKI-MORI-SAN.
Chapter 81
I'VE BEEN MAINLINING PANDA VIDEOS BECAUSE I'M SO EXCITED FOR THIS...
AND IT'S BEEN A WHILE SINCE SHIKIMORI-SAN AND I WENT ON A GOOD DATE, TOO!
BOO!
AAAH!!
ポンッ Pap

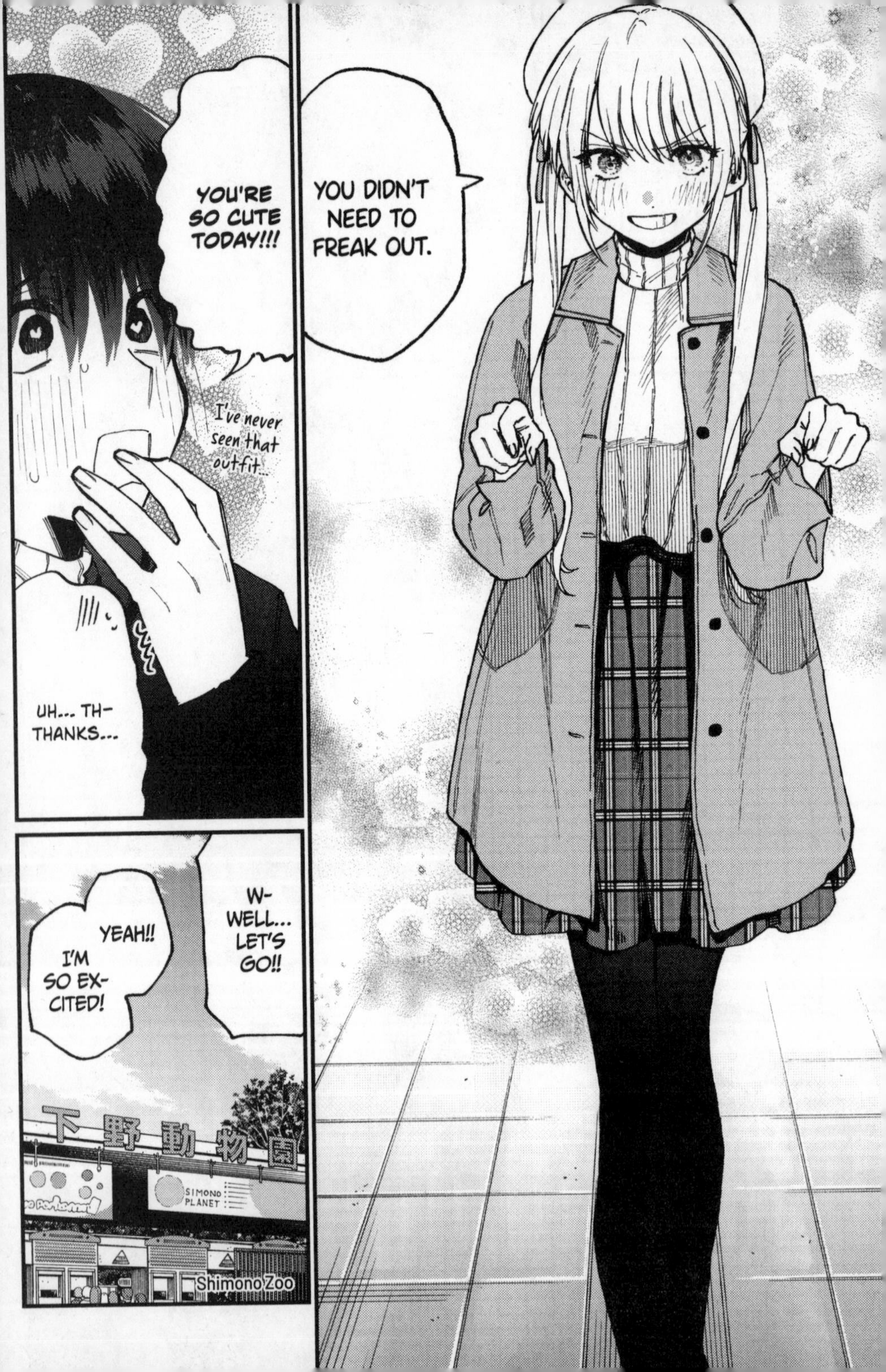
YOU DIDN'T NEED TO FREAK OUT.
YOU'RE SO CUTE TODAY!!!
I've never seen that outfit...
UH... TH- THANKS...
W- WELL... LET'S GO!!
YEAH!! I'M SO EX- CITED!
下野動物園
SIMONO PLANET
Shimono Zoo

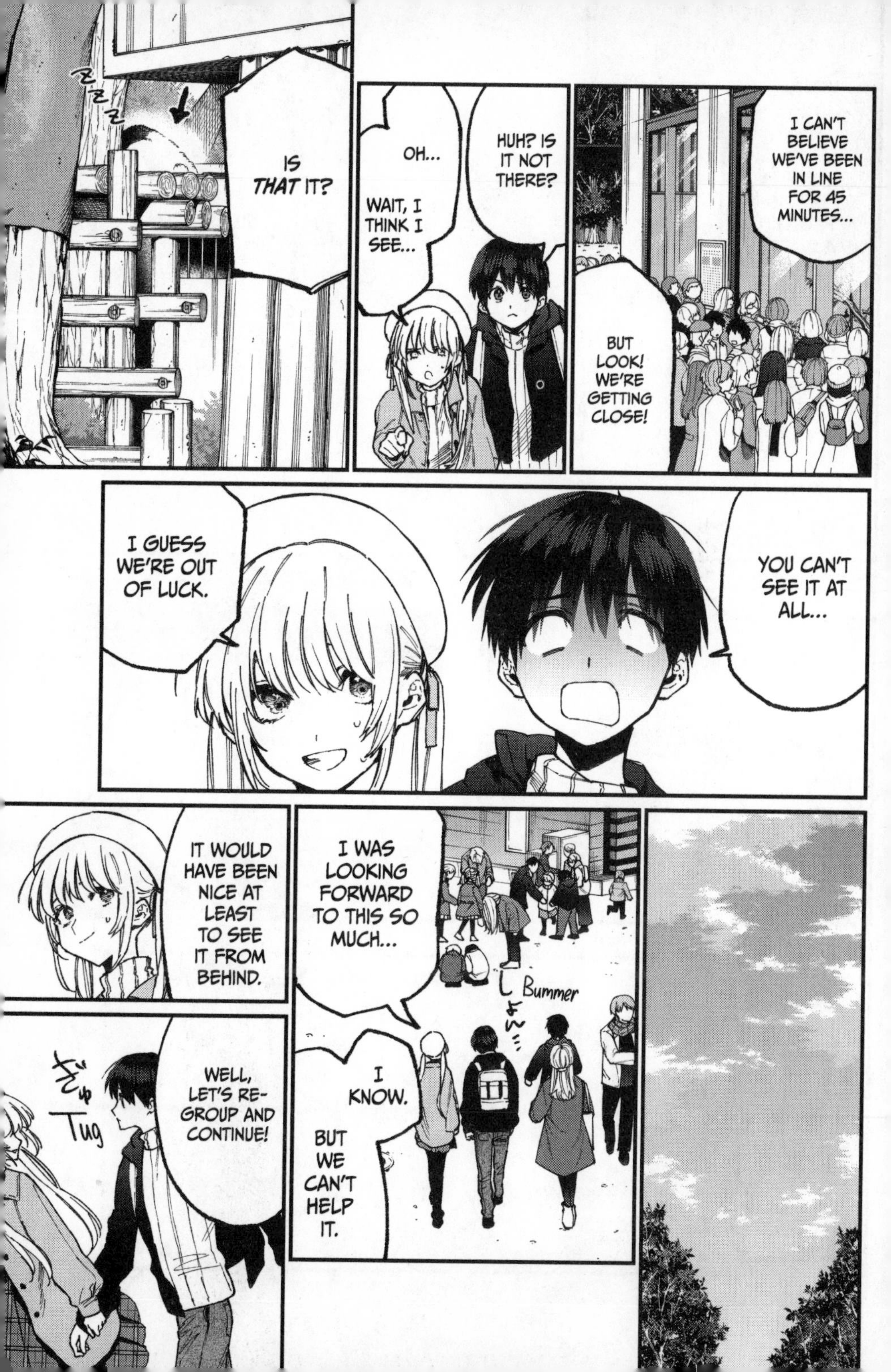

I CAN'T BELIEVE WE'VE BEEN IN LINE FOR 45 MINUTES...
BUT LOOK! WE'RE GETTING CLOSE!
HUH? IS IT NOT THERE?
OH...
WAIT, I THINK I SEE...
IS *THAT* IT?
YOU CAN'T SEE IT AT ALL...
I GUESS WE'RE OUT OF LUCK.
I WAS LOOKING FORWARD TO THIS SO MUCH...
Bummer
I KNOW.
BUT WE CAN'T HELP IT.
IT WOULD HAVE BEEN NICE AT LEAST TO SEE IT FROM BEHIND.
WELL, LET'S RE-GROUP AND CONTINUE!
Tug

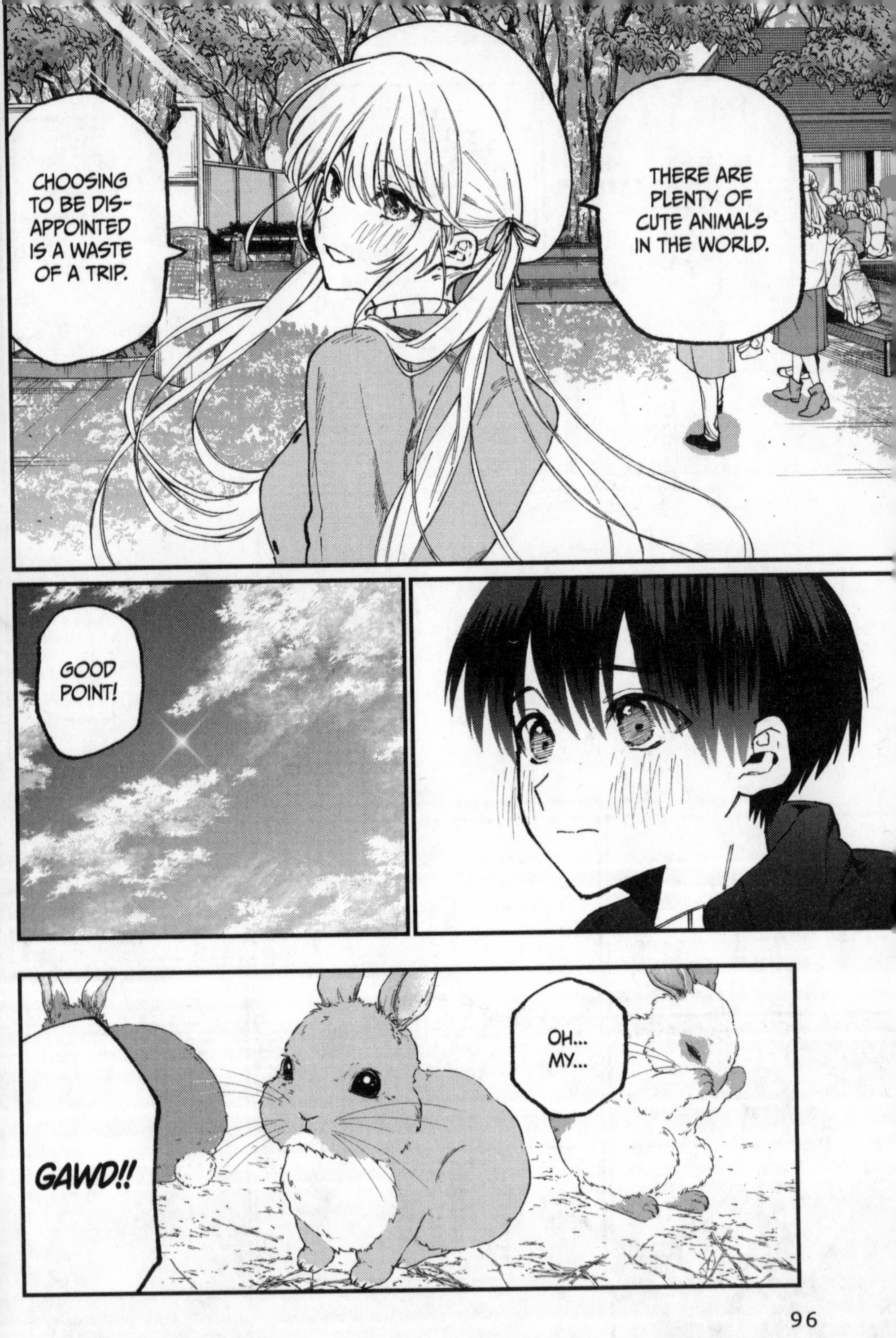
THERE ARE PLENTY OF CUTE ANIMALS IN THE WORLD.
CHOOSING TO BE DIS-APPOINTED IS A WASTE OF A TRIP.
GOOD POINT!
OH... MY...
GAWD!!

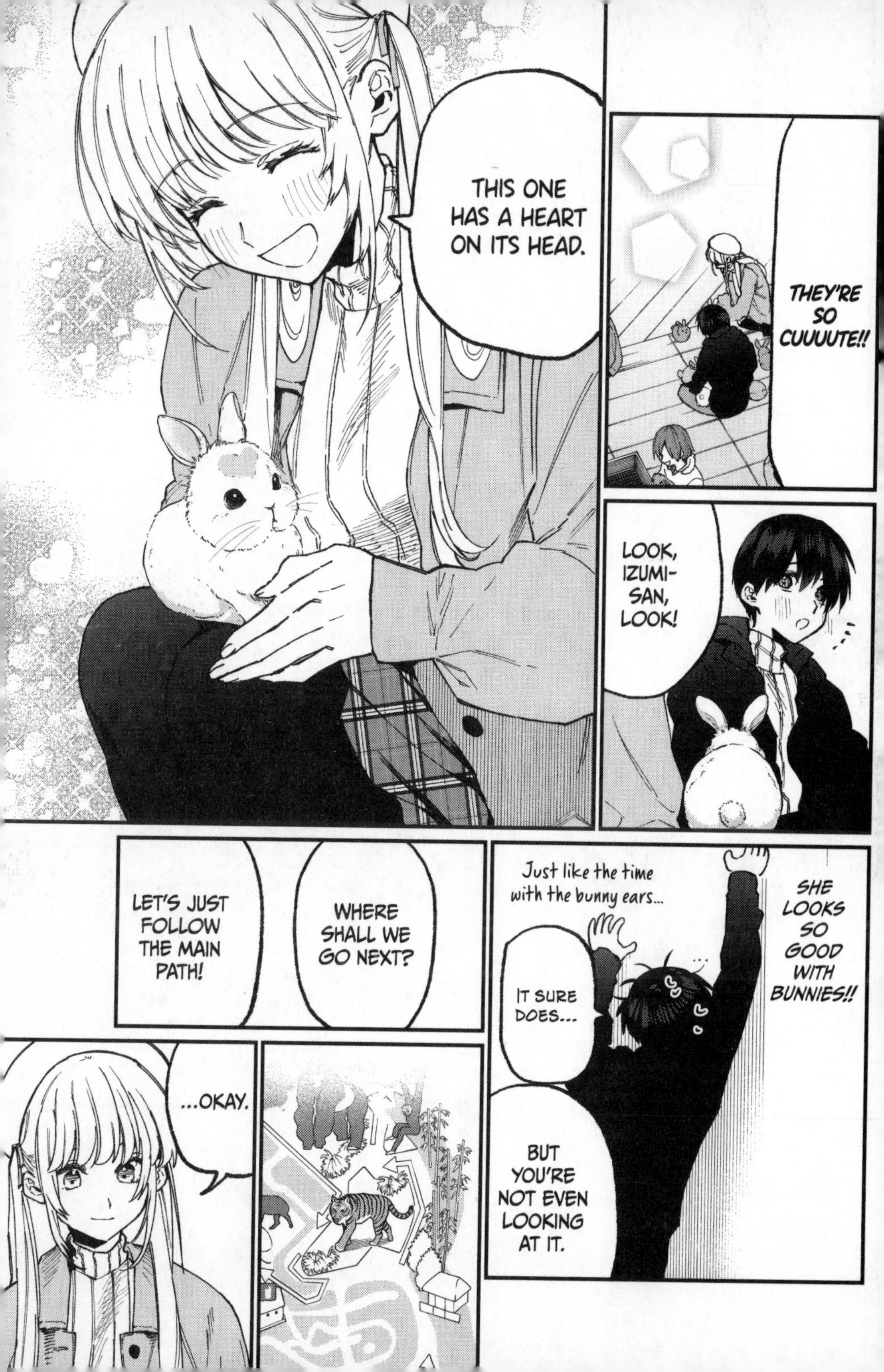

THEY'RE SO CUUUUTE!!
LOOK, IZUMI-SAN, LOOK!
THIS ONE HAS A HEART ON ITS HEAD.
SHE LOOKS SO GOOD WITH BUNNIES!!
Just like the time with the bunny ears...
...
IT SURE DOES...
BUT YOU'RE NOT EVEN LOOKING AT IT.
WHERE SHALL WE GO NEXT?
LET'S JUST FOLLOW THE MAIN PATH!
...OKAY.

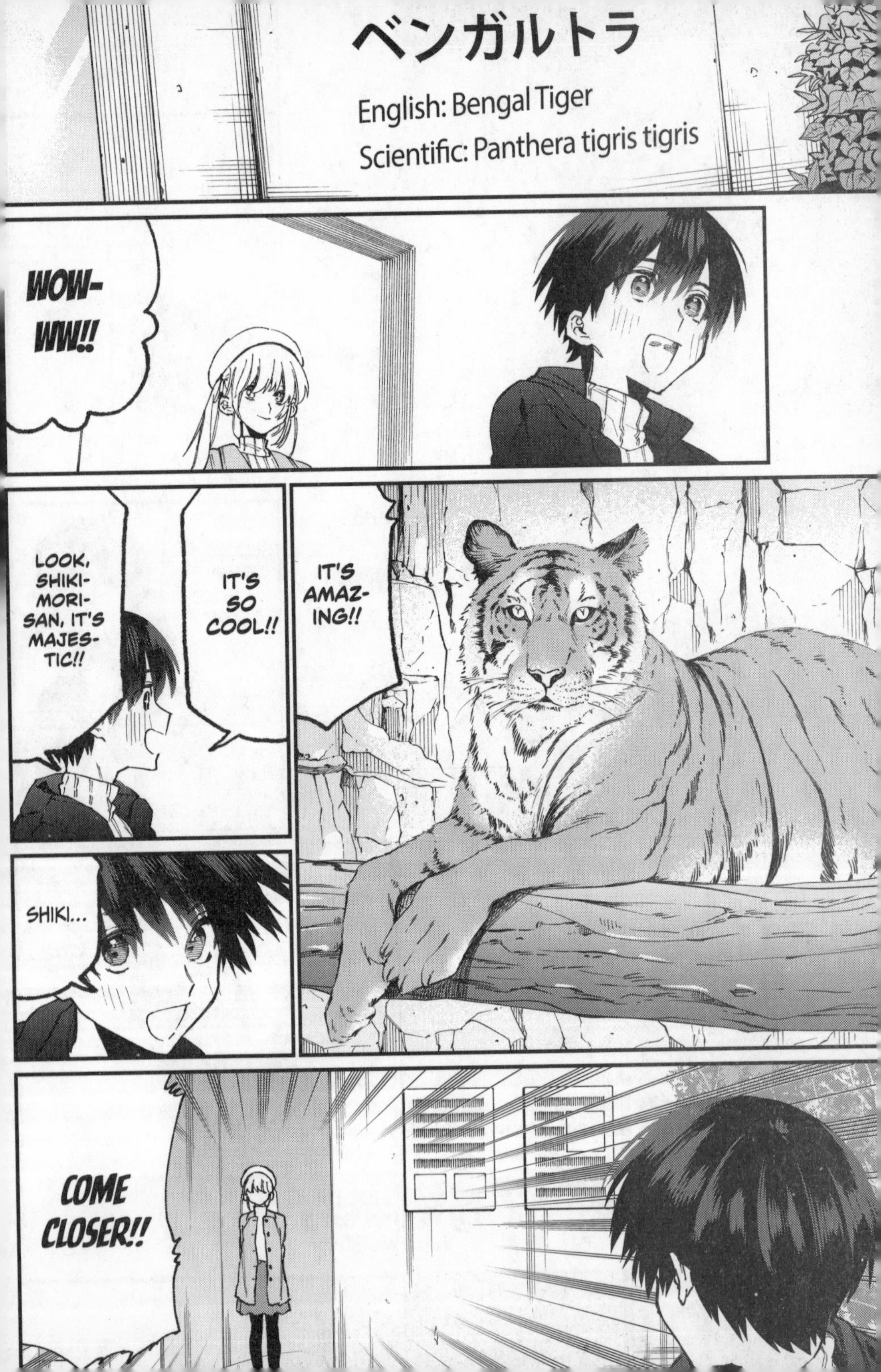
ベンガルトラ
English: Bengal Tiger
Scientific: Panthera tigris tigris
WOW-WW!!
IT'S AMAZ-ING!!
IT'S SO COOL!!
LOOK, SHIKI-MORI-SAN, IT'S MAJES-TIC!!
SHIKI...
COME CLOSER!!

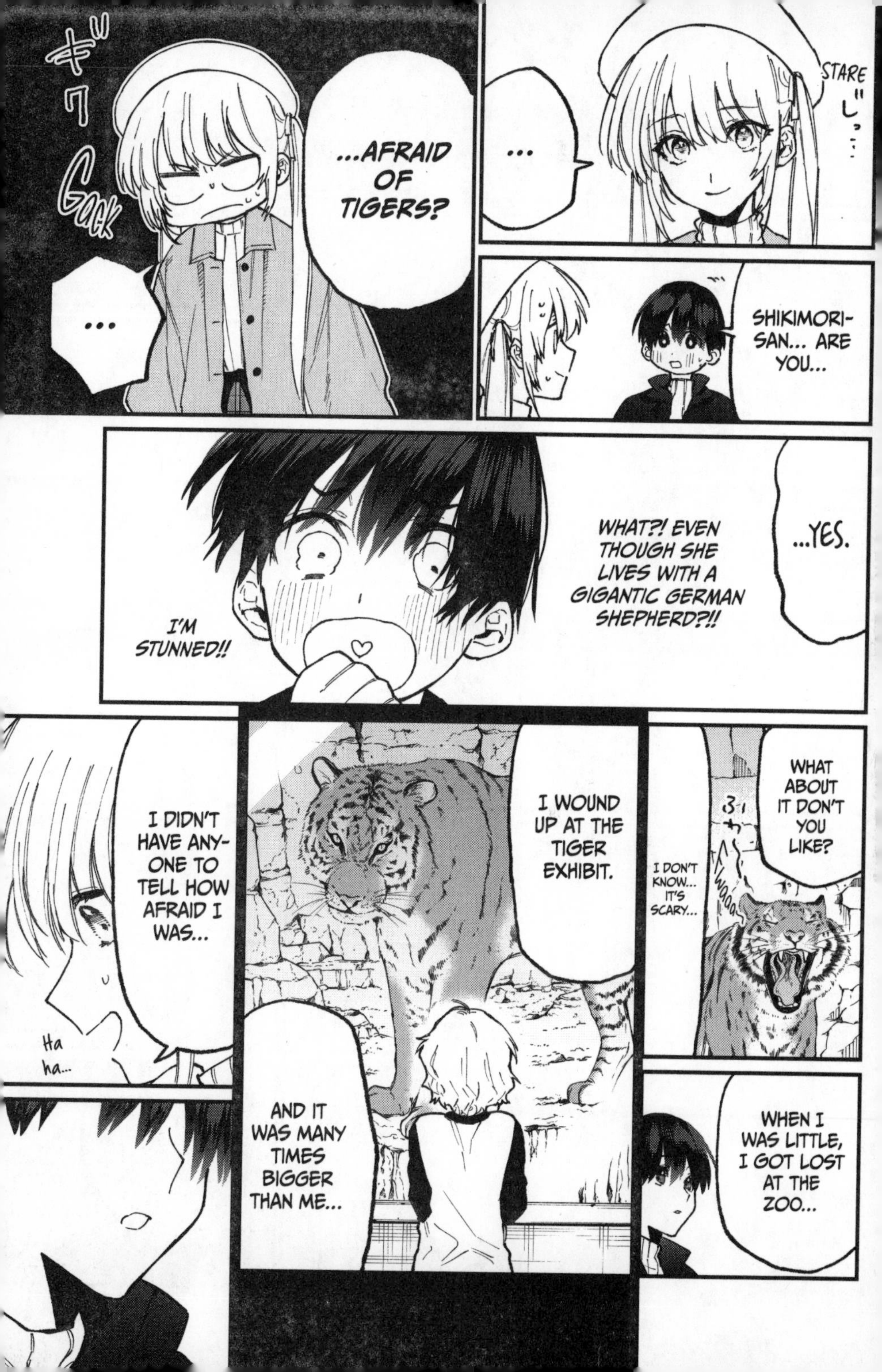
STARE
じっ…
...
SHIKIMORI-SAN... ARE YOU...
...AFRAID OF TIGERS?
ギク
Gack
...
...YES.
WHAT?! EVEN THOUGH SHE LIVES WITH A GIGANTIC GERMAN SHEPHERD?!!
I'M STUNNED!!
WHAT ABOUT IT DON'T YOU LIKE?
ふわ
Fwaaa
I DON'T KNOW... IT'S SCARY...
WHEN I WAS LITTLE, I GOT LOST AT THE ZOO...
I WOUND UP AT THE TIGER EXHIBIT.
AND IT WAS MANY TIMES BIGGER THAN ME...
I DIDN'T HAVE ANYONE TO TELL HOW AFRAID I WAS...
Ha ha...

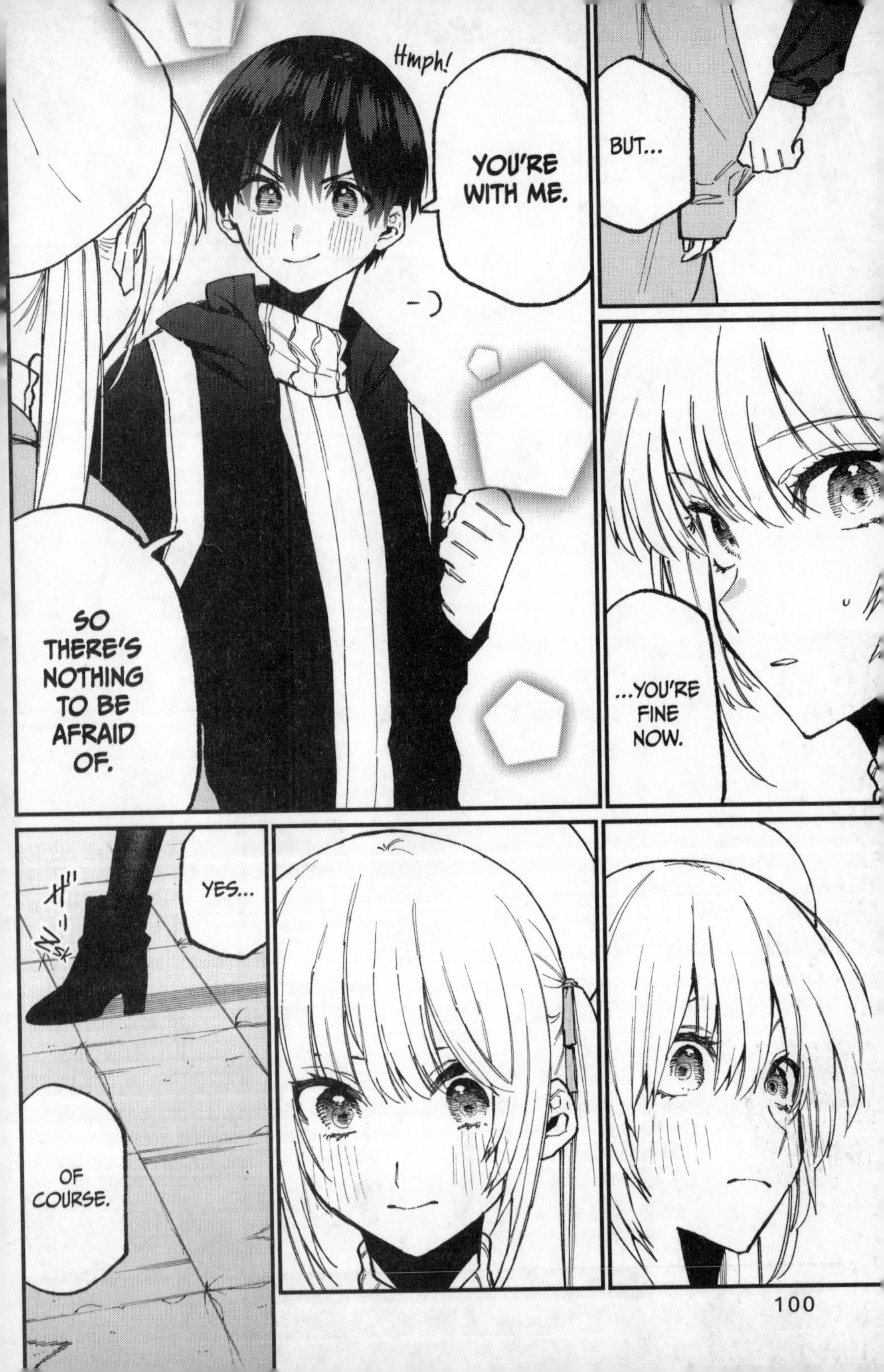
BUT...
...YOU'RE FINE NOW.
Hmph!
YOU'RE WITH ME.
SO THERE'S NOTHING TO BE AFRAID OF.
YES...
ZSK
OF COURSE.

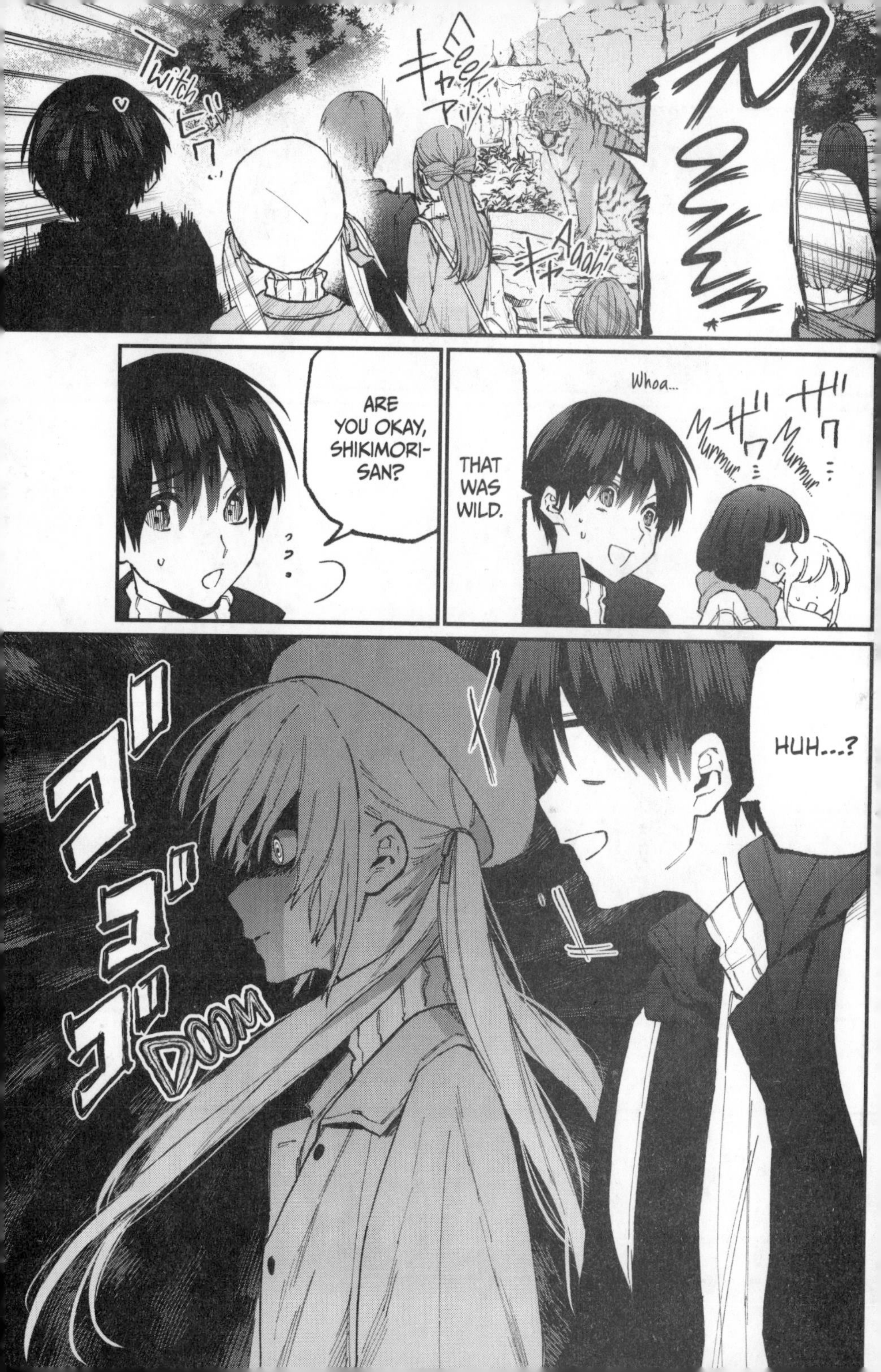
Eeek!
キャアッ
Aaah!
キャ
Twitch
ビクッ
Whoa...
THAT WAS WILD.
Murmur
ザワ
Murmur
ザワ
ARE YOU OKAY, SHIKIMORI-SAN?
HUH...?
ゴゴゴゴ
DOOM

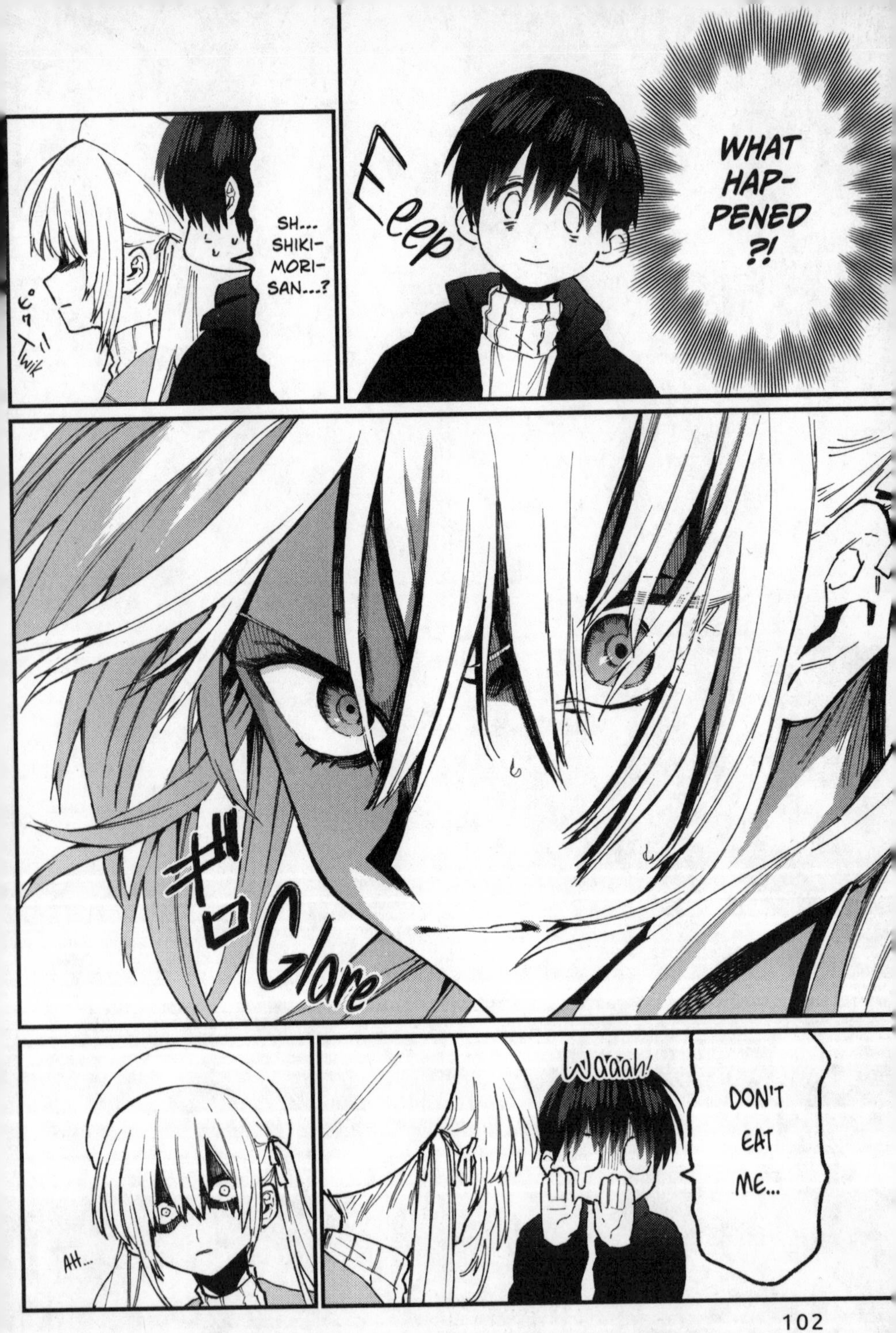
WHAT HAP-PENED?!
Eeep
SH... SHIKI-MORI-SAN...?
ピク
Twik
ギロ
Glare
Waaah!
DON'T EAT ME...
AH...

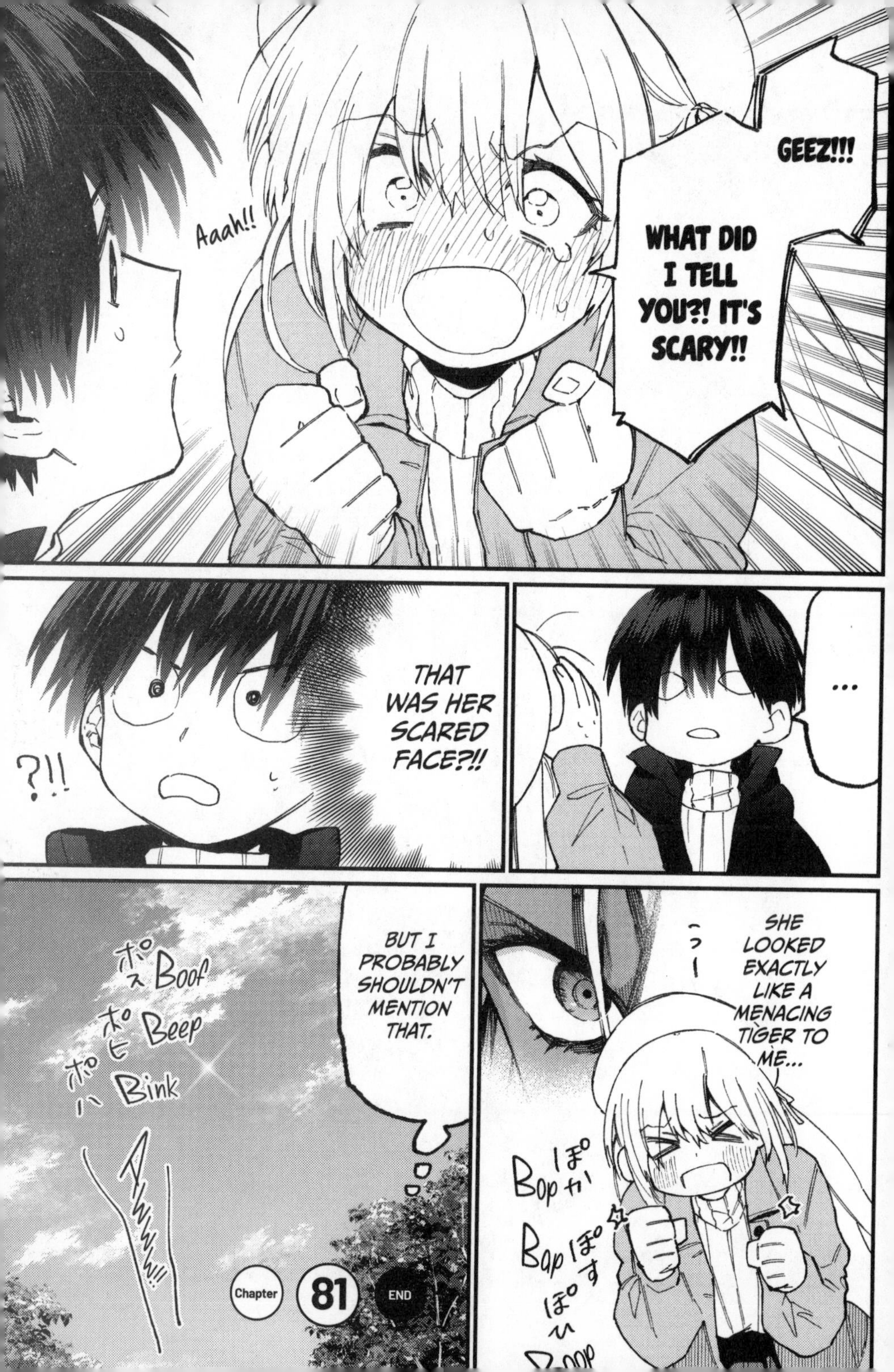
GEEZ!!!
WHAT DID I TELL YOU?! IT'S SCARY!!
Aaah!!
...
THAT WAS HER SCARED FACE?!!
?!!
SHE LOOKED EXACTLY LIKE A MENACING TIGER TO ME...
Bop ぽか
Bap ぽす
ぽひ
BUT I PROBABLY SHOULDN'T MENTION THAT.
ポス Boof
ポピ Beep
ポハ Bink
Awww!!!
Chapter 81 END

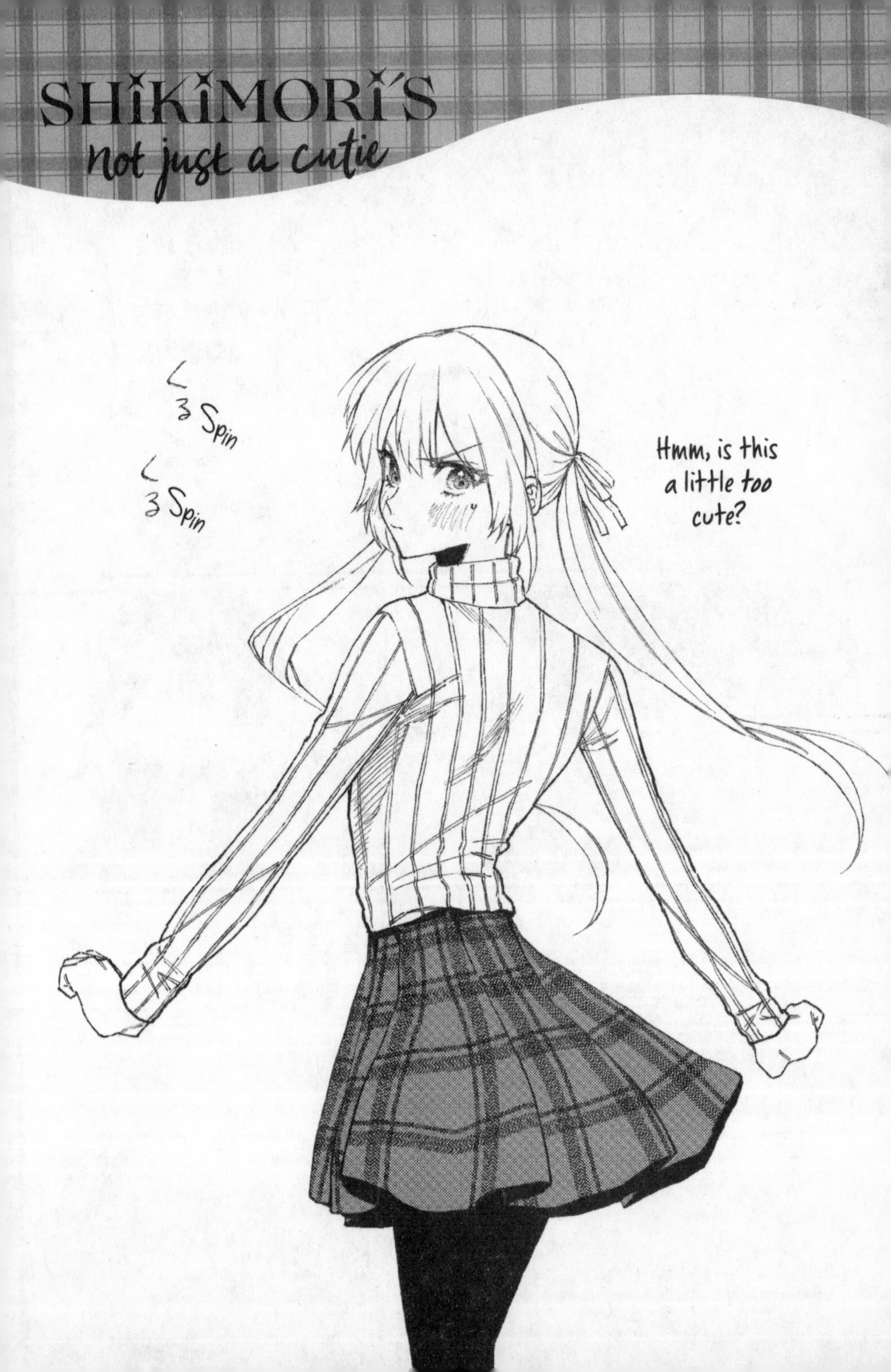
SHIKIMORI'S
not just a cutie
Hmm, is this a little too cute?
Spin
Spin

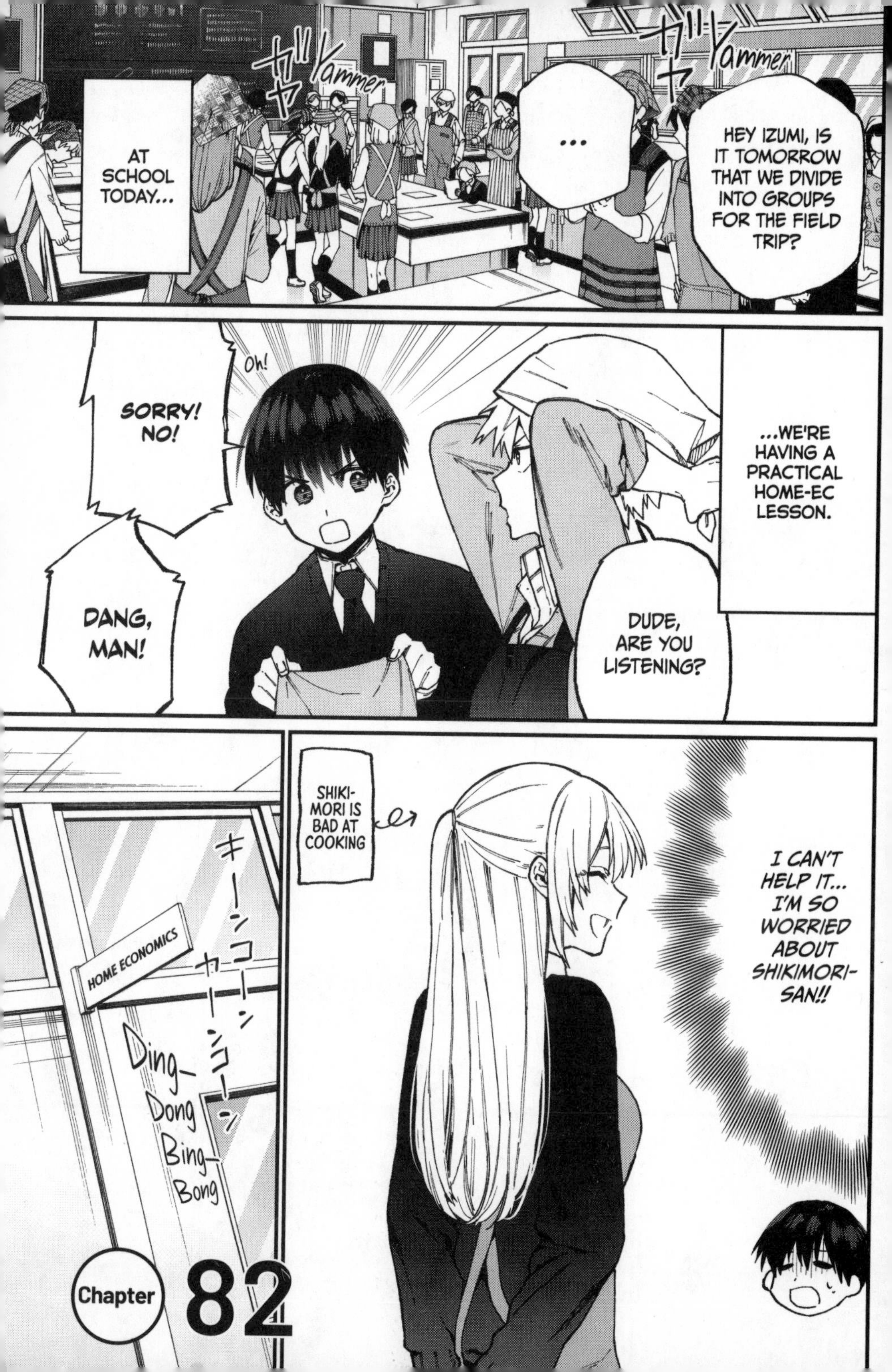
ガヤ Yammer
HEY IZUMI, IS IT TOMORROW THAT WE DIVIDE INTO GROUPS FOR THE FIELD TRIP?
...
ガヤ Yammer
AT SCHOOL TODAY...
...WE'RE HAVING A PRACTICAL HOME-EC LESSON.
DUDE, ARE YOU LISTENING?
Oh!
SORRY! NO!
DANG, MAN!
I CAN'T HELP IT... I'M SO WORRIED ABOUT SHIKIMORI-SAN!!
SHIKIMORI IS BAD AT COOKING
HOME ECONOMICS
キーンコーンカーンコーン
Ding-Dong Bing-Bong
Chapter 82

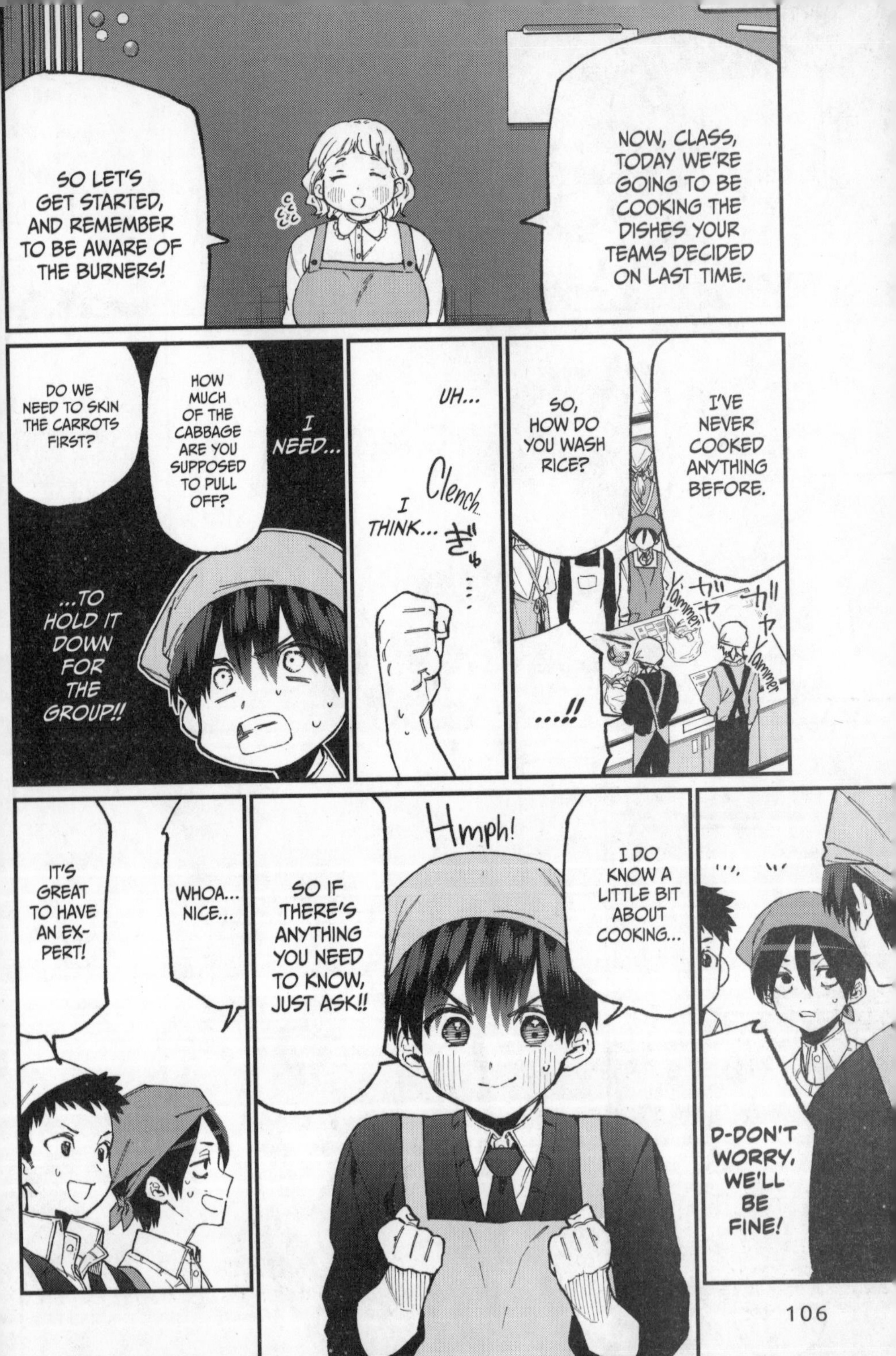
NOW, CLASS, TODAY WE'RE GOING TO BE COOKING THE DISHES YOUR TEAMS DECIDED ON LAST TIME.
SO LET'S GET STARTED, AND REMEMBER TO BE AWARE OF THE BURNERS!
I'VE NEVER COOKED ANYTHING BEFORE.
SO, HOW DO YOU WASH RICE?
Yammer
Yammer
...!!
UH...
I THINK...
Clench...
I NEED...
HOW MUCH OF THE CABBAGE ARE YOU SUPPOSED TO PULL OFF?
DO WE NEED TO SKIN THE CARROTS FIRST?
...TO HOLD IT DOWN FOR THE GROUP!!
D-DON'T WORRY, WE'LL BE FINE!
Hmph!
I DO KNOW A LITTLE BIT ABOUT COOKING...
SO IF THERE'S ANYTHING YOU NEED TO KNOW, JUST ASK!!
WHOA... NICE...
IT'S GREAT TO HAVE AN EXPERT!

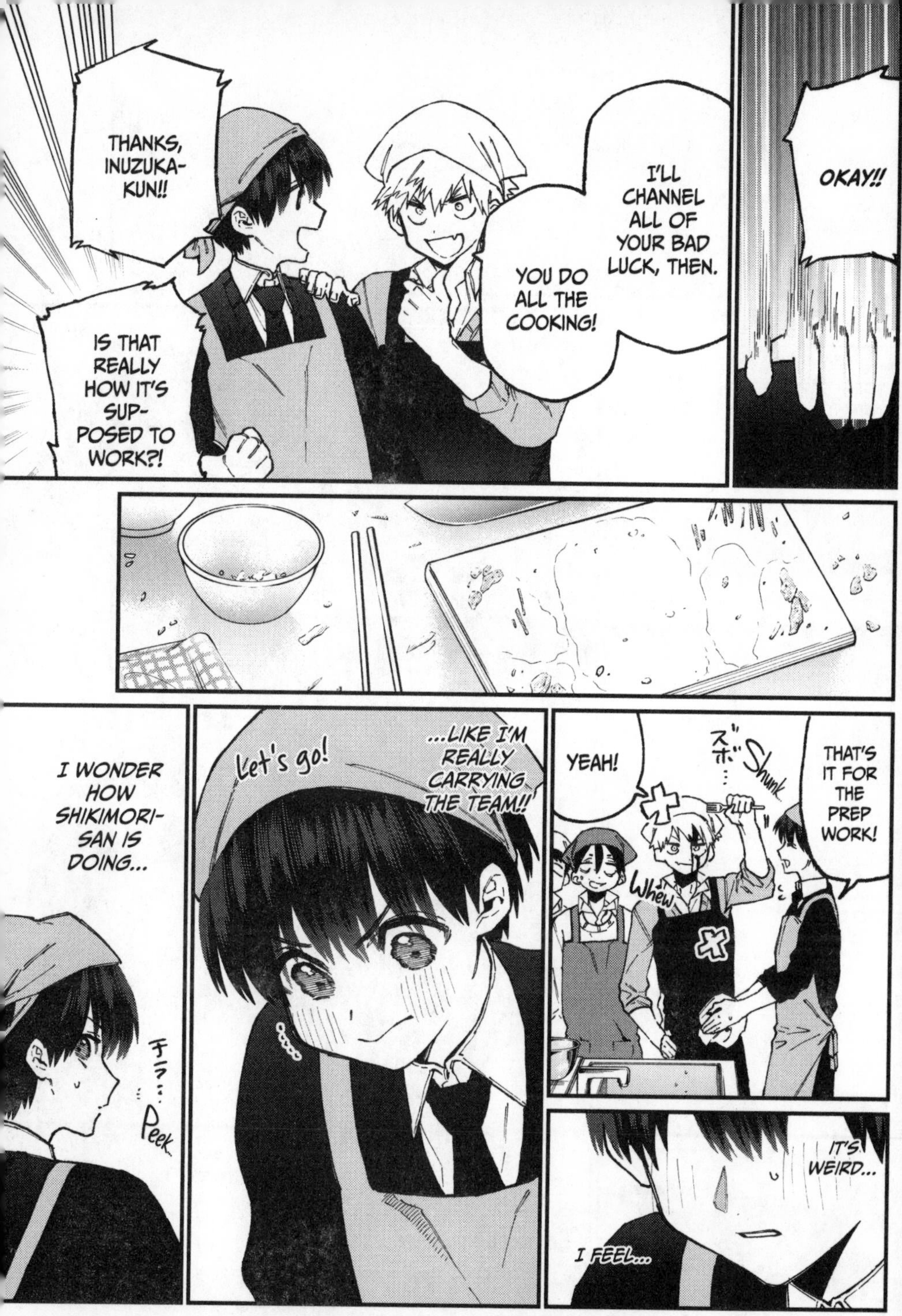
OKAY!!
I'LL CHANNEL ALL OF YOUR BAD LUCK, THEN.
YOU DO ALL THE COOKING!
THANKS, INUZUKA-KUN!!
IS THAT REALLY HOW IT'S SUP-POSED TO WORK?!
THAT'S IT FOR THE PREP WORK!
ズボ…
Shunk
YEAH!
Whew
IT'S WEIRD...
I FEEL...
...LIKE I'M REALLY CARRYING THE TEAM!!
Let's go!
I WONDER HOW SHIKIMORI-SAN IS DOING...
チラ…
Peek

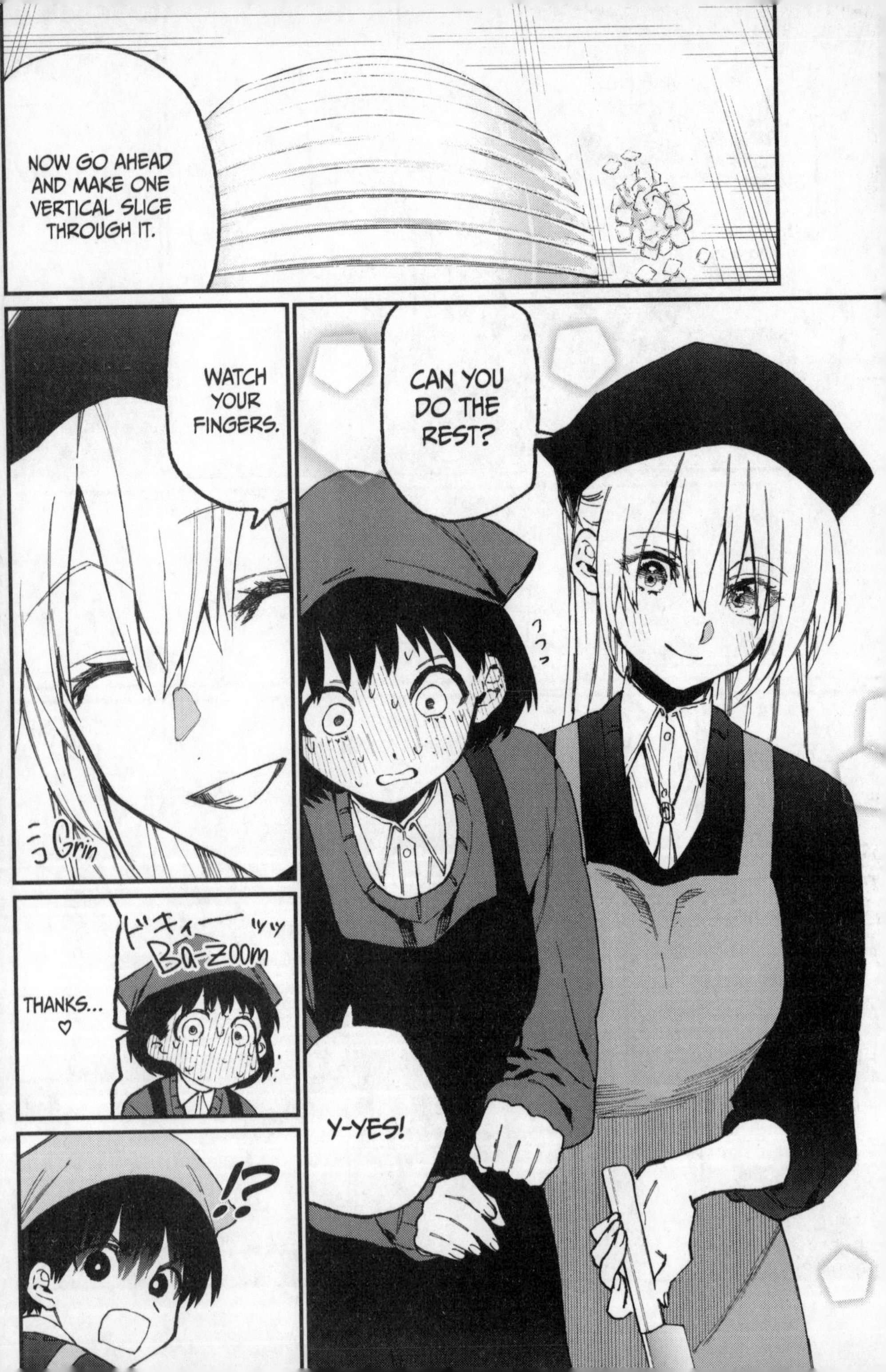
NOW GO AHEAD AND MAKE ONE VERTICAL SLICE THROUGH IT.
CAN YOU DO THE REST?
Y-YES!
WATCH YOUR FINGERS.
ニコ Grin
ドキィーッッ Ba-Zoom
THANKS... ♡
!?

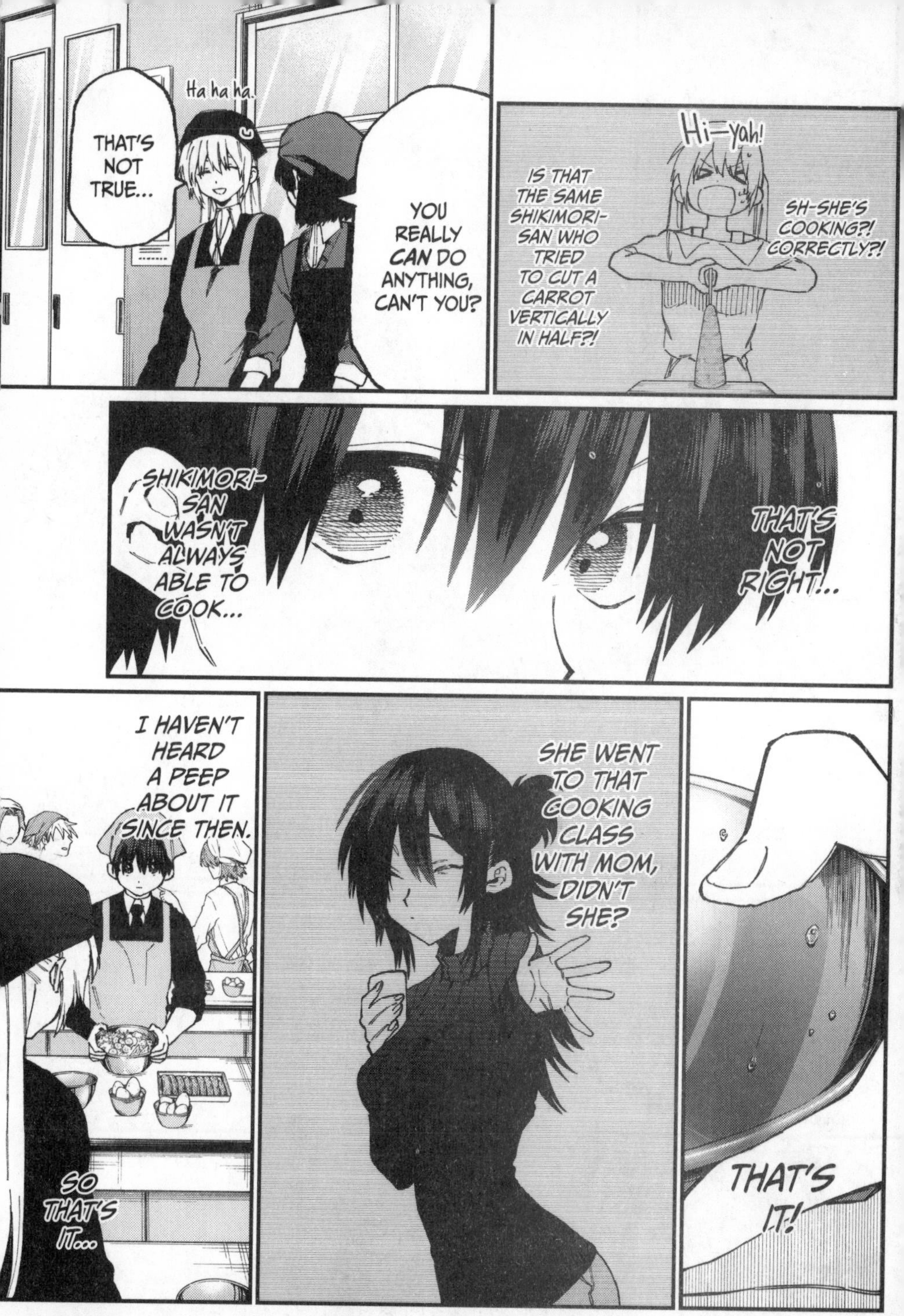
Hi—yah!
SH-SHE'S COOKING?! CORRECTLY?!
IS THAT THE SAME SHIKIMORI-SAN WHO TRIED TO CUT A CARROT VERTICALLY IN HALF?!
YOU REALLY CAN DO ANYTHING, CAN'T YOU?
Ha ha ha.
THAT'S NOT TRUE...
THAT'S NOT RIGHT...
SHIKIMORI-SAN WASN'T ALWAYS ABLE TO COOK...
THAT'S IT!
SHE WENT TO THAT COOKING CLASS WITH MOM, DIDN'T SHE?
I HAVEN'T HEARD A PEEP ABOUT IT SINCE THEN.
SO THAT'S IT...

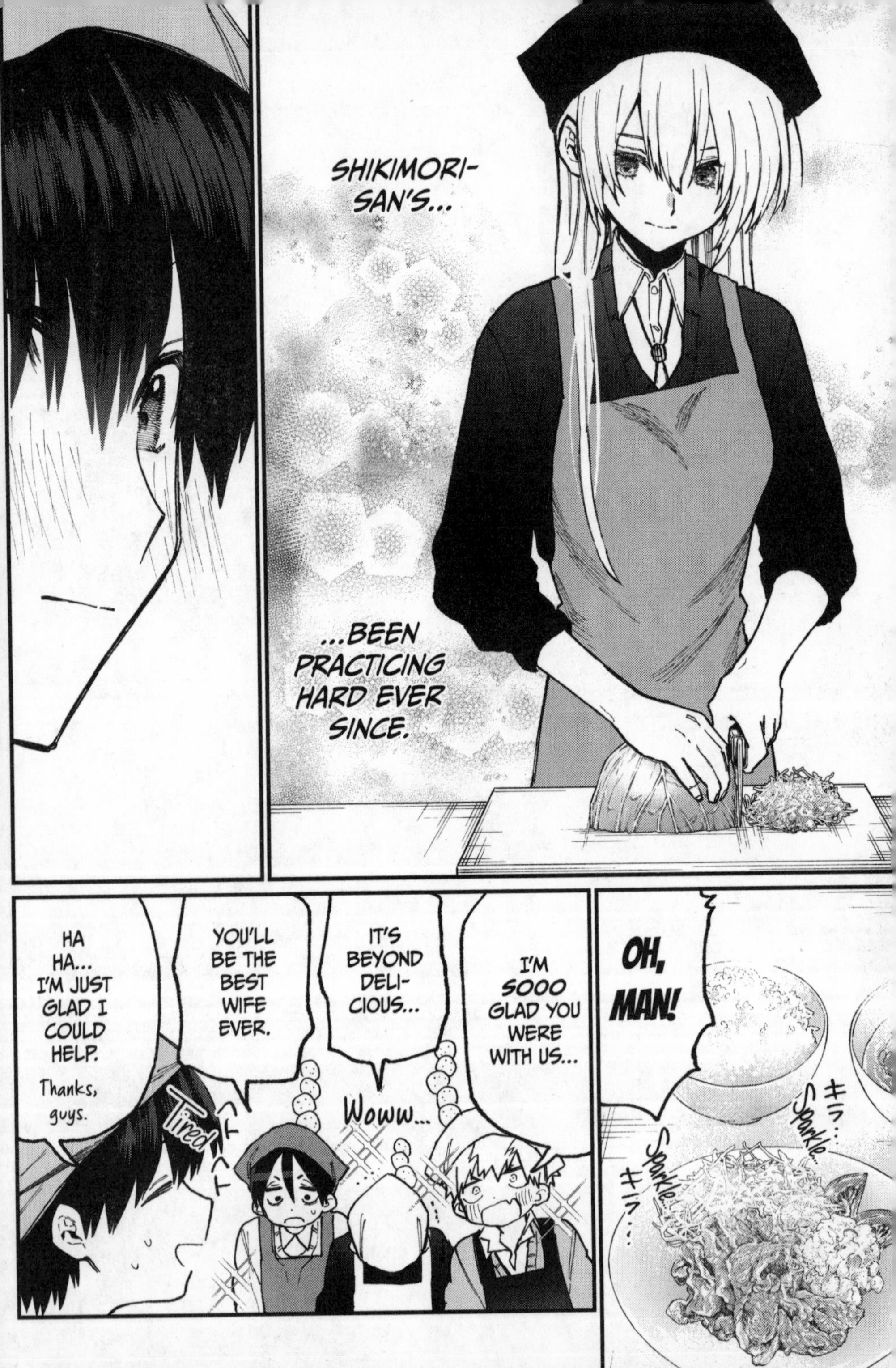
SHIKIMORI-SAN'S...
...BEEN PRACTICING HARD EVER SINCE.
OH, MAN!
キラ… Sparkle...
Sparkle... キラ…
I'M SOOO GLAD YOU WERE WITH US...
IT'S BEYOND DELI-CIOUS...
Woww...
YOU'LL BE THE BEST WIFE EVER.
Tired
HA HA... I'M JUST GLAD I COULD HELP.
Thanks, guys.

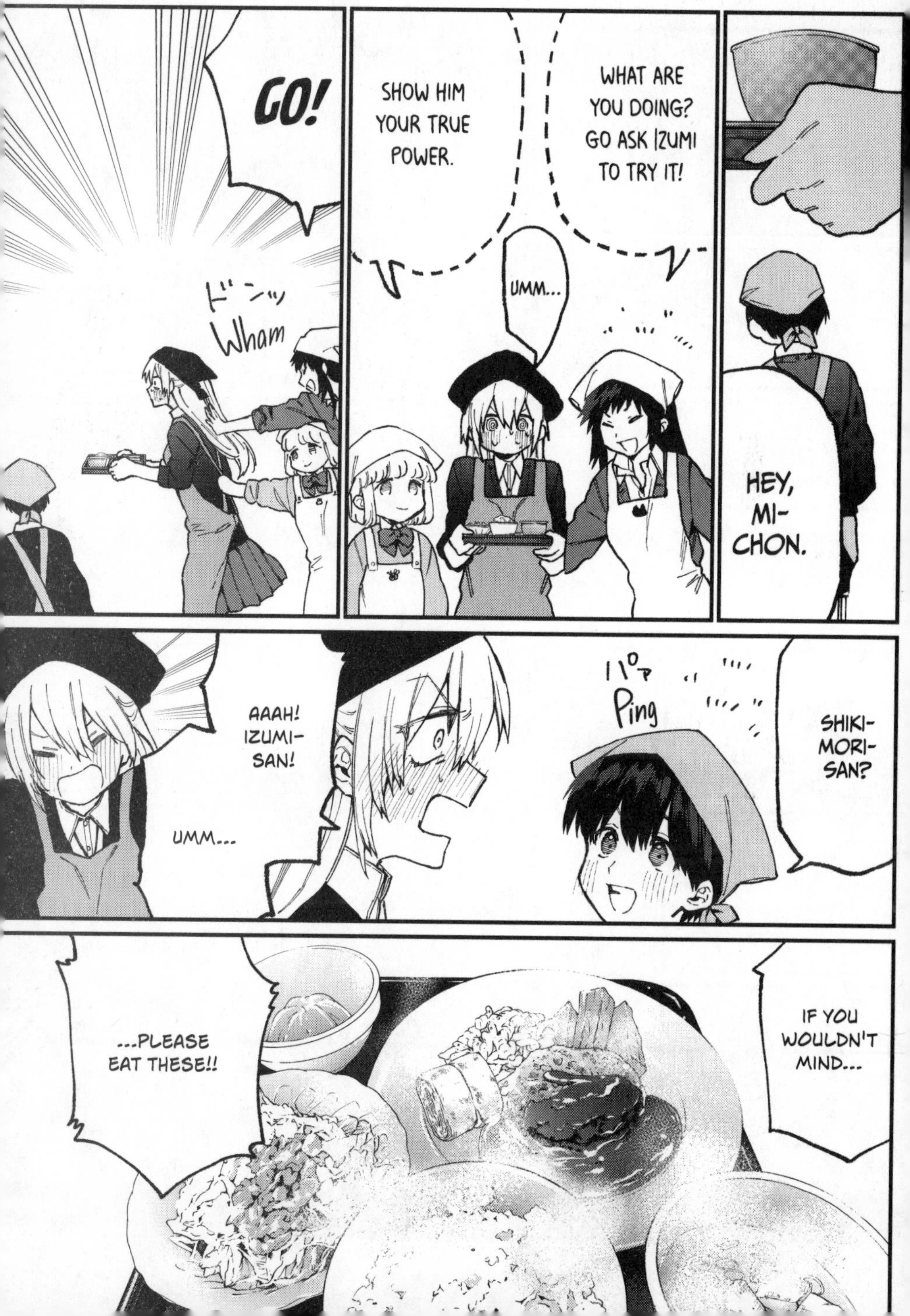
HEY, MI-CHON.
WHAT ARE YOU DOING? GO ASK IZUMI TO TRY IT!
SHOW HIM YOUR TRUE POWER.
UMM...
GO!
ドンッ
Wham
SHIKI-MORI-SAN?
パァ
Ping
AAAH! IZUMI-SAN!
UMM...
IF YOU WOULDN'T MIND...
...PLEASE EAT THESE!!

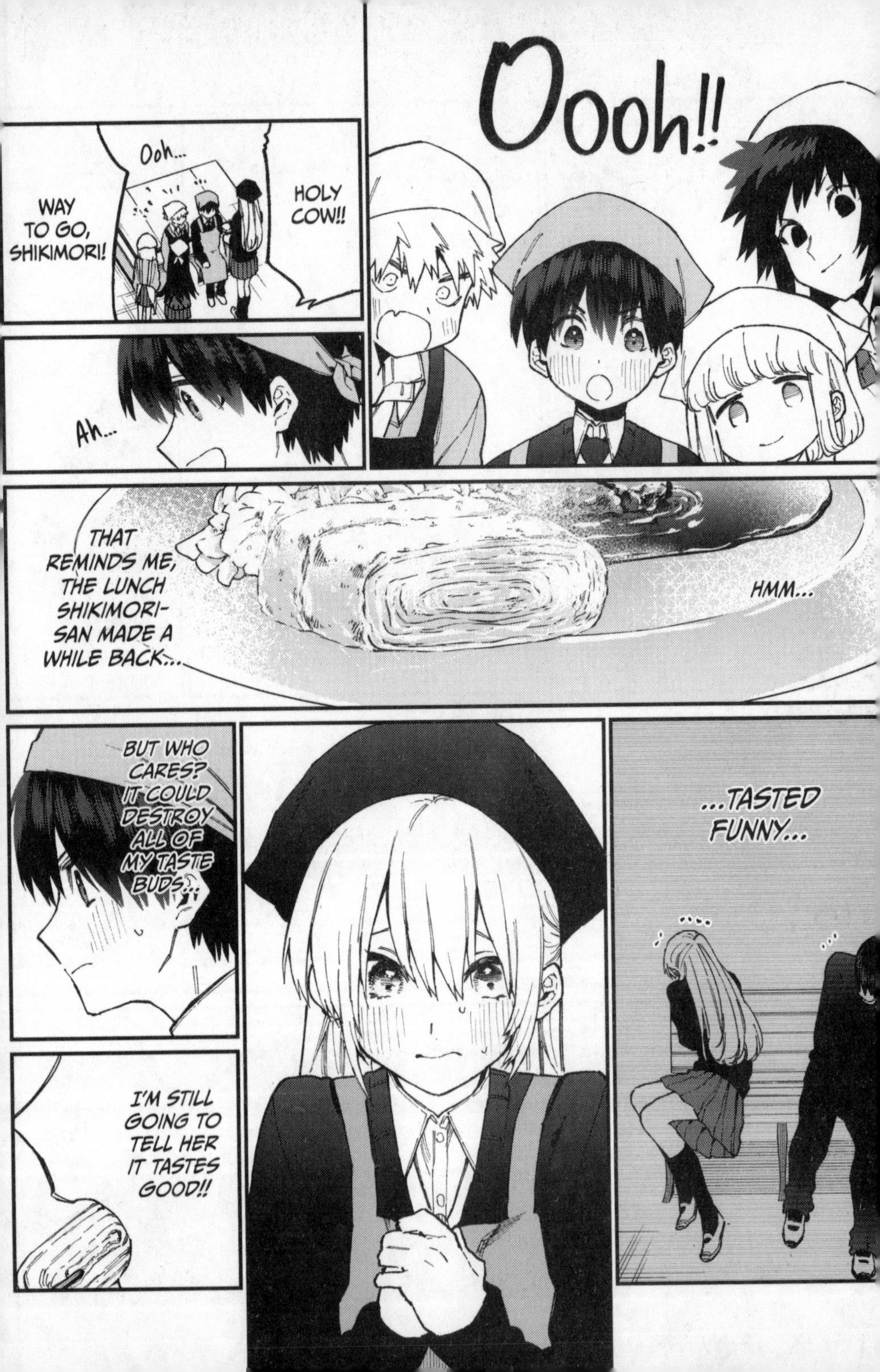
Oooh!!
Ooh...
HOLY COW!!
WAY TO GO, SHIKIMORI!
Ah...
HMM...
THAT REMINDS ME, THE LUNCH SHIKIMORI-SAN MADE A WHILE BACK...
...TASTED FUNNY...
BUT WHO CARES? IT COULD DESTROY ALL OF MY TASTE BUDS...
I'M STILL GOING TO TELL HER IT TASTES GOOD!!

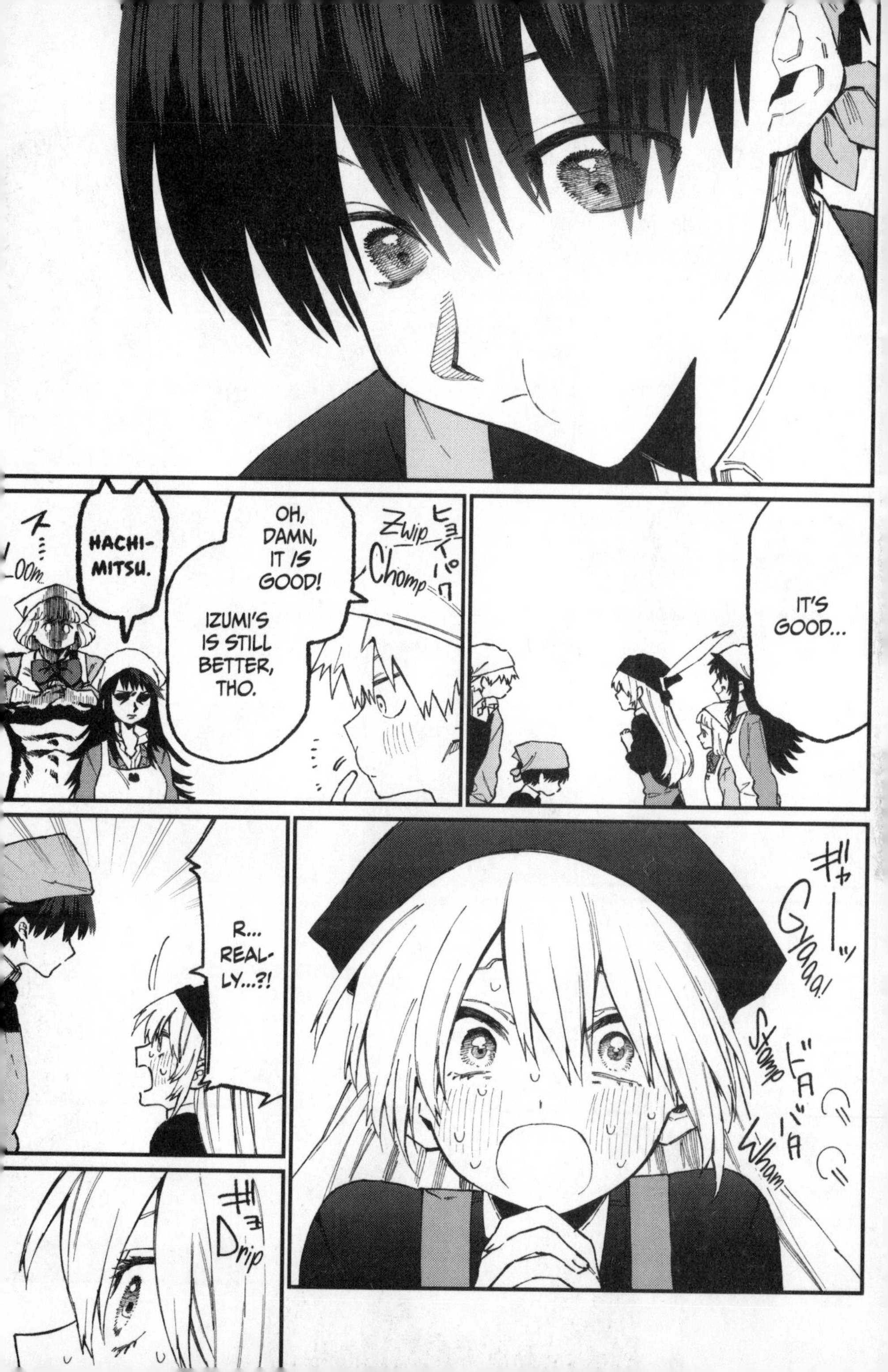
IT'S GOOD...
OH, DAMN, IT IS GOOD!
IZUMI'S IS STILL BETTER, THO.
Zwip
Chomp
HACHI-MITSU.
Gyaaa!
Stamp
Wham
R... REALLY...?!
Drip

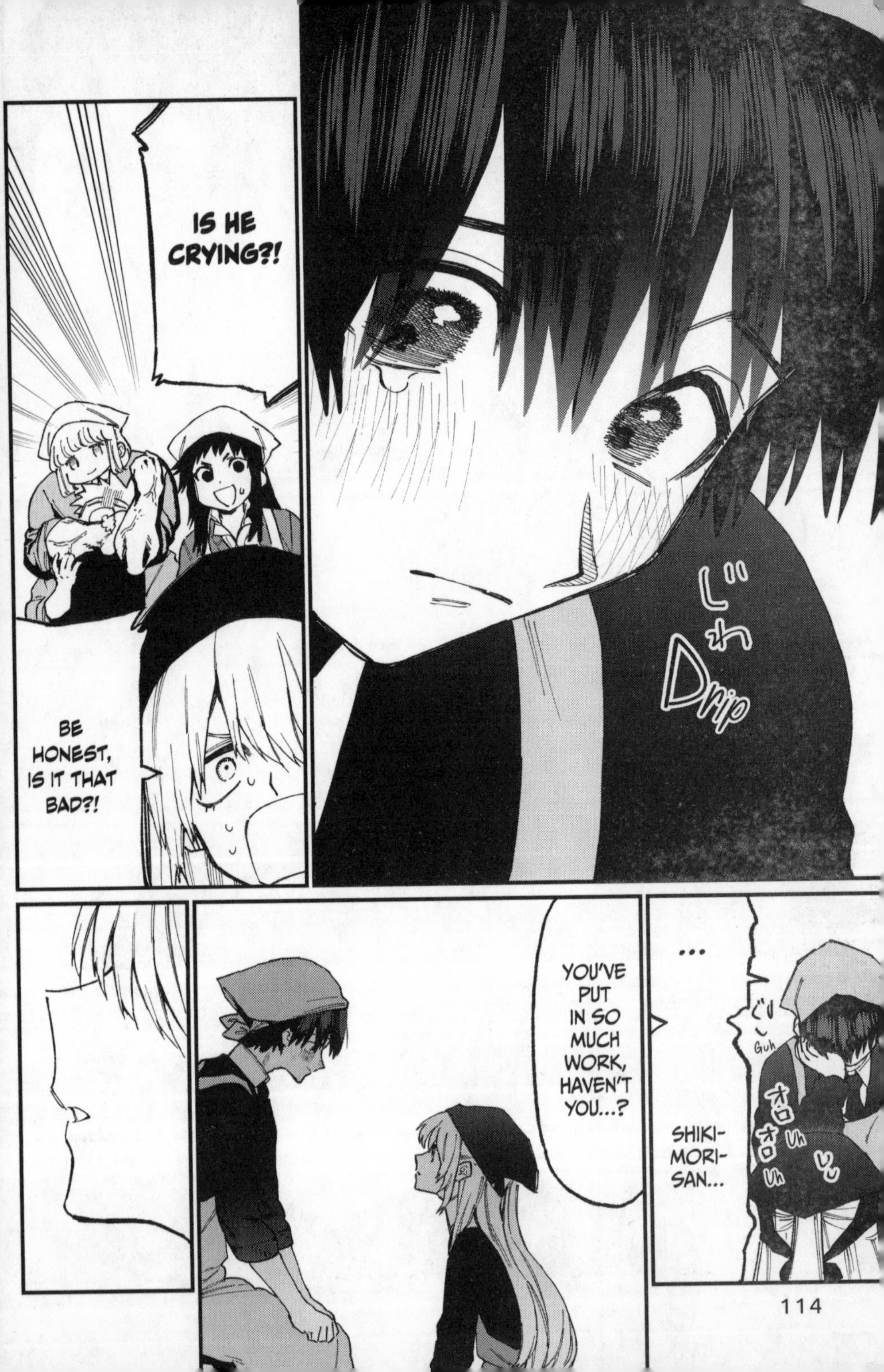
じわ
Drip
IS HE CRYING?!
BE HONEST, IS IT THAT BAD?!
...
ぐ
Guh
SHIKI-MORI-SAN...
オロ uh オロ uh
YOU'VE PUT IN SO MUCH WORK, HAVEN'T YOU...?

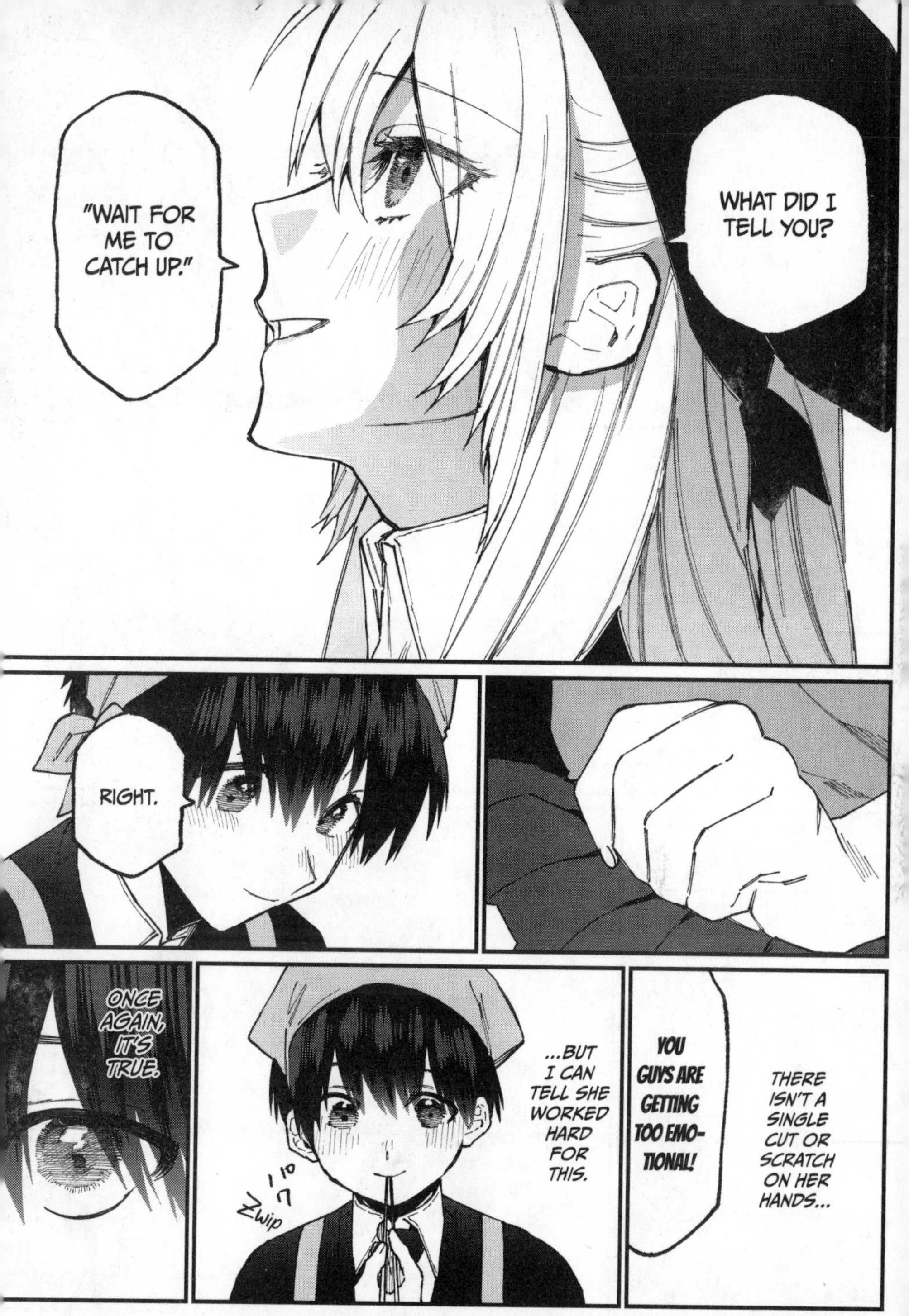

WHAT DID I TELL YOU?
"WAIT FOR ME TO CATCH UP."
RIGHT.
THERE ISN'T A SINGLE CUT OR SCRATCH ON HER HANDS...
YOU GUYS ARE GETTING TOO EMOTIONAL!
...BUT I CAN TELL SHE WORKED HARD FOR THIS.
ZWIP
ONCE AGAIN, IT'S TRUE.

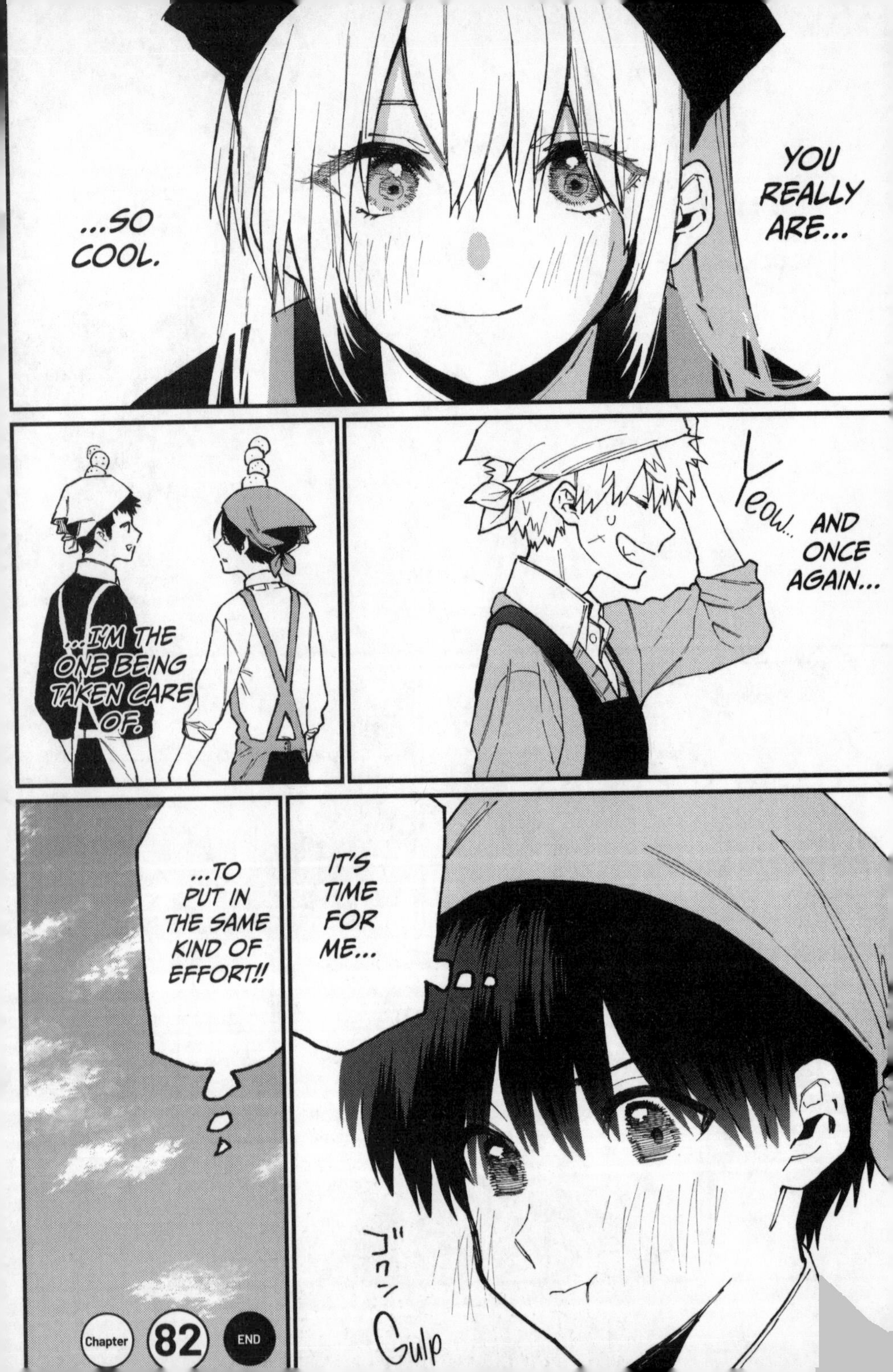
YOU REALLY ARE...
...SO COOL.
Yeow...
AND ONCE AGAIN...
...I'M THE ONE BEING TAKEN CARE OF.
IT'S TIME FOR ME...
...TO PUT IN THE SAME KIND OF EFFORT!!
ゴクン
Gulp
Chapter 82 END

SHIKIMORI'S not just a cutie

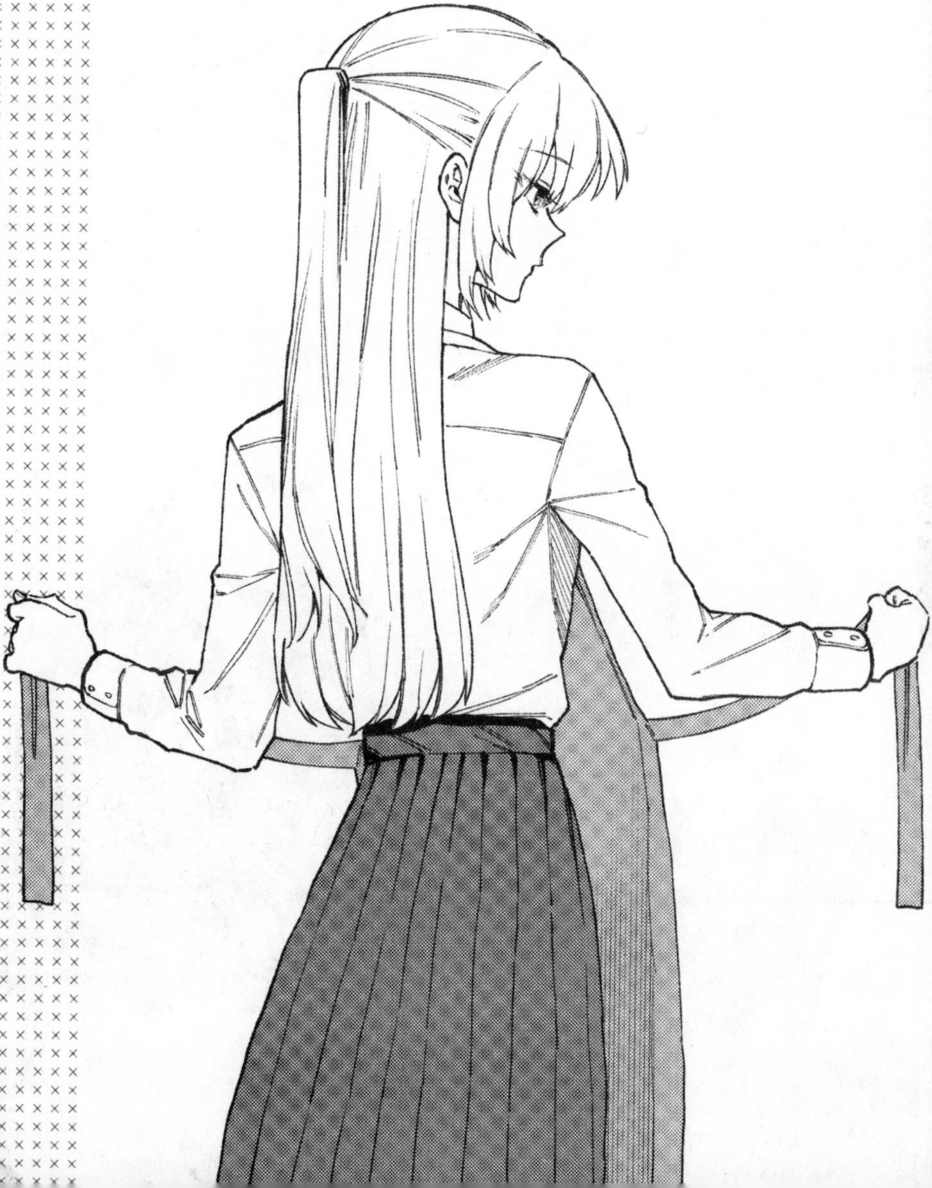

SHIKIMORI'S
not just a cutie

PRACTICING

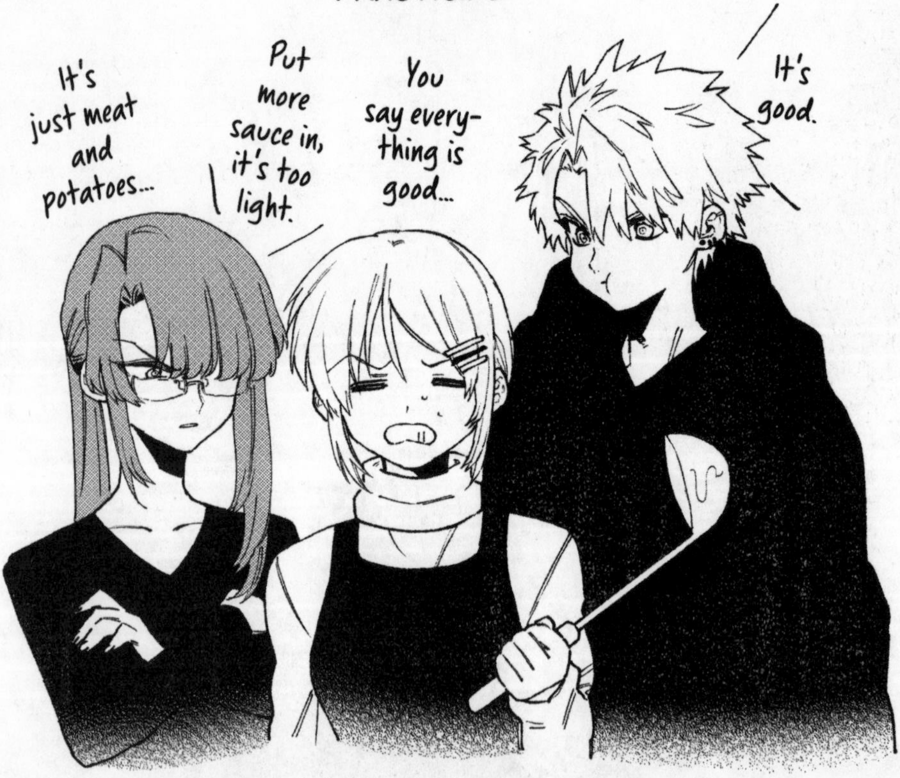
It's good.
You say every-thing is good...
Put more sauce in, it's too light.
It's just meat and potatoes...

Chapter 83

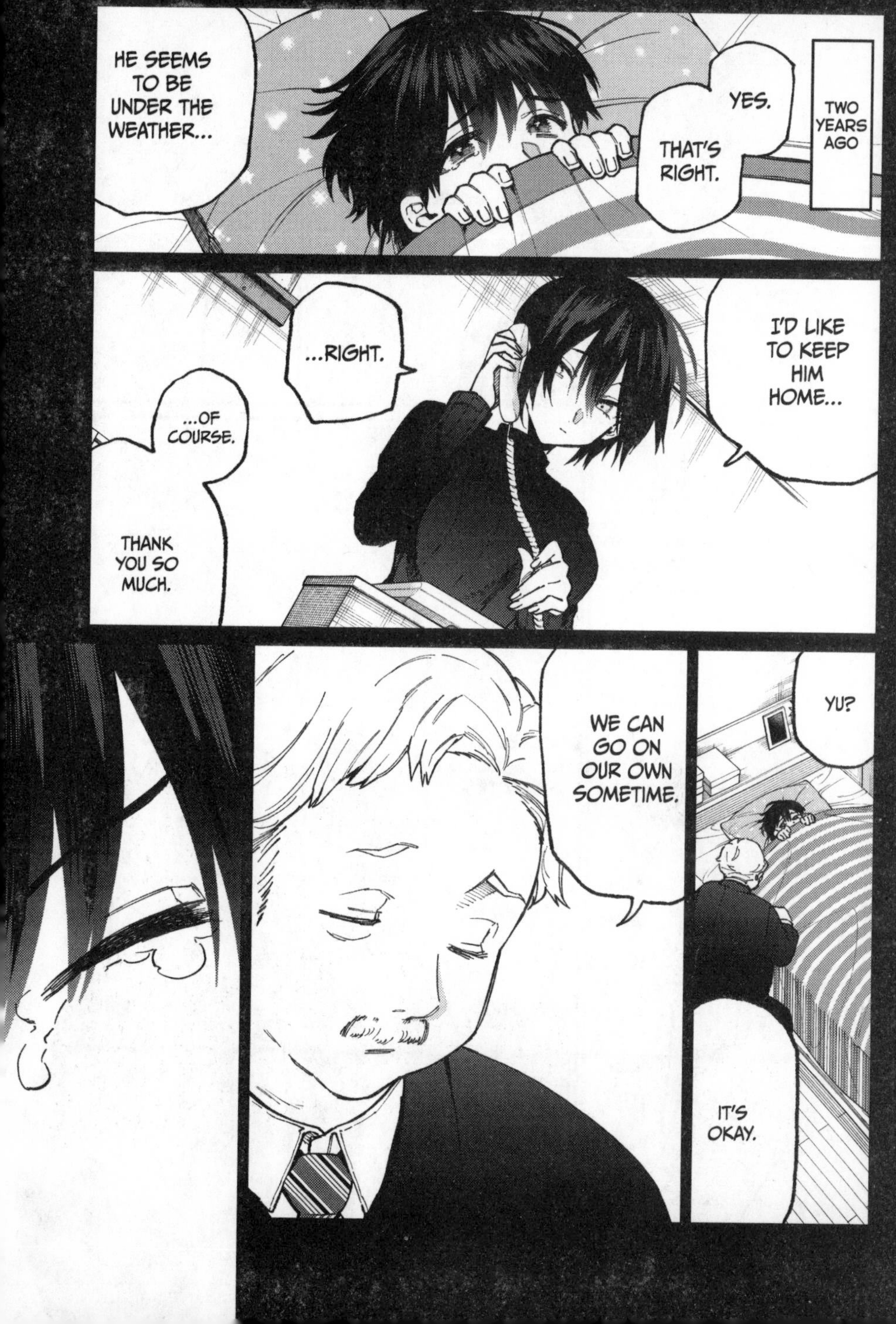
TWO YEARS AGO
YES.
THAT'S RIGHT.
HE SEEMS TO BE UNDER THE WEATHER...
I'D LIKE TO KEEP HIM HOME...
...RIGHT.
...OF COURSE.
THANK YOU SO MUCH.
YU?
IT'S OKAY.
WE CAN GO ON OUR OWN SOMETIME.

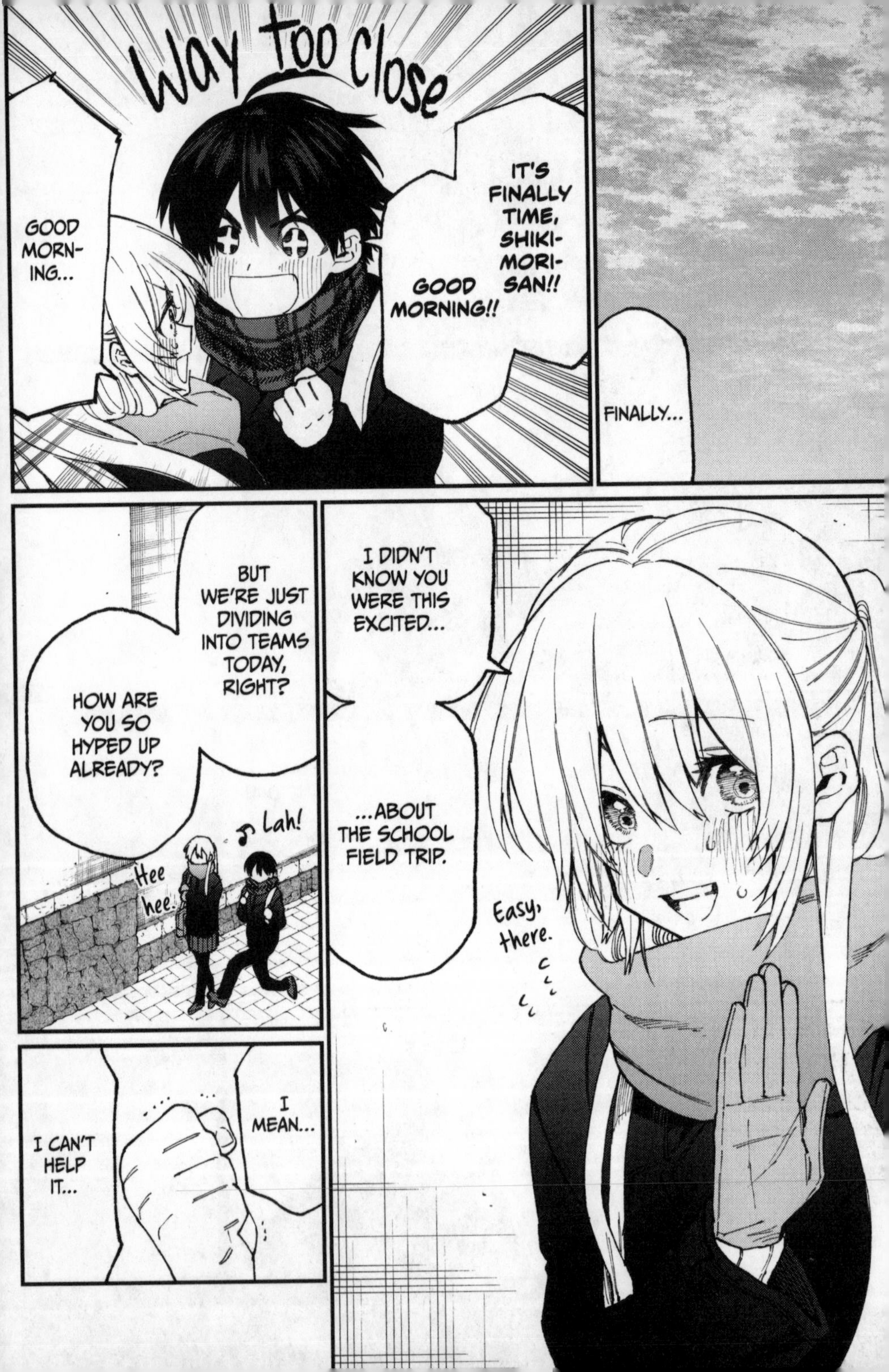
FINALLY...
Way too close
IT'S FINALLY TIME, SHIKI-MORI-SAN!!
GOOD MORNING!!
GOOD MORN-ING...
I DIDN'T KNOW YOU WERE THIS EXCITED...
...ABOUT THE SCHOOL FIELD TRIP.
Easy, there.
BUT WE'RE JUST DIVIDING INTO TEAMS TODAY, RIGHT?
HOW ARE YOU SO HYPED UP ALREADY?
Lah!
Hee hee.
I MEAN...
I CAN'T HELP IT...

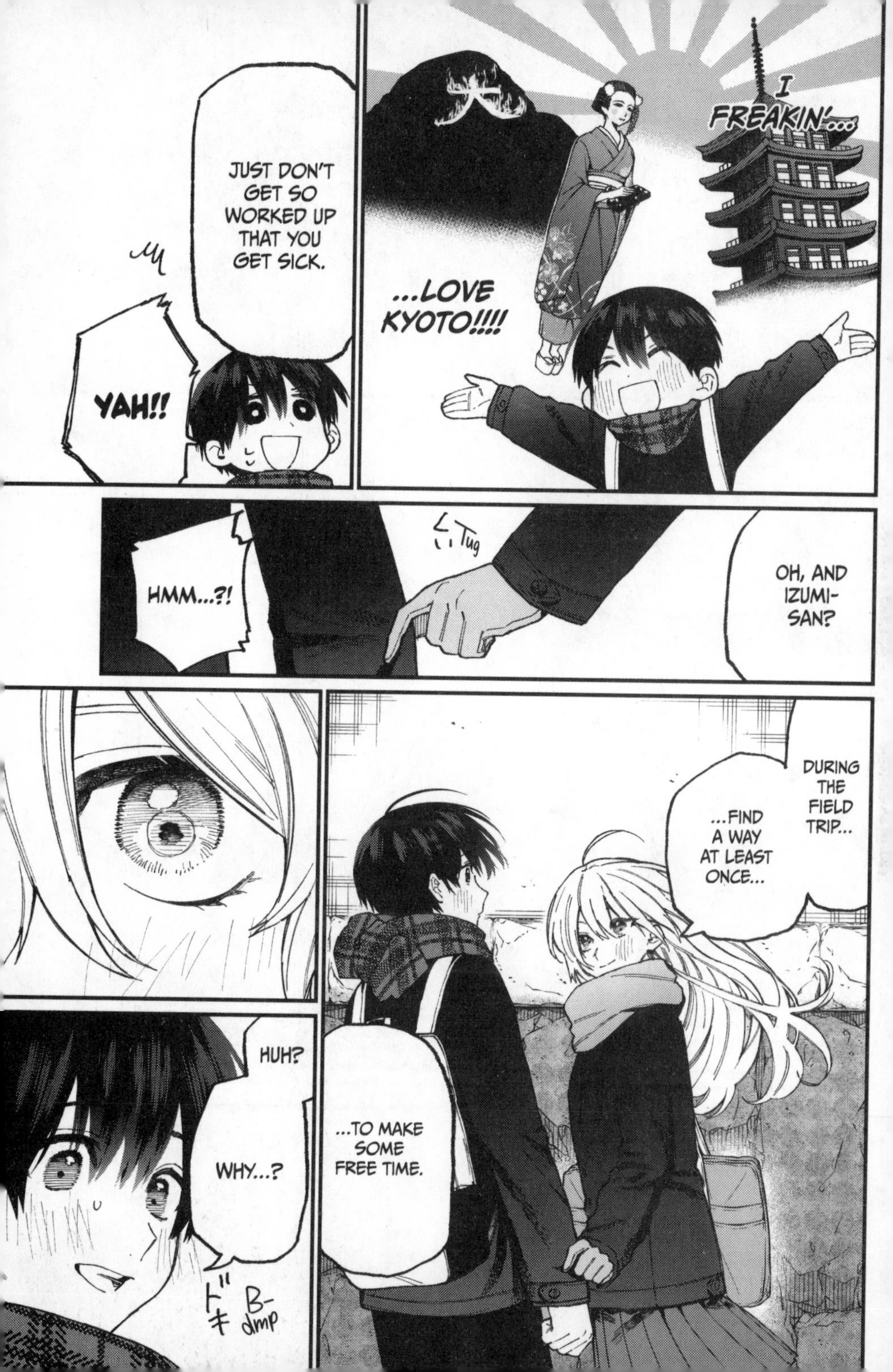
I FREAKIN'...
...LOVE KYOTO!!!!
JUST DON'T GET SO WORKED UP THAT YOU GET SICK.
YAH!!
OH, AND IZUMI-SAN?
Tug
HMM...?!
DURING THE FIELD TRIP...
...FIND A WAY AT LEAST ONCE...
...TO MAKE SOME FREE TIME.
HUH?
WHY...?
B-dmp

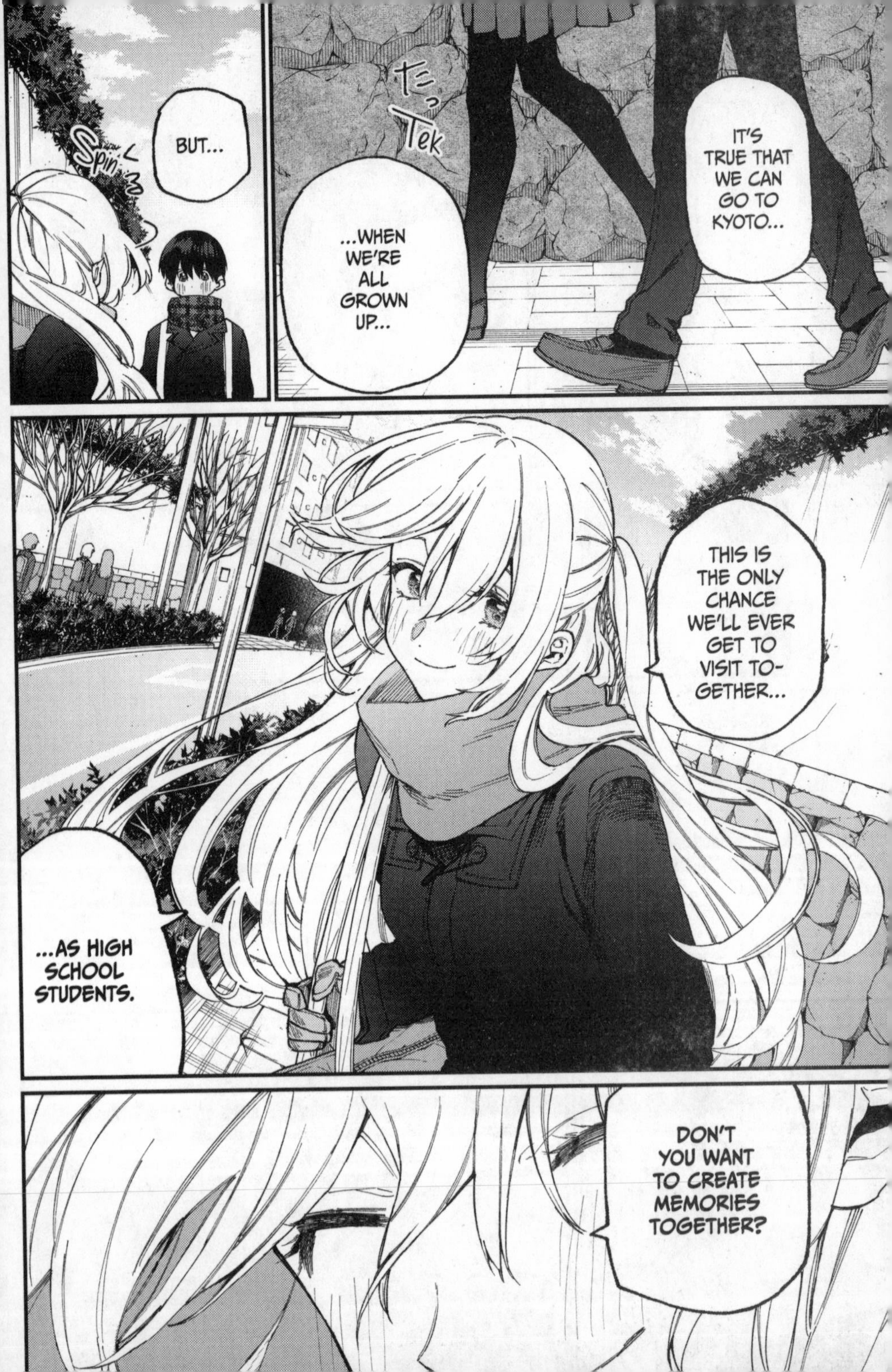
IT'S TRUE THAT WE CAN GO TO KYOTO...
たっ
Tek
...WHEN WE'RE ALL GROWN UP...
BUT...
Spin
THIS IS THE ONLY CHANCE WE'LL EVER GET TO VISIT TO-GETHER...
...AS HIGH SCHOOL STUDENTS.
DON'T YOU WANT TO CREATE MEMORIES TOGETHER?

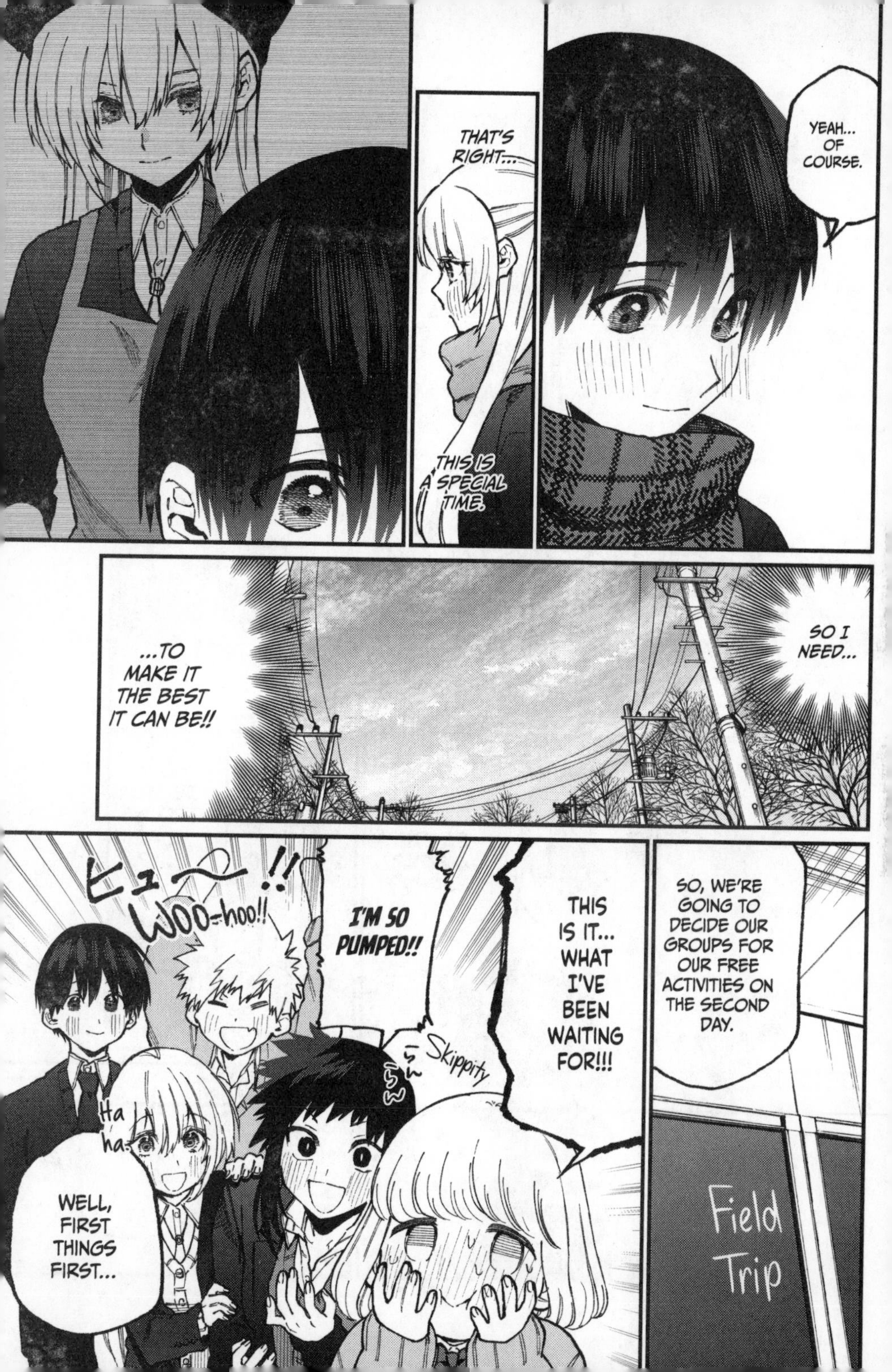
YEAH... OF COURSE.
THAT'S RIGHT...
THIS IS A SPECIAL TIME.
SO I NEED...
...TO MAKE IT THE BEST IT CAN BE!!
SO, WE'RE GOING TO DECIDE OUR GROUPS FOR OUR FREE ACTIVITIES ON THE SECOND DAY.
Field Trip
THIS IS IT... WHAT I'VE BEEN WAITING FOR!!!
I'M SO PUMPED!!
ヒュ〜!!
WOO-hoo!!
Skippity
Ha ha.
WELL, FIRST THINGS FIRST...

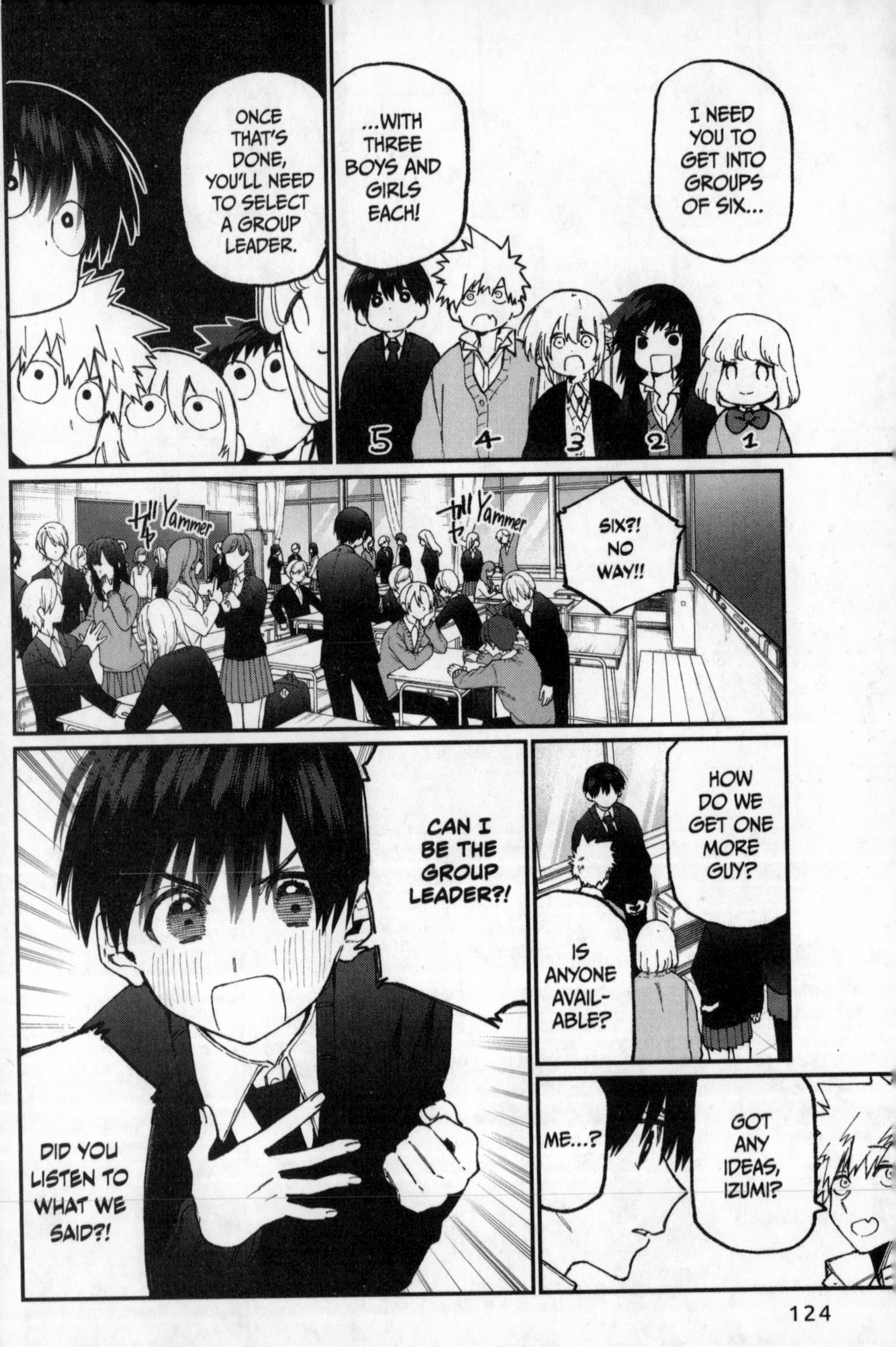
I NEED YOU TO GET INTO GROUPS OF SIX...
...WITH THREE BOYS AND GIRLS EACH!
1
2
3
4
5
ONCE THAT'S DONE, YOU'LL NEED TO SELECT A GROUP LEADER.
Yammer
Yammer
SIX?! NO WAY!!
HOW DO WE GET ONE MORE GUY?
IS ANYONE AVAIL-ABLE?
GOT ANY IDEAS, IZUMI?
ME...?
CAN I BE THE GROUP LEADER?!
DID YOU LISTEN TO WHAT WE SAID?!

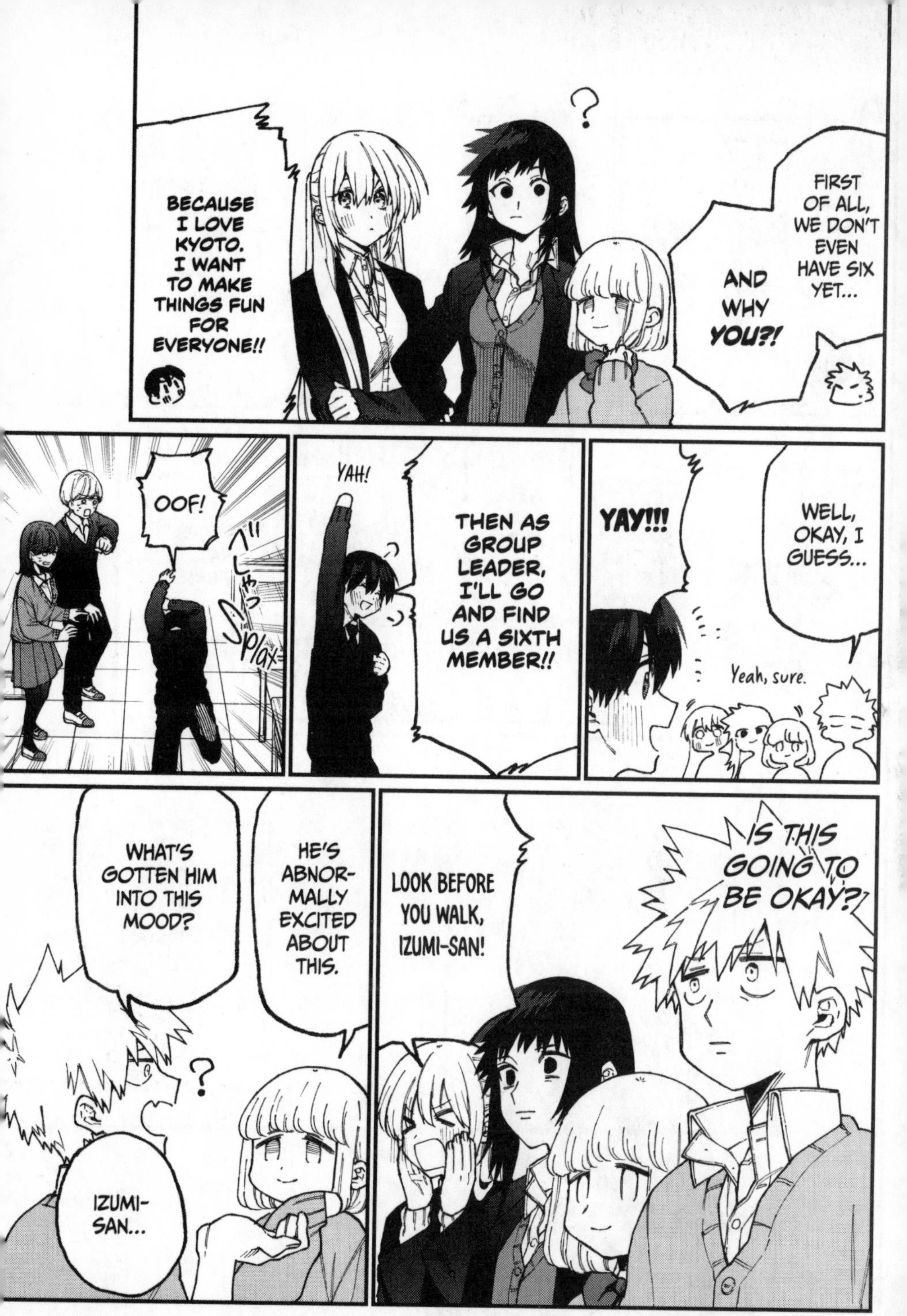

FIRST OF ALL, WE DON'T EVEN HAVE SIX YET...
AND WHY YOU?!
BECAUSE I LOVE KYOTO. I WANT TO MAKE THINGS FUN FOR EVERYONE!!
WELL, OKAY, I GUESS...
Yeah, sure.
YAY!!!
THEN AS GROUP LEADER, I'LL GO AND FIND US A SIXTH MEMBER!!
YAH!
OOF!
Splat
IS THIS GOING TO BE OKAY?
LOOK BEFORE YOU WALK, IZUMI-SAN!
HE'S ABNORMALLY EXCITED ABOUT THIS.
WHAT'S GOTTEN HIM INTO THIS MOOD?
IZUMI-SAN...

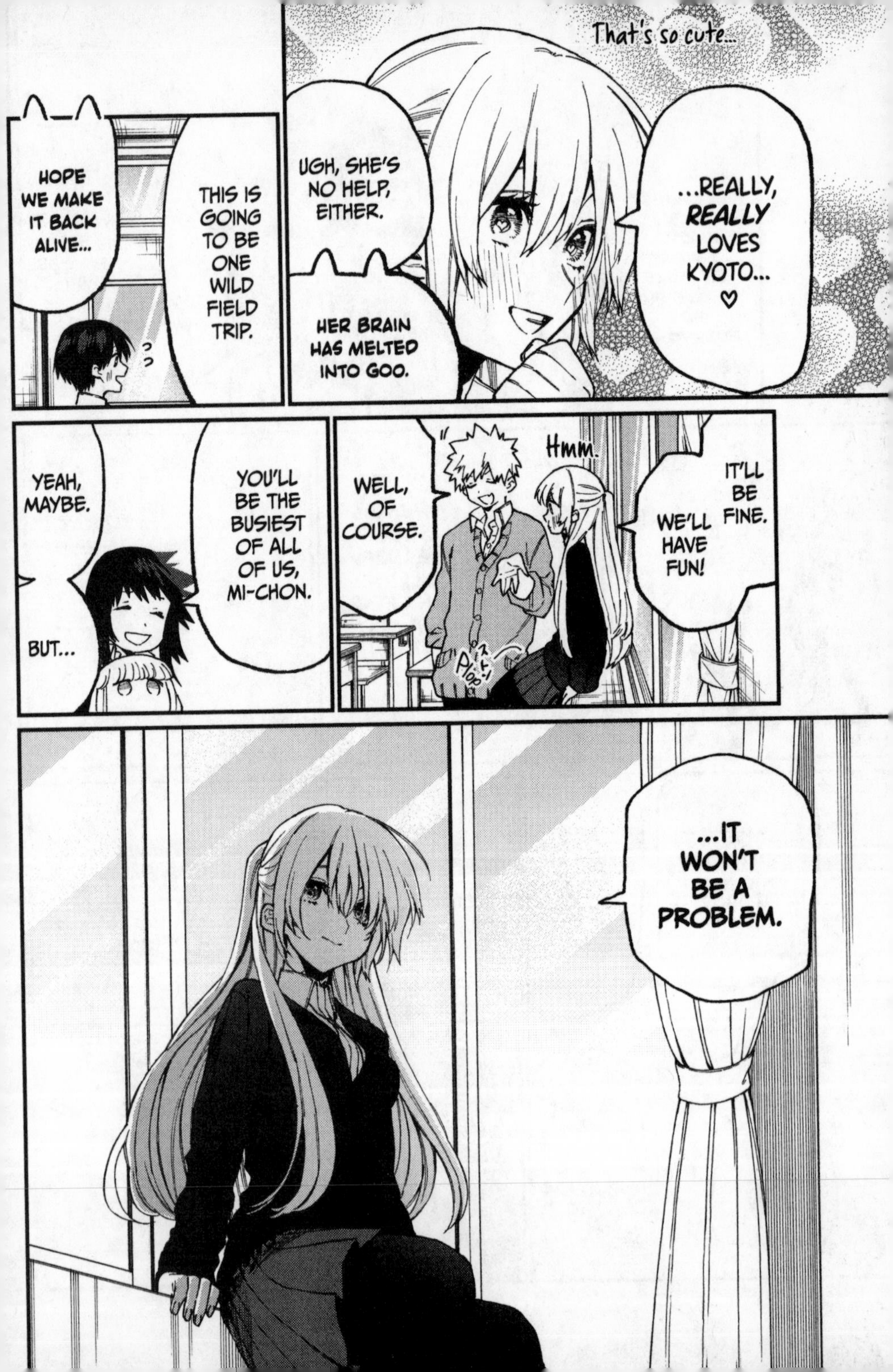
That's so cute...
...REALLY, REALLY LOVES KYOTO... ♡
UGH, SHE'S NO HELP, EITHER.
HER BRAIN HAS MELTED INTO GOO.
THIS IS GOING TO BE ONE WILD FIELD TRIP.
HOPE WE MAKE IT BACK ALIVE...
IT'LL BE FINE.
WE'LL HAVE FUN!
Hmm.
WELL, OF COURSE.
Plop
YOU'LL BE THE BUSIEST OF ALL OF US, MI-CHON.
YEAH, MAYBE.
BUT...
...IT WON'T BE A PROBLEM.

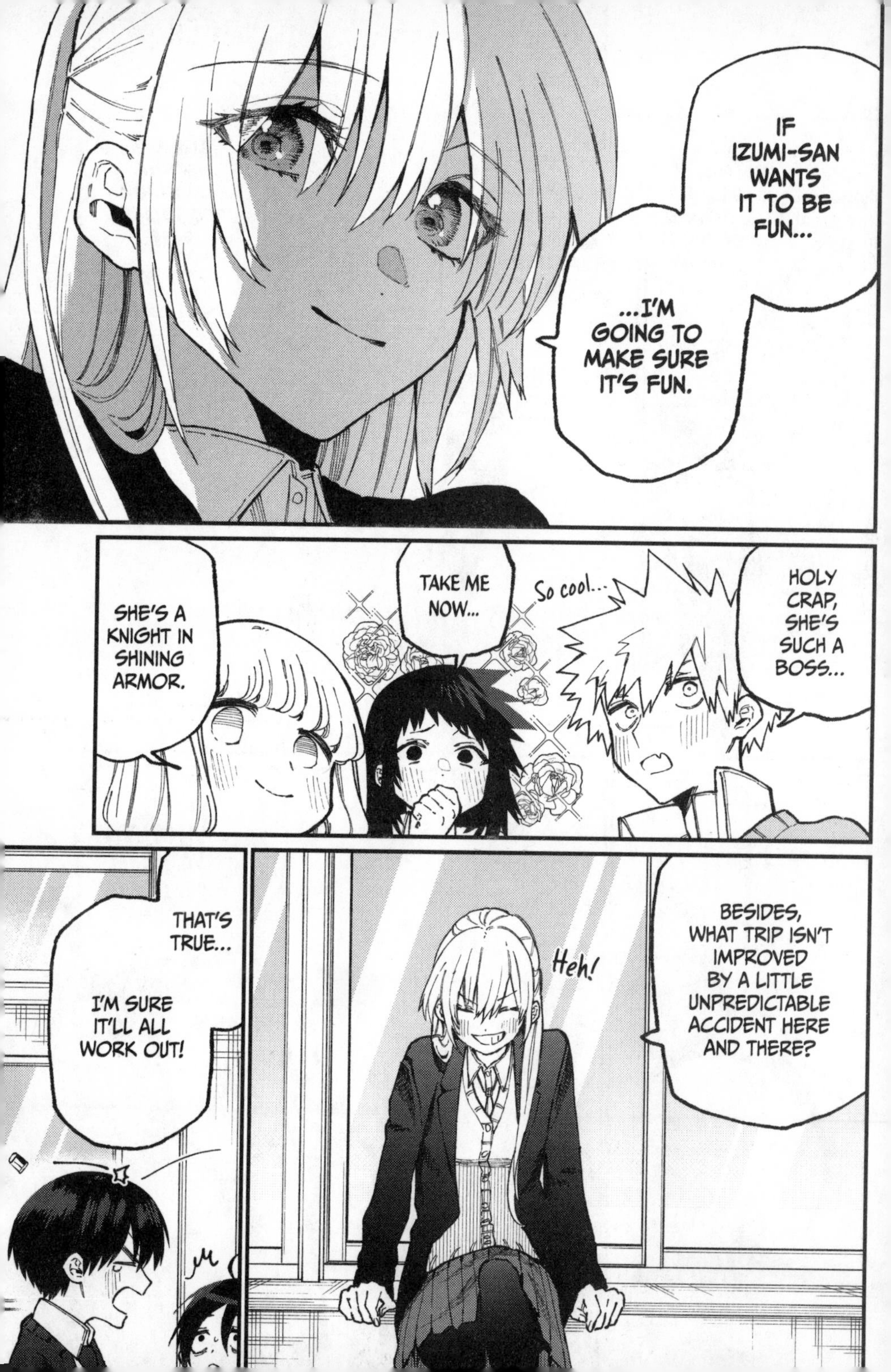
IF IZUMI-SAN WANTS IT TO BE FUN...
...I'M GOING TO MAKE SURE IT'S FUN.
HOLY CRAP, SHE'S SUCH A BOSS...
So cool...
TAKE ME NOW...
SHE'S A KNIGHT IN SHINING ARMOR.
BESIDES, WHAT TRIP ISN'T IMPROVED BY A LITTLE UNPREDICTABLE ACCIDENT HERE AND THERE?
Heh!
THAT'S TRUE...
I'M SURE IT'LL ALL WORK OUT!

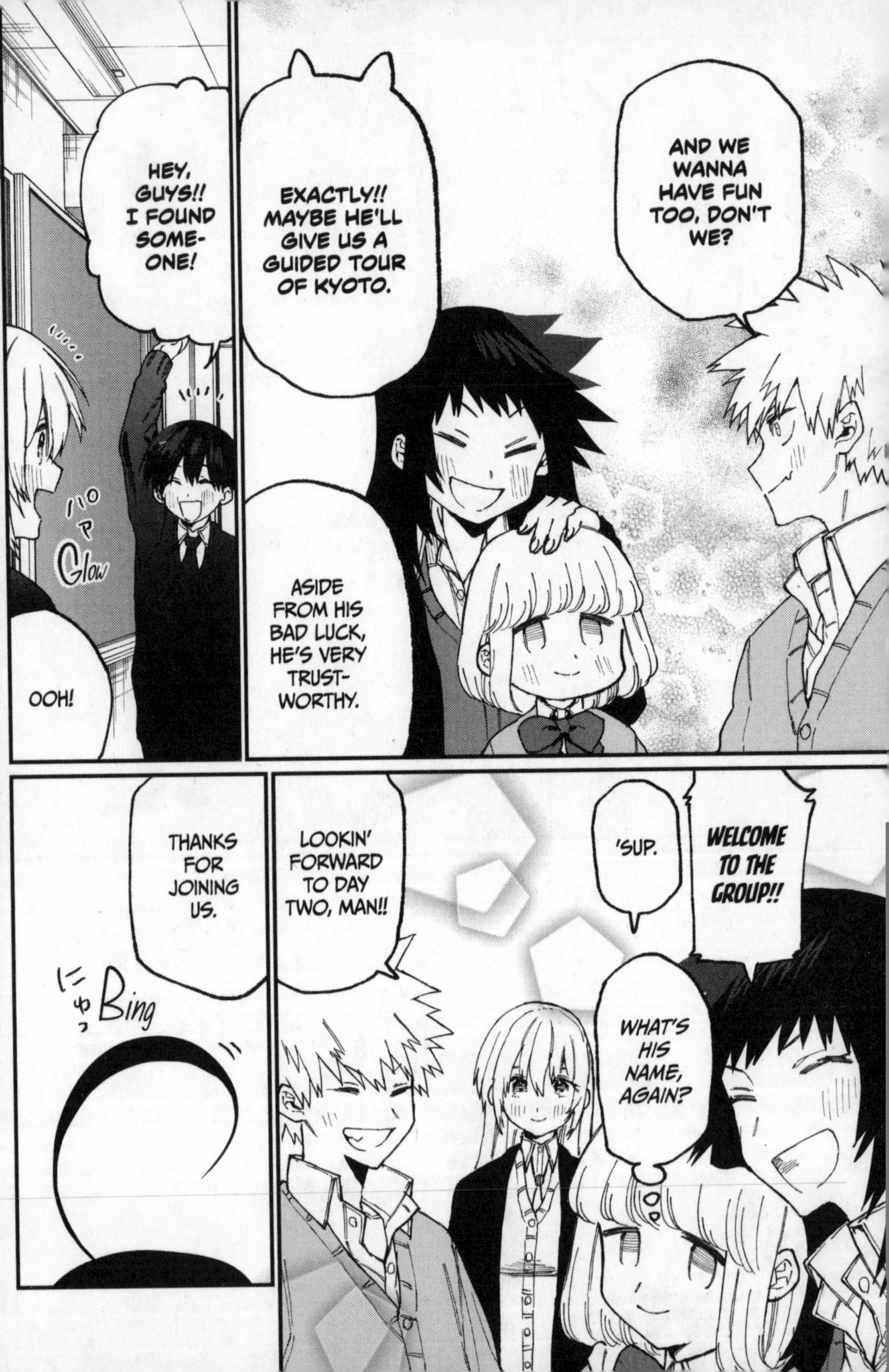
AND WE WANNA HAVE FUN TOO, DON'T WE?
EXACTLY!! MAYBE HE'LL GIVE US A GUIDED TOUR OF KYOTO.
ASIDE FROM HIS BAD LUCK, HE'S VERY TRUST-WORTHY.
HEY, GUYS!! I FOUND SOME-ONE!
Glow
OOH!
WELCOME TO THE GROUP!!
'SUP.
WHAT'S HIS NAME, AGAIN?
LOOKIN' FORWARD TO DAY TWO, MAN!!
THANKS FOR JOINING US.
Bing

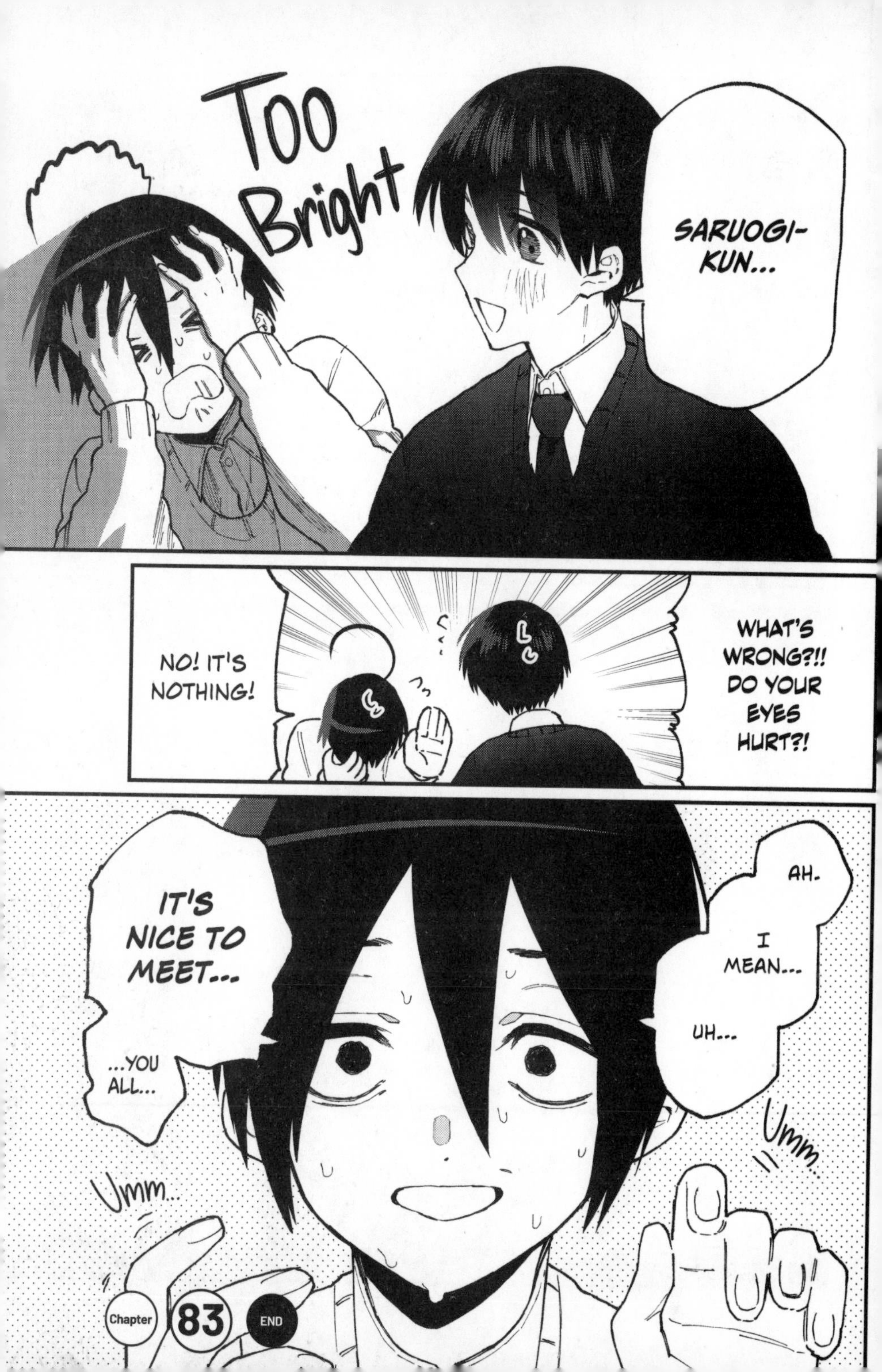
SARUOGI-KUN...
Too Bright
WHAT'S WRONG?!! DO YOUR EYES HURT?!
NO! IT'S NOTHING!
AH.
I MEAN...
UH...
Umm...
IT'S NICE TO MEET...
...YOU ALL...
Umm...
Chapter 83 END

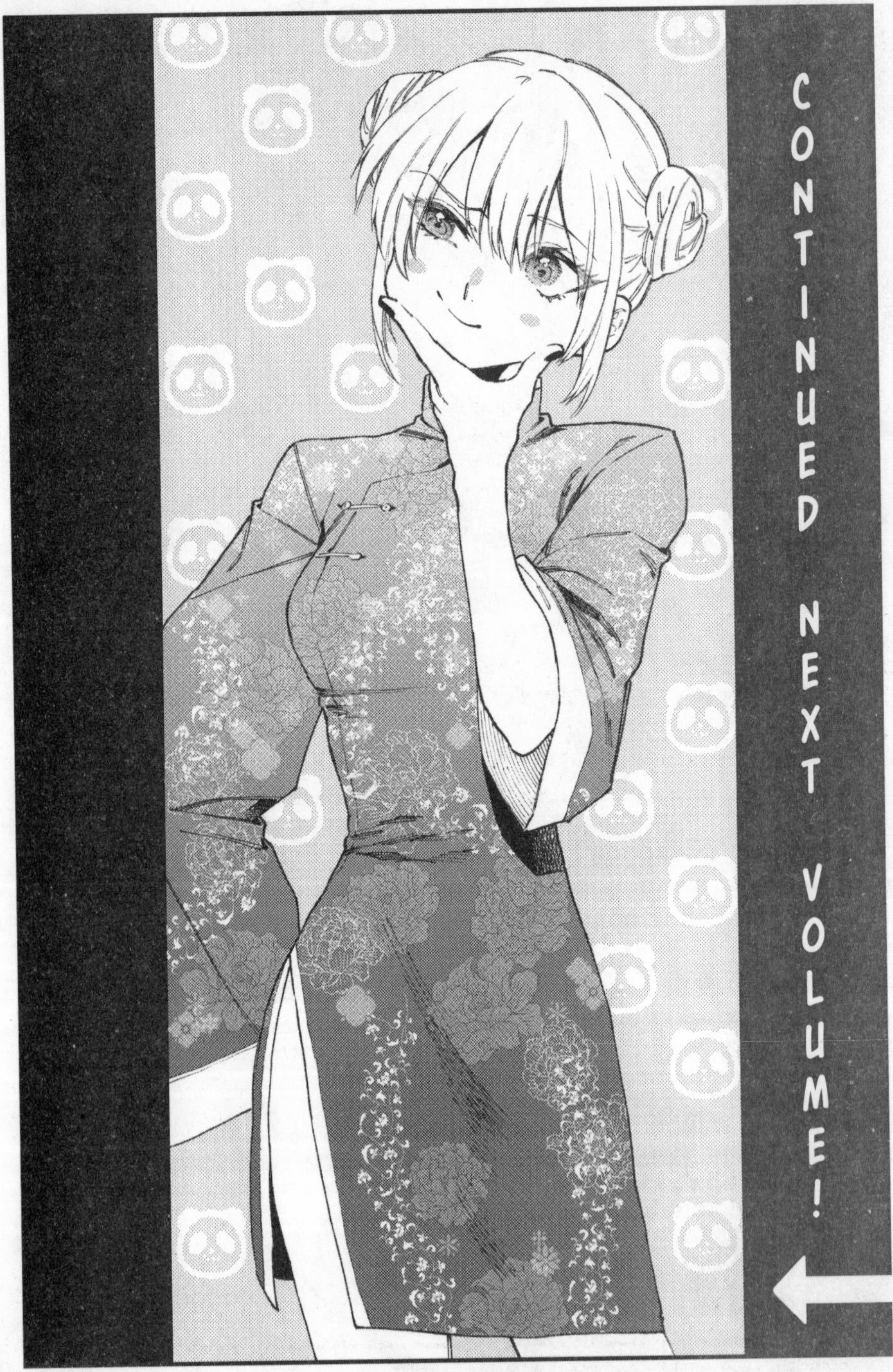
CONTINUED NEXT VOLUME!

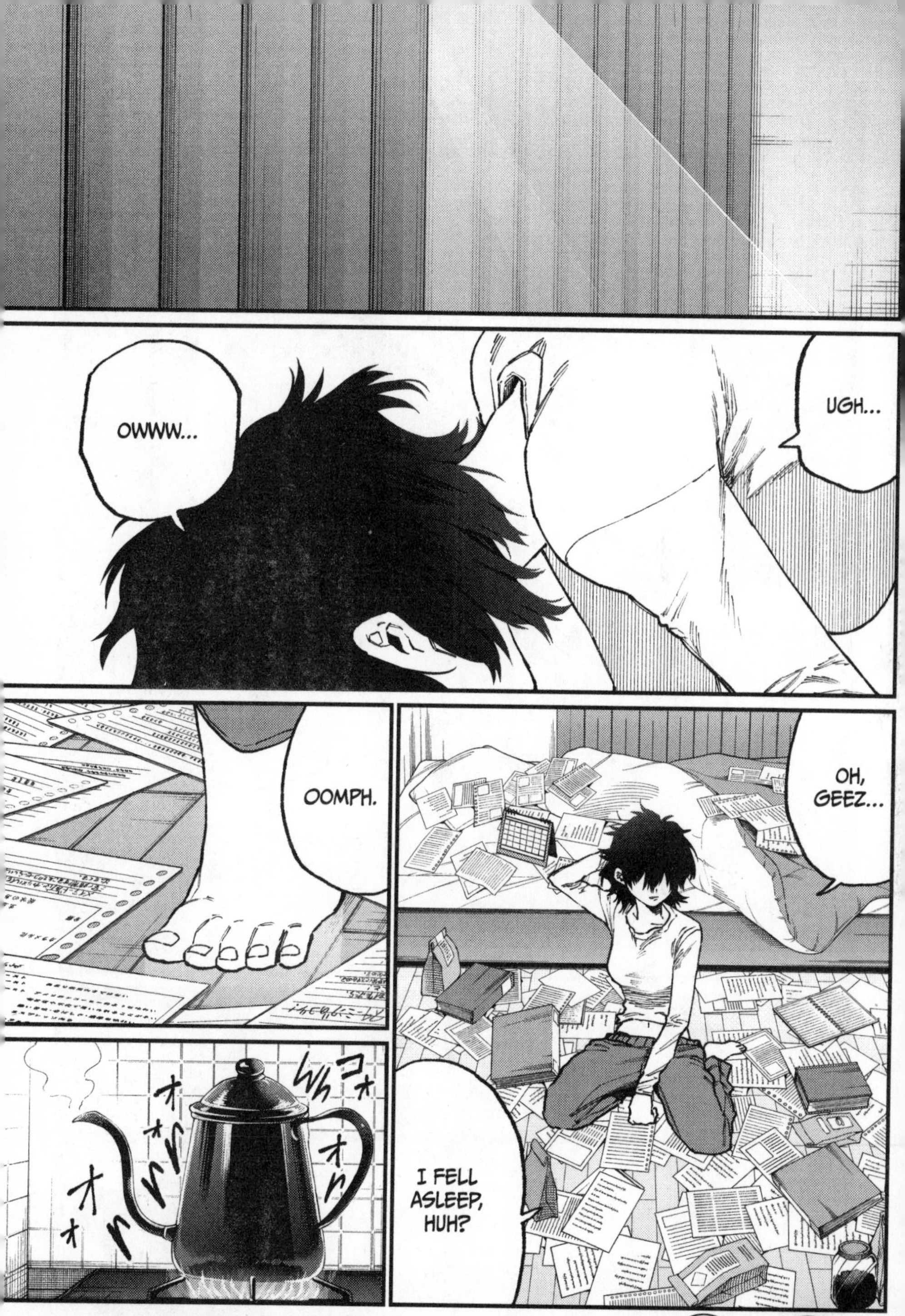
UGH...
OWWW...
OH, GEEZ...
I FELL ASLEEP, HUH?
OOMPH.

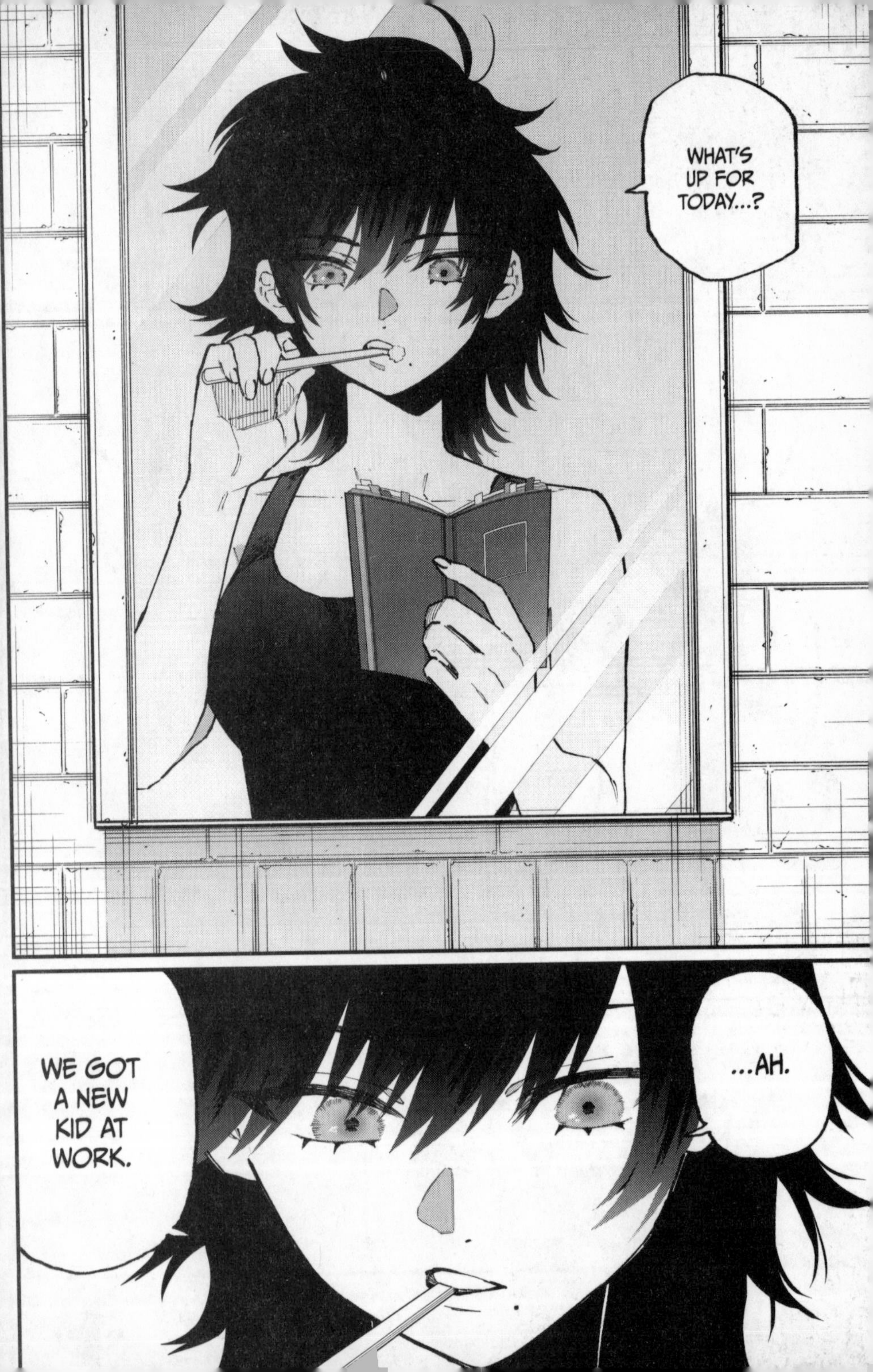
WHAT'S UP FOR TODAY...?
...AH.
WE GOT A NEW KID AT WORK.

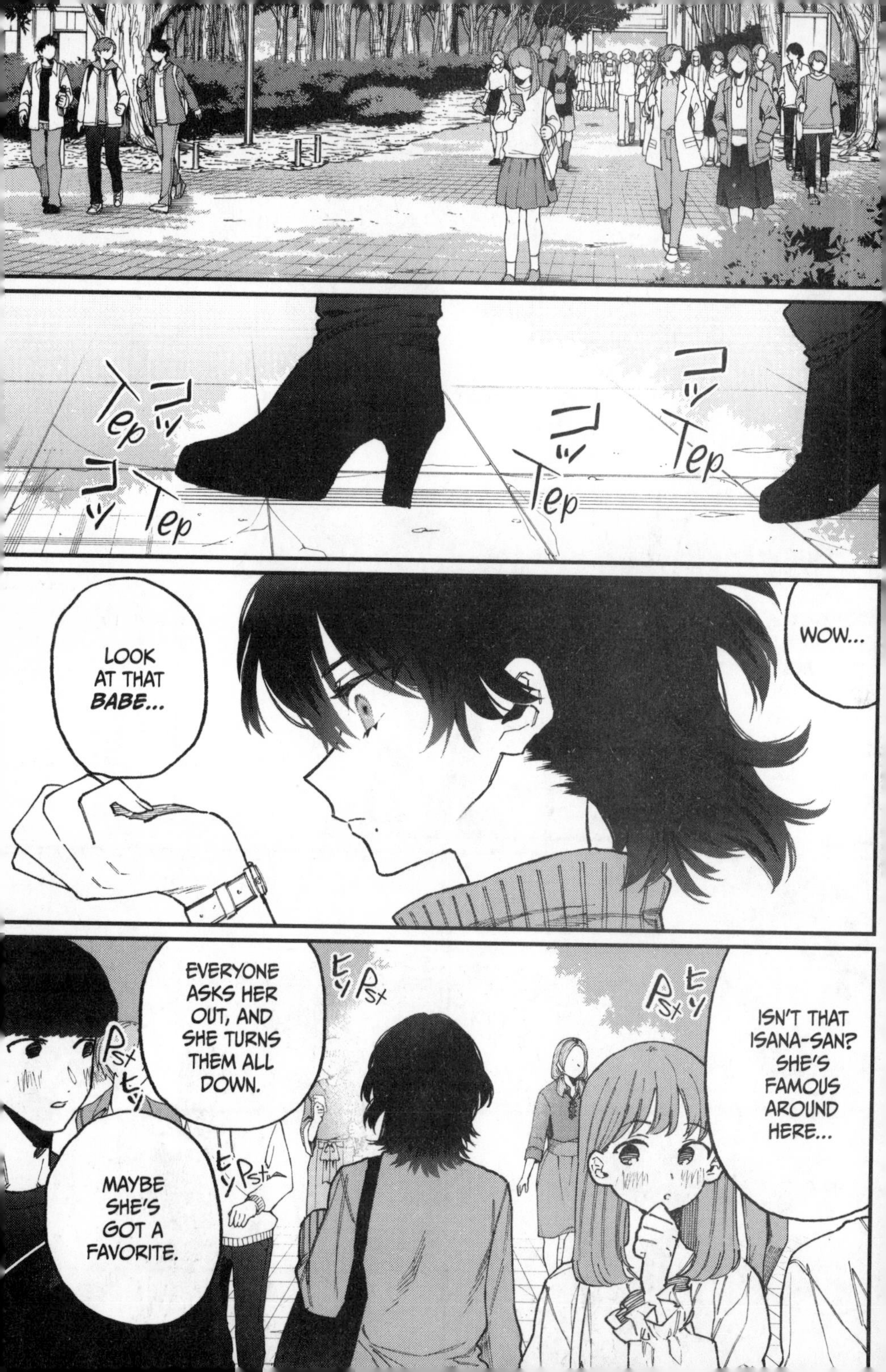

コッ
Tep
コッ
Tep
コッ
Tep
コッ
Tep
WOW...
LOOK AT THAT *BABE*...
ヒソ
Psst
ISN'T THAT ISANA-SAN? SHE'S FAMOUS AROUND HERE...
ヒソ
Psst
EVERYONE ASKS HER OUT, AND SHE TURNS THEM ALL DOWN.
ヒソ
Psst
ヒソ
Psst
MAYBE SHE'S GOT A FAVORITE.

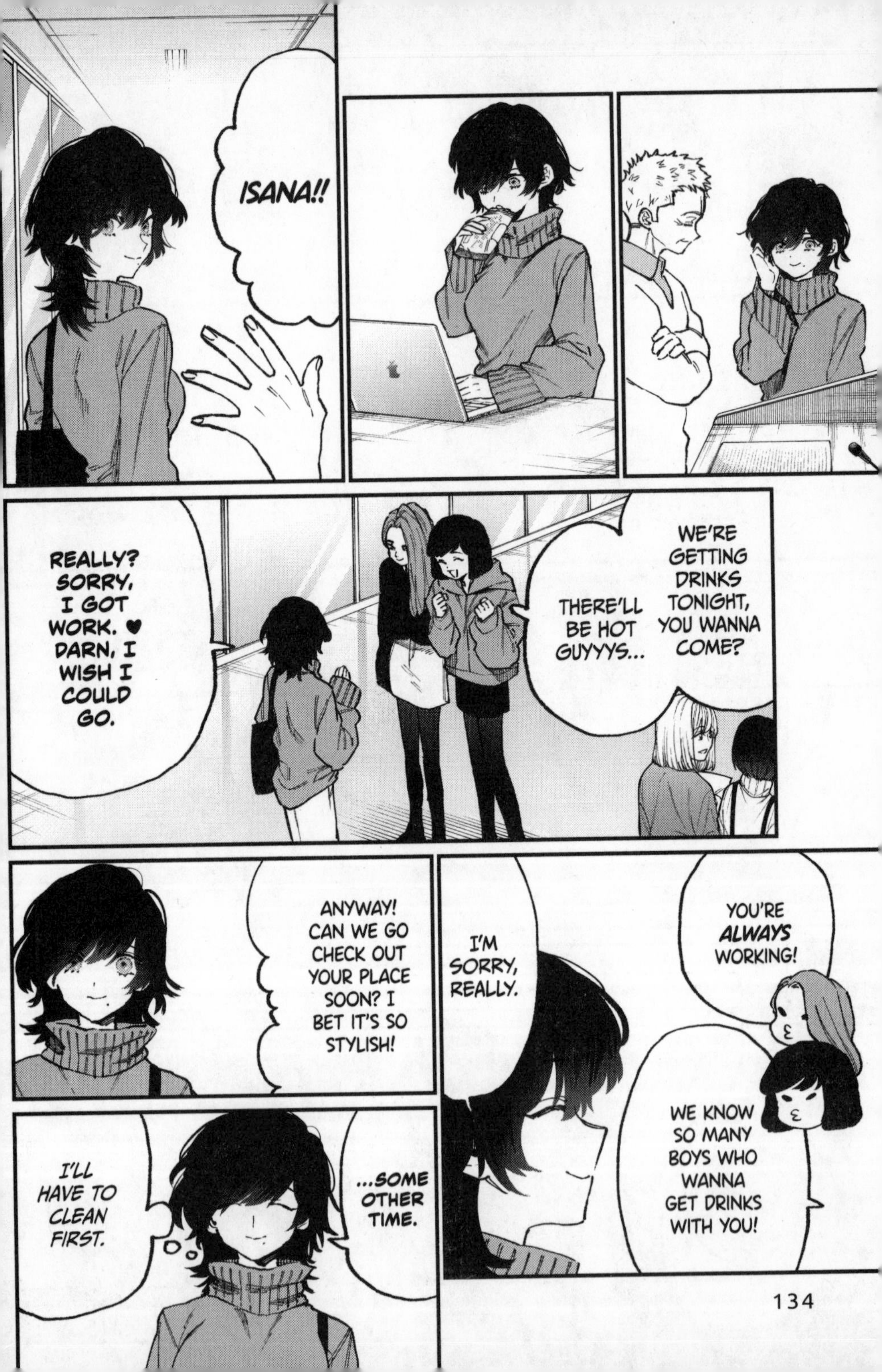
ISANA!!
WE'RE GETTING DRINKS TONIGHT, YOU WANNA COME?
THERE'LL BE HOT GUYYYS...
REALLY? SORRY, I GOT WORK. ♥ DARN, I WISH I COULD GO.
YOU'RE ***ALWAYS*** WORKING!
WE KNOW SO MANY BOYS WHO WANNA GET DRINKS WITH YOU!
I'M SORRY, REALLY.
ANYWAY! CAN WE GO CHECK OUT YOUR PLACE SOON? I BET IT'S SO STYLISH!
...SOME OTHER TIME.
I'LL HAVE TO CLEAN FIRST.

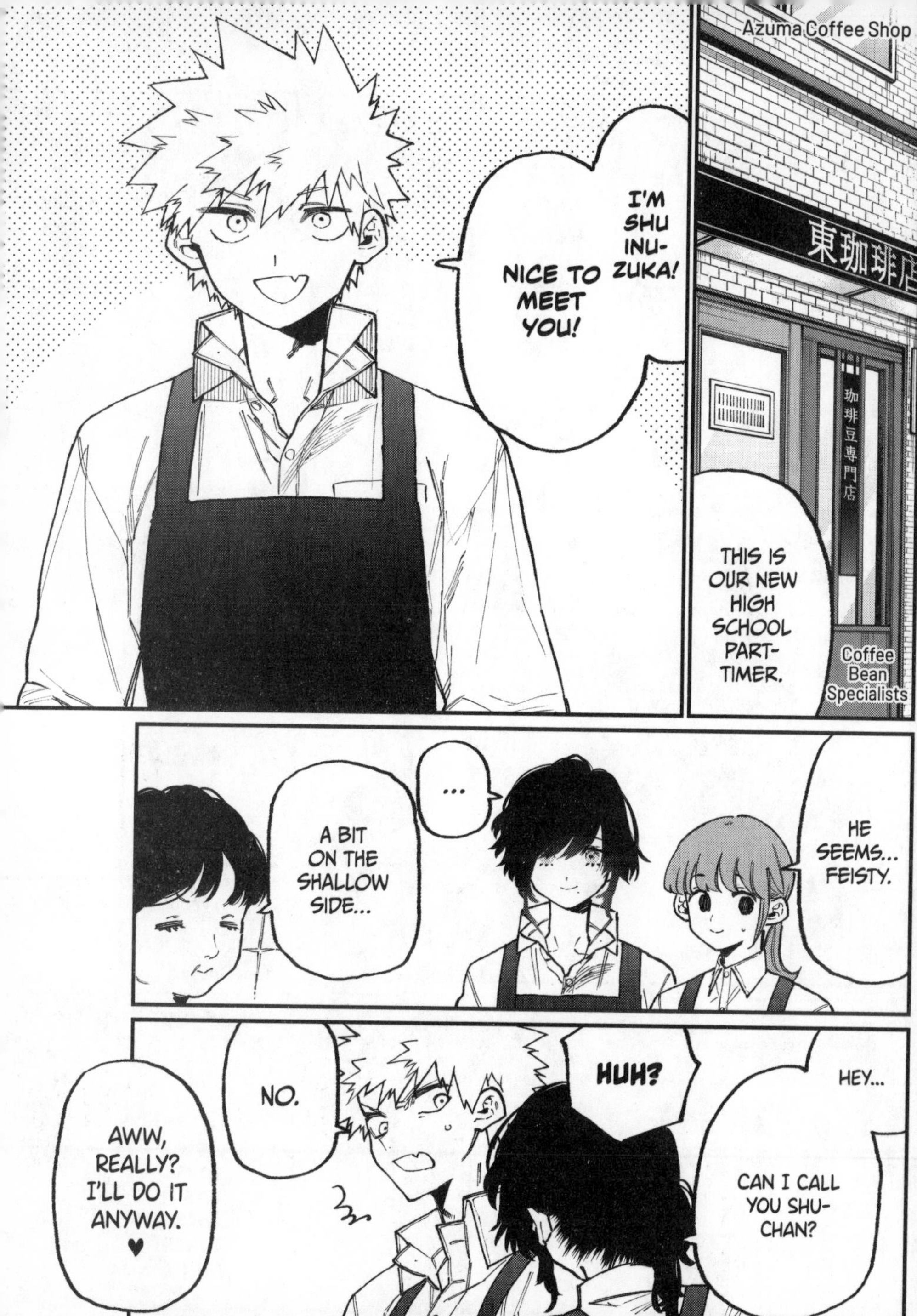
Azuma Coffee Shop
東珈琲店
珈琲豆専門店
THIS IS OUR NEW HIGH SCHOOL PART-TIMER.
Coffee Bean Specialists
I'M SHU INUZUKA!
NICE TO MEET YOU!
HE SEEMS... FEISTY.
...
A BIT ON THE SHALLOW SIDE...
HEY...
CAN I CALL YOU SHU-CHAN?
HUH?
NO.
AWW, REALLY? I'LL DO IT ANYWAY. ♥

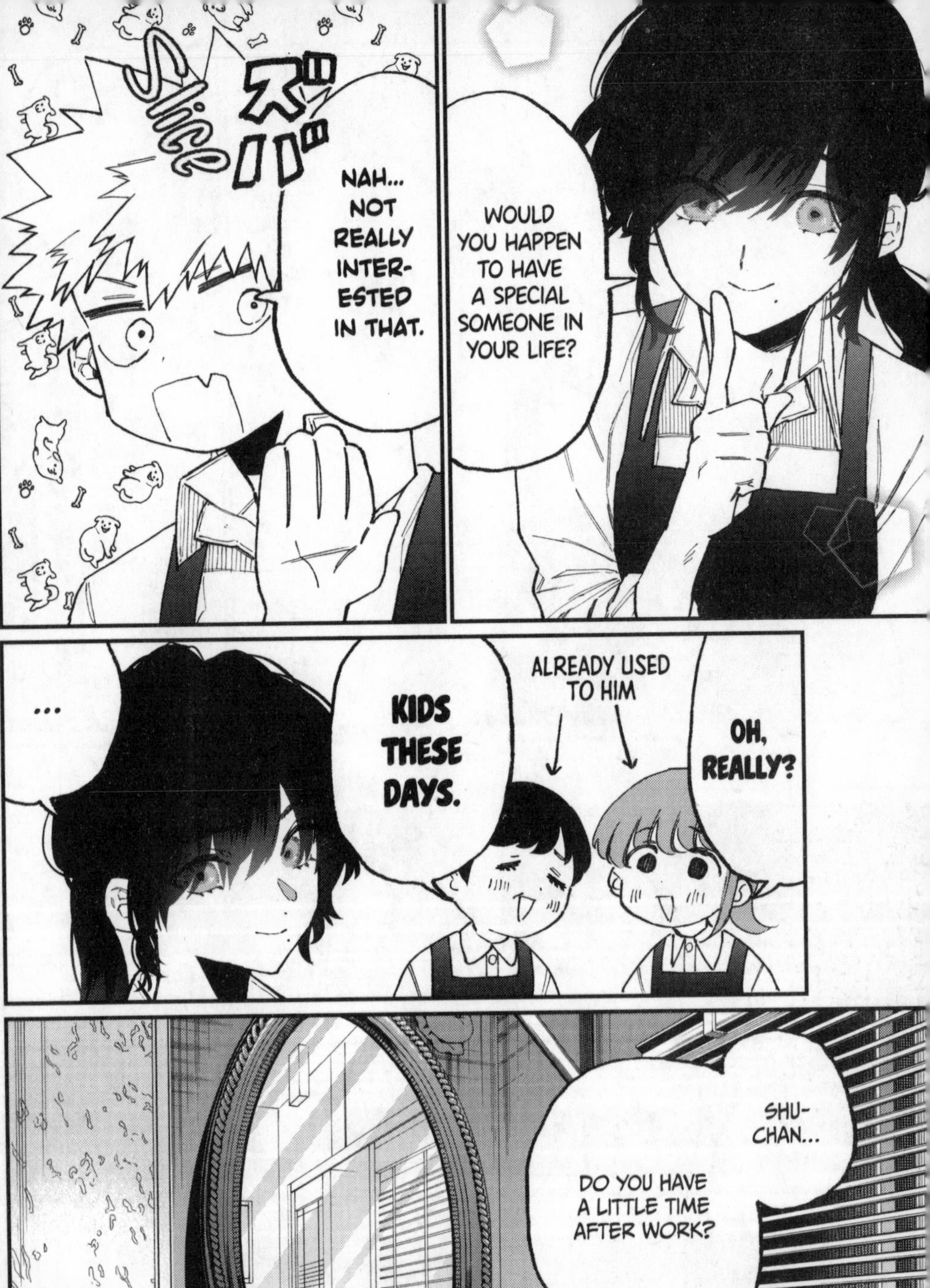
WOULD YOU HAPPEN TO HAVE A SPECIAL SOMEONE IN YOUR LIFE?
NAH... NOT REALLY INTER-ESTED IN THAT.
Slice
OH, REALLY?
ALREADY USED TO HIM
KIDS THESE DAYS.
...
SHU-CHAN...
DO YOU HAVE A LITTLE TIME AFTER WORK?

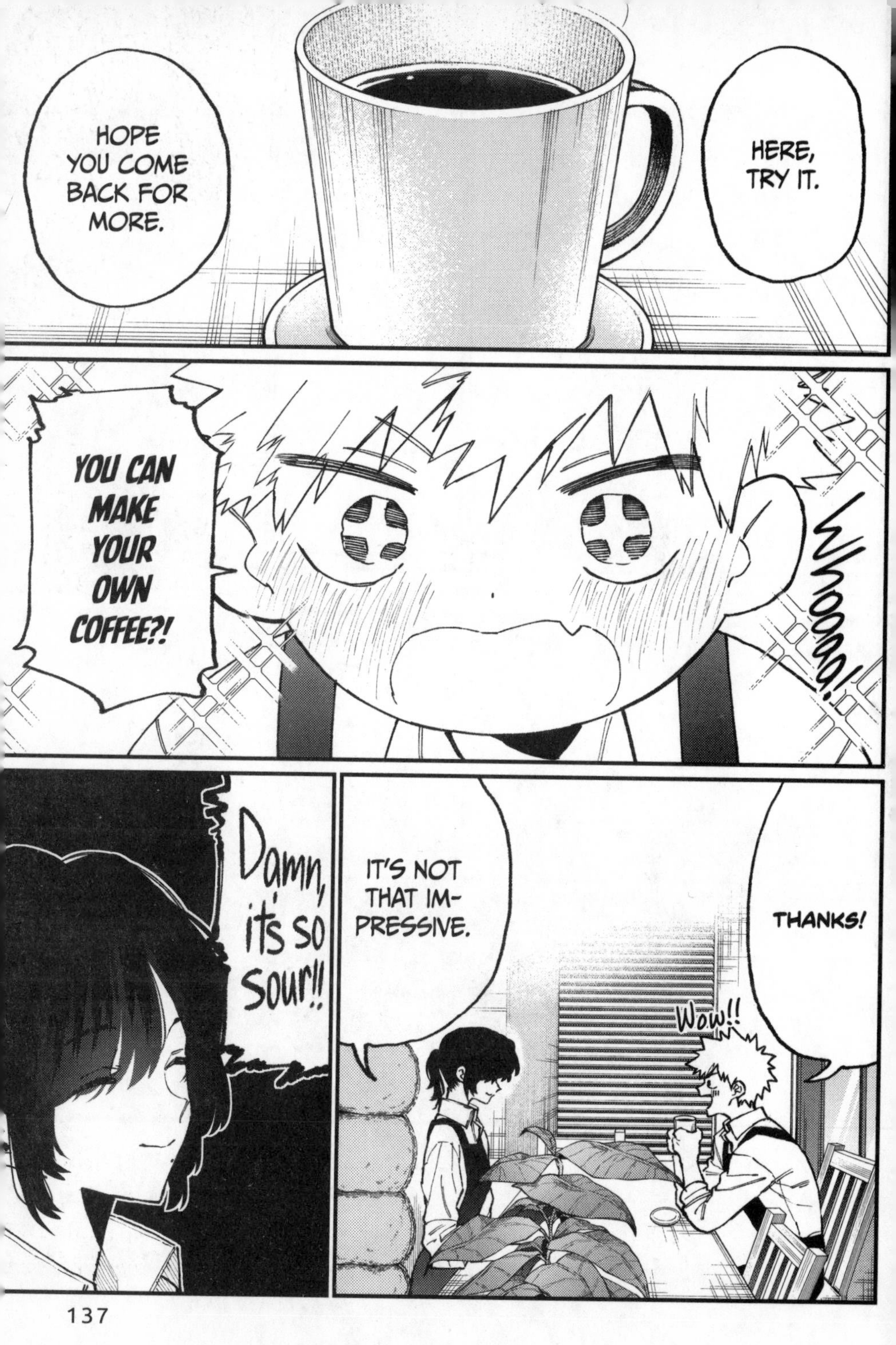
HERE, TRY IT.
HOPE YOU COME BACK FOR MORE.
WHOOOA!
YOU CAN MAKE YOUR OWN COFFEE?!
THANKS!
IT'S NOT THAT IM-PRESSIVE.
Wow!!
Damn, it's so sour!!

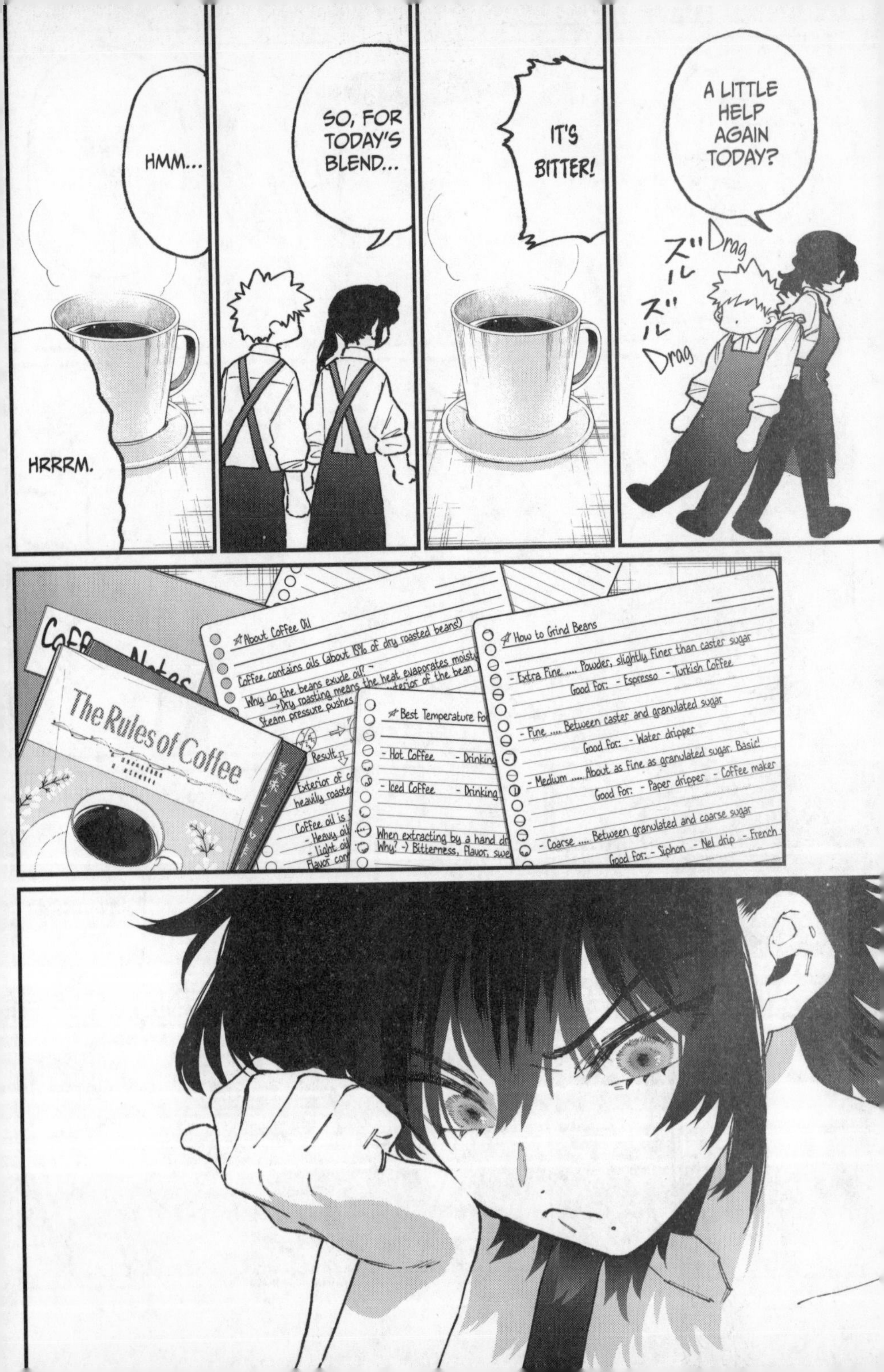
A LITTLE HELP AGAIN TODAY?
ズルズル
Drag
Drag
IT'S BITTER!
SO, FOR TODAY'S BLEND...
HMM...
HRRRM.
How to Grind Beans
- Extra Fine .... Powder, slightly finer than caster sugar
Good for: - Espresso - Turkish Coffee
- Fine .... Between caster and granulated sugar
Good for: - Water dripper
- Medium .... About as fine as granulated sugar. Basic!
Good for: - Paper dripper - Coffee maker
- Coarse .... Between granulated and coarse sugar
Good for: - Siphon - Nel drip - French
Best Temperature for
- Hot Coffee - Drinking
- Iced Coffee - Drinking
When extracting by a hand dr
Why? -) Bitterness, Flavor, swe
About Coffee Oil
Coffee contains oils (about 15% of dry roasted beans!)
Why do the beans exude oil? ~
→Dry roasting means the heat evaporates moist
Steam pressure pushes
Result
Exterior of c
heavily roaste
Coffee oil is
- Heavy oil
- light oil
Flavor con
The Rules of Coffee

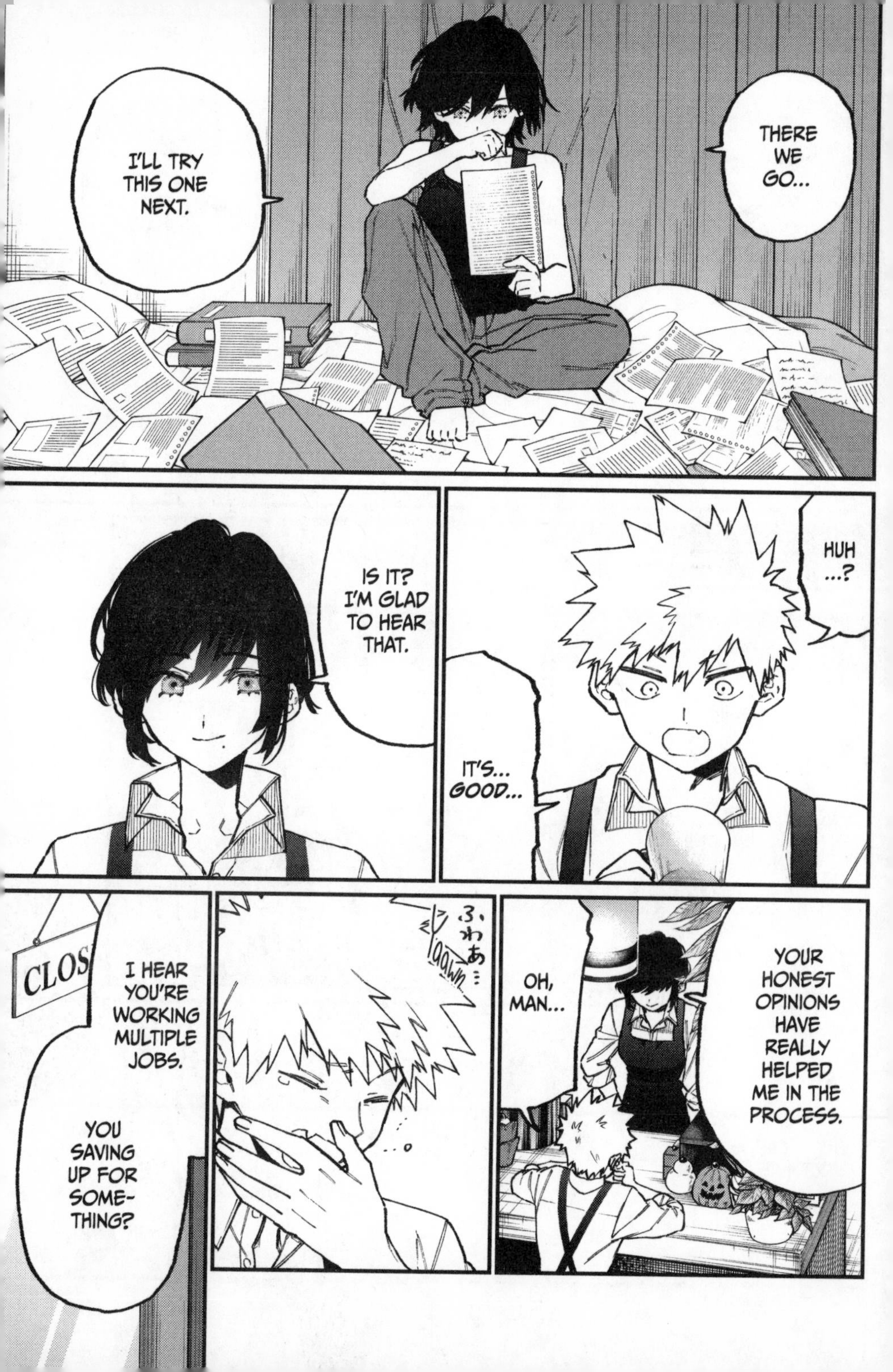
THERE WE GO...
I'LL TRY THIS ONE NEXT.
HUH ...?
IT'S... GOOD...
IS IT? I'M GLAD TO HEAR THAT.
YOUR HONEST OPINIONS HAVE REALLY HELPED ME IN THE PROCESS.
OH, MAN...
ふわあ…
yaawn
I HEAR YOU'RE WORKING MULTIPLE JOBS.
YOU SAVING UP FOR SOME-THING?
CLOS

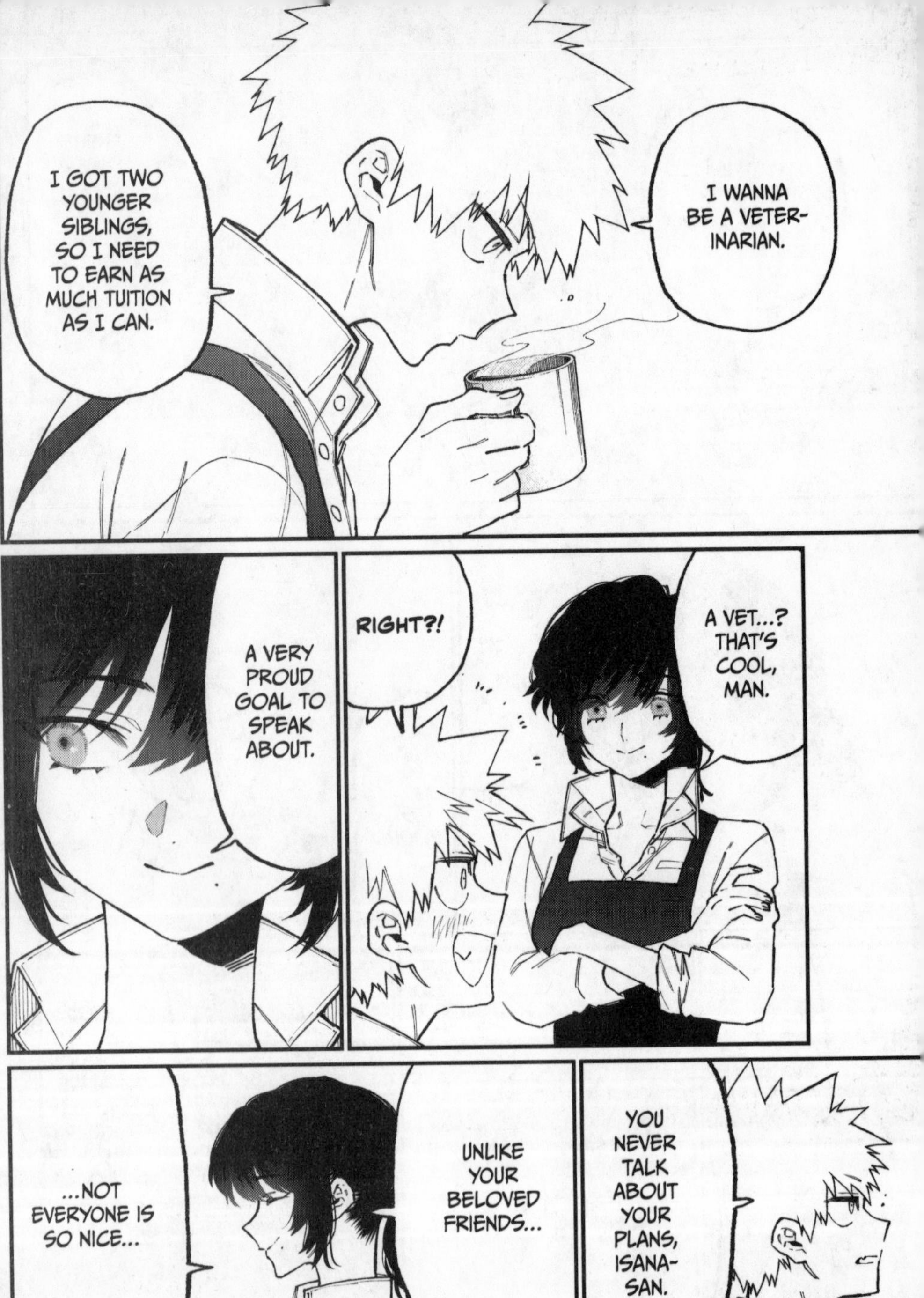
I WANNA BE A VETER-INARIAN.
I GOT TWO YOUNGER SIBLINGS, SO I NEED TO EARN AS MUCH TUITION AS I CAN.
A VET...? THAT'S COOL, MAN.
RIGHT?!
A VERY PROUD GOAL TO SPEAK ABOUT.
YOU NEVER TALK ABOUT YOUR PLANS, ISANA-SAN.
UNLIKE YOUR BELOVED FRIENDS...
...NOT EVERYONE IS SO NICE...

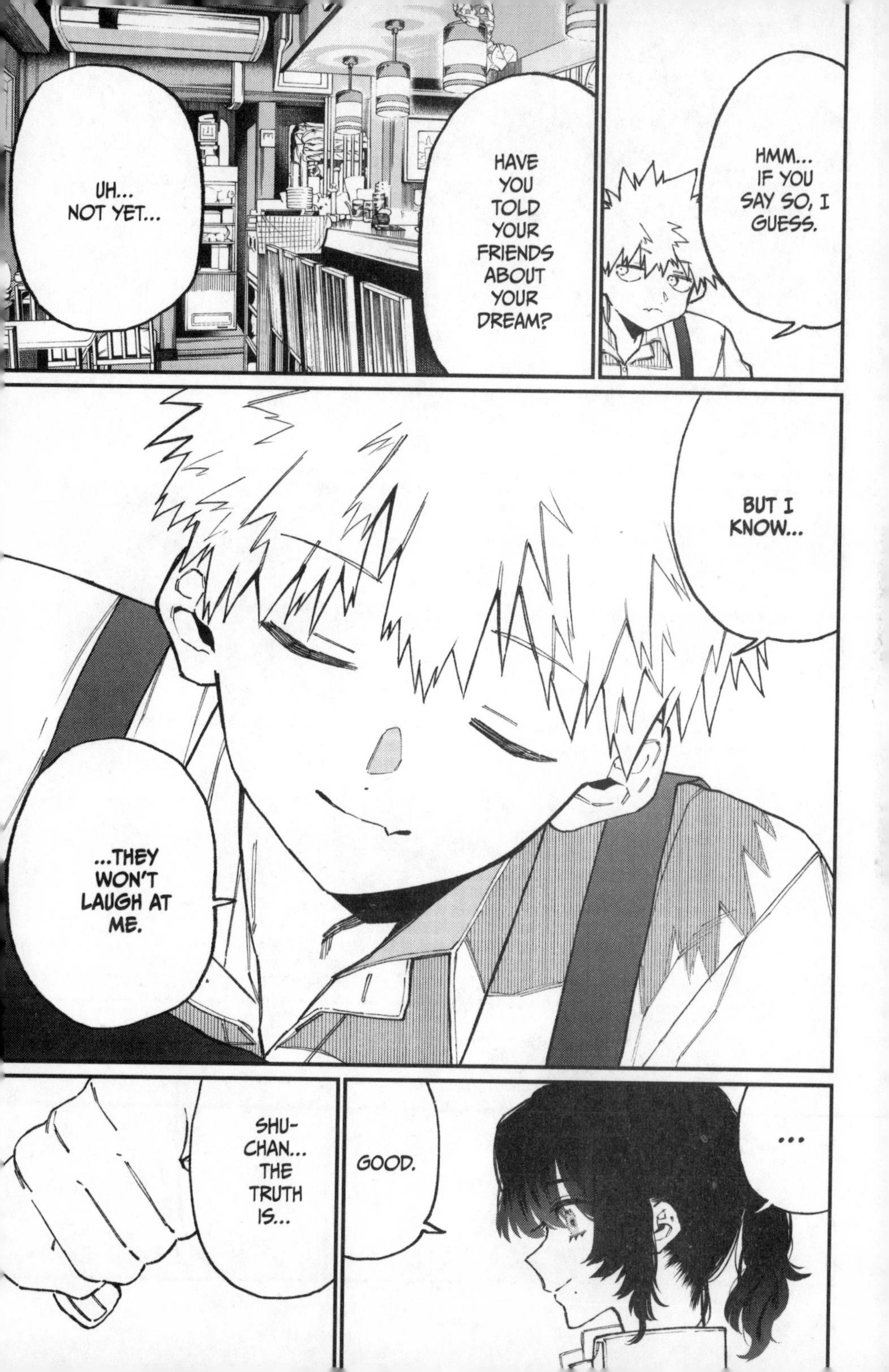
HMM... IF YOU SAY SO, I GUESS.
HAVE YOU TOLD YOUR FRIENDS ABOUT YOUR DREAM?
UH... NOT YET...
BUT I KNOW...
...THEY WON'T LAUGH AT ME.
...
GOOD.
SHU-CHAN... THE TRUTH IS...

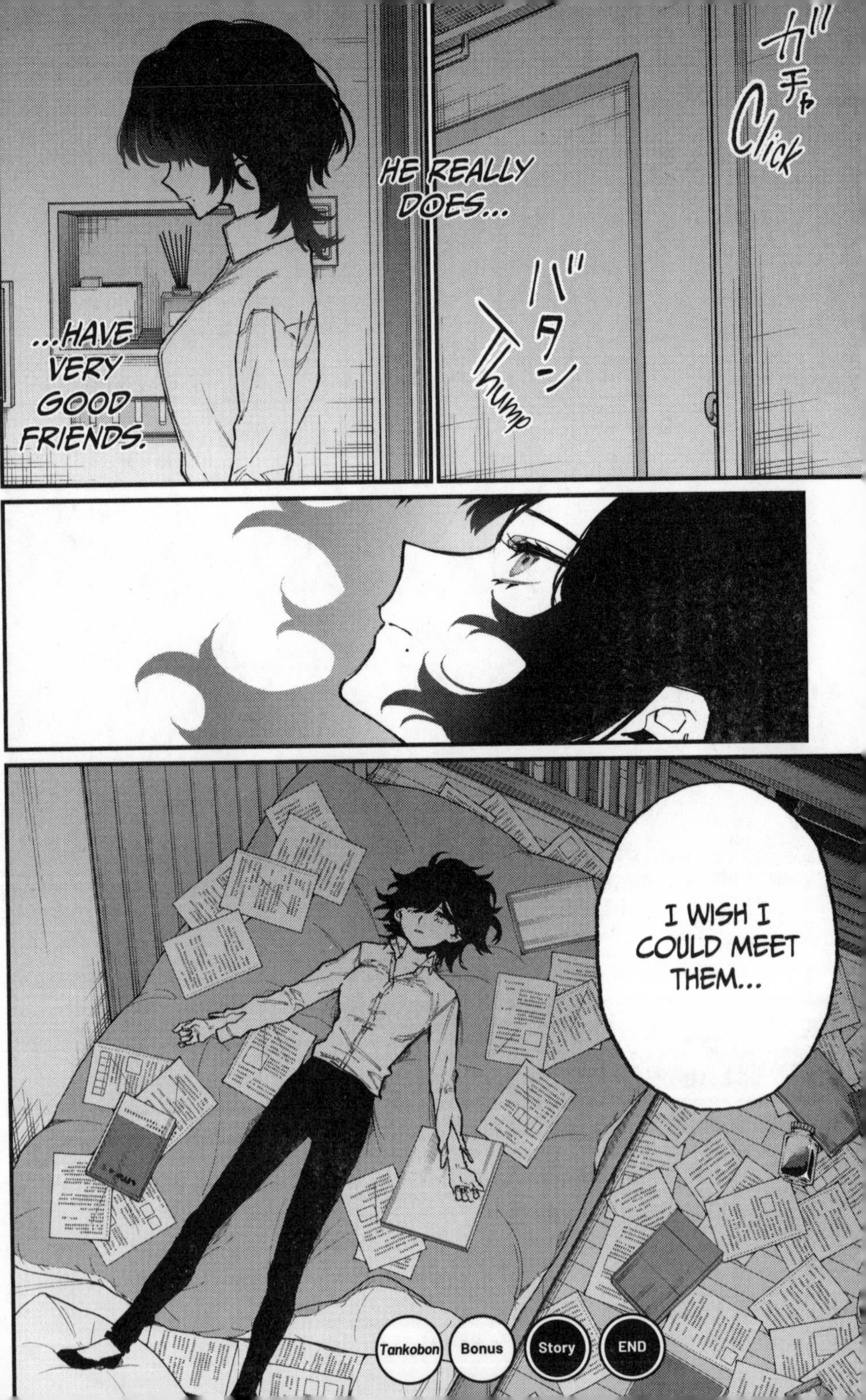
ガチャ
Click
HE REALLY DOES...
バタン
Thump
...HAVE VERY GOOD FRIENDS.
I WISH I COULD MEET THEM...
Tankobon
Bonus
Story
END

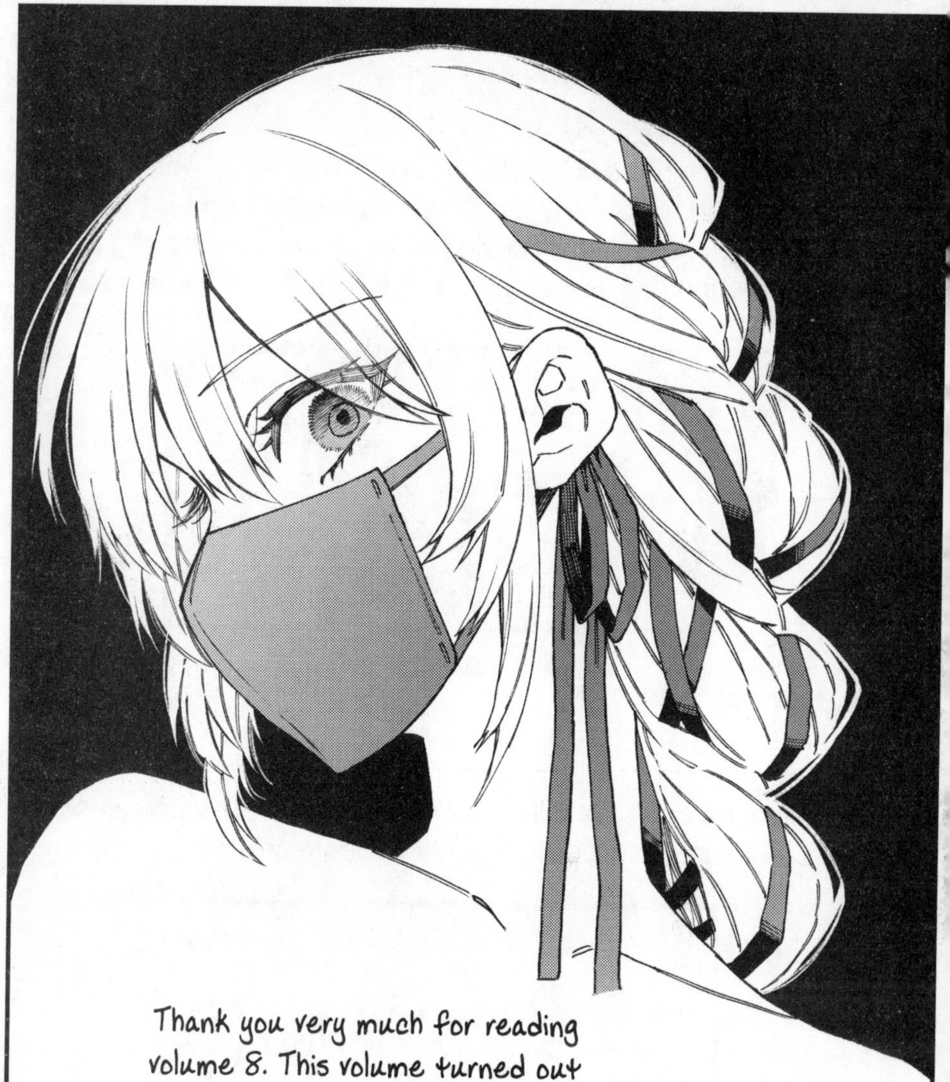

Thank you very much for reading volume 8. This volume turned out to be about everyday life.

Staff

Naa-san

Uchida-san

Santo-san

Design: Kurachi-san

Editor: Hiraoka-san

TRANSLATOR'S NOTES

First trip to the temple, page 19

A Japanese tradition known as *hatsumôde,* in which people visit a temple or shrine within the first few days of the year to pray for good fortune in the year ahead. It's an occasion for buying new good luck charms and drawing ceremonial fortunes, and is often done with family and/or friends.

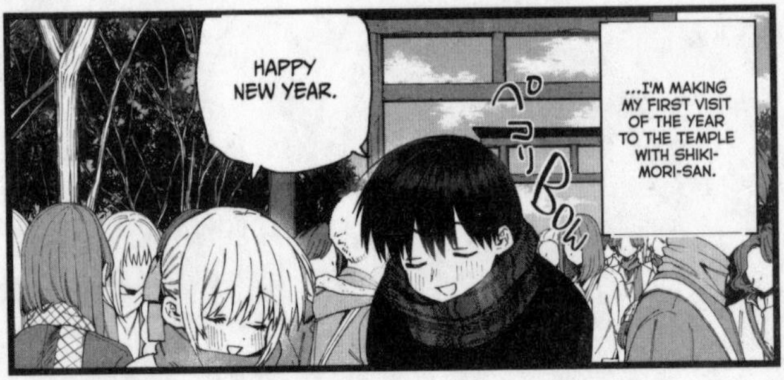
...I'M MAKING MY FIRST VISIT OF THE YEAR TO THE TEMPLE WITH SHIKI-MORI-SAN.
BOW
HAPPY NEW YEAR.

Sweet sake, page 20

Amazake ("sweet sake") is a traditional version of *sake* that uses the rice pulp (lees) from *sake* production. The result is lightly sweet and has a porridge-like texture. It naturally contains less than one percent alcohol by volume, so it's not classified as an alcoholic beverage.

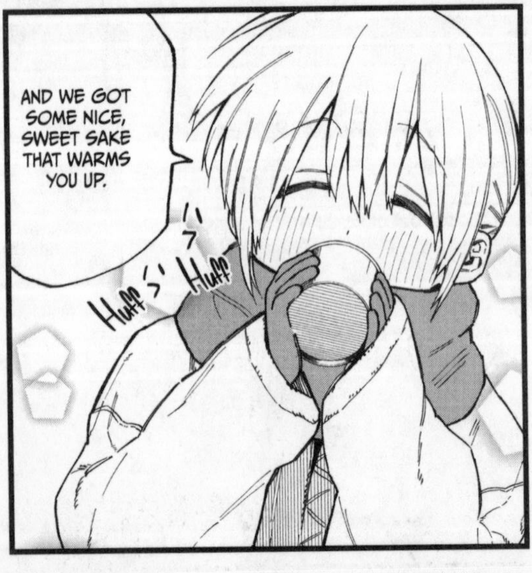
AND WE GOT SOME NICE, SWEET SAKE THAT WARMS YOU UP.
Huff
Huff

Omikuji, page 24
A New Year's custom at temples and shrines in Japan. *Omikuji* are paper fortunes that can be purchased at a window (or machine) that purport to tell one's luck for the year ahead, ranging from "very bad" to "very good," including more specific information in a variety of categories. If a bad fortune is pulled, it is customarily tied to a tree or special wall of wires, which supposedly keeps the bad fortune tied there, rather than with the original person.

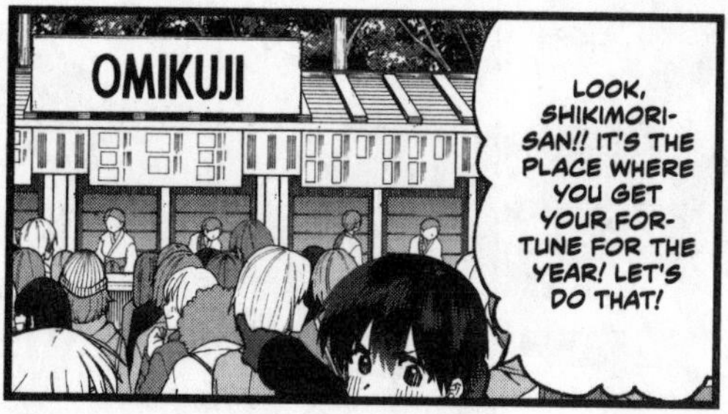
LOOK, SHIKIMORI-SAN!! IT'S THE PLACE WHERE YOU GET YOUR FOR-TUNE FOR THE YEAR! LET'S DO THAT!
OMIKUJI

Hopping vampires, page 34
An element of Chinese folklore called *jiangshi*, a corpse dressed in old-fashioned clothes with a paper talisman stuck to the forehead containing a magic seal. The nickname "hopping vampire" comes from their rigor mortis, which leaves them too inflexible to do anything but hop. The *jiangshi* image was popularized globally through Hong Kong films. In Japan they are known as *kyonshi*, and in this illustration the "kyo" from *kyonshi* is combined with the "kyo" from "bad luck" as seen on *omikuji*.

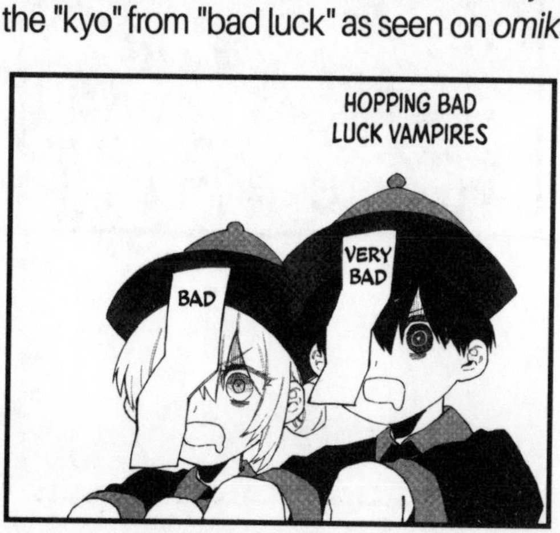
HOPPING BAD LUCK VAMPIRES
VERY BAD
BAD

Lucky bag, page 35

A typical tactic used by retail stores during the New Year's shopping period. A lucky bag, or *fukubukuro*, is a blind grab bag of the store's products, sold for a much cheaper price than it would cost to buy them individually. So while you might not know what you'll get (some businesses do make it clear) it's still guaranteed to be an excellent deal.

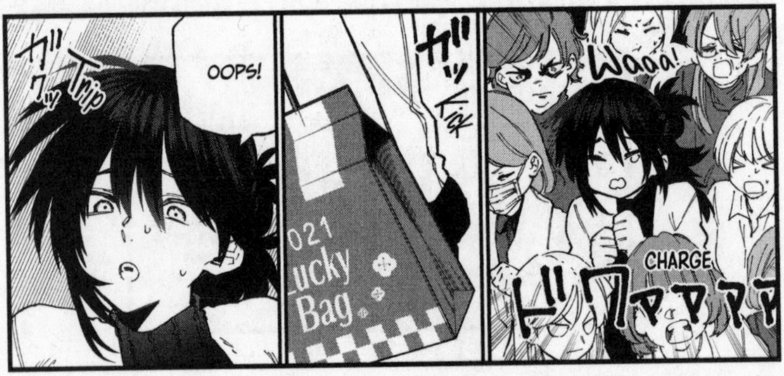
Waaa!
CHARGE
ドワァァァァ
ガッ
Kick
021
Lucky
Bag
ガクッ
Trip
OOPS!

Taiyaki, page 43

A type of pastry consisting of a fluffy, waffle-like batter surrounding a center of *anko*, a sweet red bean paste. The pastry is cooked in a fish-shaped mold. They are particularly popular at festivals and holidays.

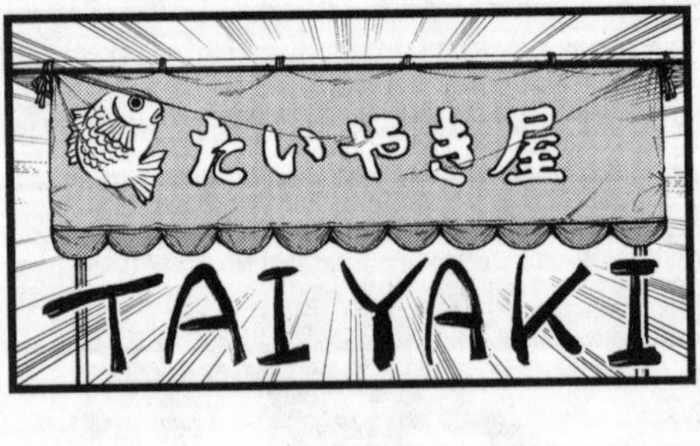
たいやき屋
TAIYAKI

Hanetsuki, page 51

A traditional game often played in the New Year's season that resembles badminton. Instead of rackets, players use solid paddles that are elongated and rectangular, and rather than using a net, players simply attempt to go back and forth, keeping the shuttlecock aloft. If you miss and let it drop to the ground, the punishment is an ink marking on the face.

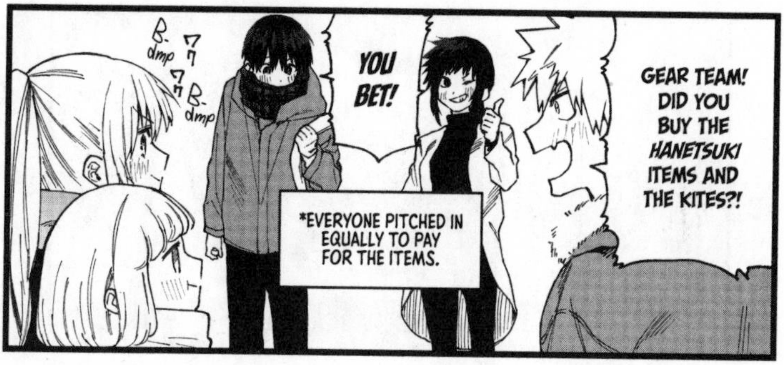
GEAR TEAM! DID YOU BUY THE *HANETSUKI* ITEMS AND THE KITES?!
YOU BET!
*EVERYONE PITCHED IN EQUALLY TO PAY FOR THE ITEMS.
B-dmp
B-dmp

Natsume Soseki, page 86

One of the most revered of Japanese novelists, known for his classic works *Bocchan, I Am a Cat,* and the story referenced in this scene, *Kokoro* ("Heart"). *Kokoro* is a story about the unnamed narrator and his memories of a mentor or teacher named "Sensei," and the complicated history that Sensei had with a close friend who died.

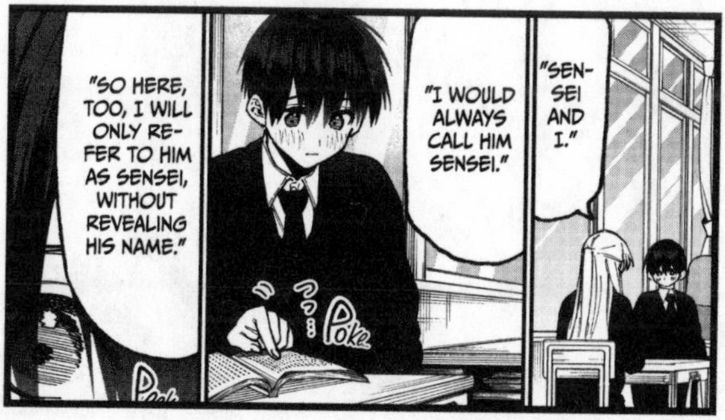
"SEN-SEI AND I."
"I WOULD ALWAYS CALL HIM SENSEI."
Poke
"SO HERE, TOO, I WILL ONLY RE-FER TO HIM AS SENSEI, WITHOUT REVEALING HIS NAME."

Shimono Zoo, page 93

A play on the famous Ueno Zoo in Tokyo. The district of Ueno contains many cultural sites and museums, including Ueno Zoo. The name Ueno means "upper field," so "Shimono" is a parody meaning "lower field." It's an obvious enough parody that more than one manga has named a zoo this, to discreetly avoid using the real zoo.

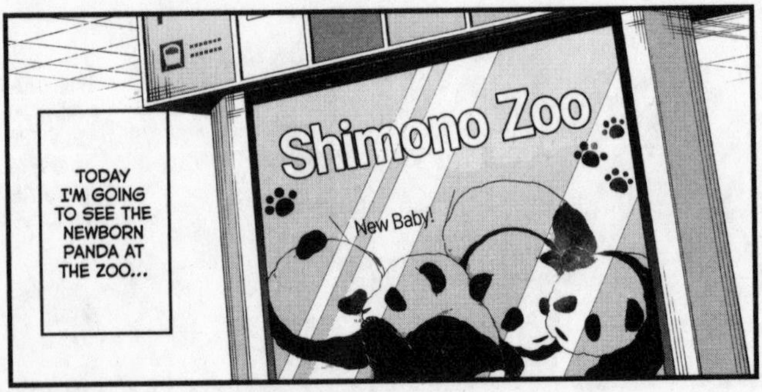
Shimono Zoo
New Baby!
TODAY I'M GOING TO SEE THE NEWBORN PANDA AT THE ZOO...

Saruogi, page 129

In keeping with some other members of the friend group (Nekozaki = cat, Inuzuka = dog), Saruogi's name contains the kanji for "monkey" (*saru*).

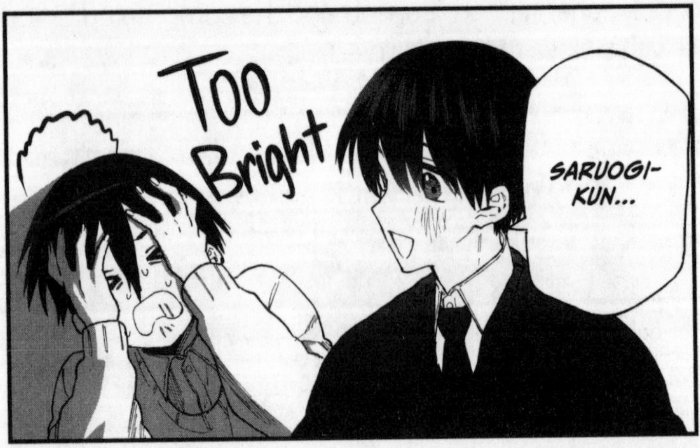
SARUOGI-KUN...
Too Bright

PERFECT WORLD

Rie Aruga

A TOUCHING NEW SERIES ABOUT LOVE AND COPING WITH DISABILITY

An office party reunites Tsugumi with her high school crush Itsuki. He's realized his dream of becoming an architect, but along the way, he experienced a spinal injury that put him in a wheelchair. Now Tsugumi's rekindled feelings will butt up against prejudices she never considered — and Itsuki will have to decide if he's ready to let someone into his heart...

"Depicts with great delicacy and courage the difficulties some with disabilities experience getting involved in romantic relationships... Rie Aruga refuses to romanticize, pushing her heroine to face the reality of disability. She invites her readers to the same tasks of empathy, knowledge and recognition."
—Slate.fr

"An important entry [in manga romance]... The emotional core of both plot and characters indicates thoughtfulness... [Aruga's] research is readily apparent in the text and artwork, making this feel like a real story."
—Anime News Network

KC KODANSHA COMICS

Perfect World © Rie Aruga/Kodansha Ltd.

A SMART, NEW ROMANTIC COMEDY FOR FANS OF *SHORTCAKE CAKE* AND *TERRACE HOUSE!*

Living-Room Matsunaga-san © Keiko Iwashita / Kodansha Ltd.

KC KODANSHA COMICS

A romance manga starring high school girl Meeko, who learns to live on her own in a boarding house whose living room is home to the odd (but handsome) Matsunaga-san. She begins to adjust to her new life away from her parents, but Meeko soon learns that no matter how far away from home she is, she's still a young girl at heart — especially when she finds herself falling for Matsunaga-san.

Knight of the Ice ©Yayoi Ogawa/Kodansha Ltd.

SKATING THRILLS AND ICY CHILLS WITH THIS NEW TINGLY ROMANCE SERIES!

A rom-com on ice, perfect for fans of *Princess Jellyfish* and *Wotakoi*. Kokoro is the talk of the figure-skating world, winning trophies and hearts. But little do they know... he's actually a huge nerd! From the beloved creator of *You're My Pet* (*Tramps Like Us*).

Chitose is a serious young woman, working for the health magazine *SASSO*. Or at least, she would be, if she wasn't constantly getting distracted by her childhood friend, international figure skating star Kokoro Kijinami! In the public eye and on the ice, Kokoro is a gallant, flawless knight, but behind his glittery costumes and breathtaking spins lies a secret: He's actually a hopelessly romantic otaku, who can only land his quad jumps when Chitose is on hand to recite a spell from his favorite magical girl anime!

KC
KODANSHA
COMICS

The adorable new odd-couple cat comedy manga from the creator of the beloved *Chi's Sweet Home*, in full color!

Praise for Chi's Sweet Home

"Nearly impossible to turn away... a true all-ages title that anyone, young or old, cat lover or not, will enjoy. The stories will bring a smile to your face and warm your heart."

~School Library Journal

Sue & Tai-chan

Konami Kanata

Sue is an aging housecat who's looking forward to living out her life in peace... but her plans change when the mischievous black tomcat Tai-chan enters the picture! Hey! Sue never signed up to be a catsitter! *Sue & Tai-chan* is the latest from the reigning meow-narch of cute kitty comics, Konami Kanata.

Sue & Tai-chan © Konami Kanata/Kodansha Ltd.

KC KODANSHA COMICS

CUTE ANIMALS AND LIFE LESSONS, PERFECT FOR ASPIRING PET VETS OF ALL AGES!

KODANSHA COMICS

YUZU THE PET VET

1

BY
MINGO ITO

In collaboration with
NIPPON COLUMBIA CO., LTD.

Yuzu the Pet Vet © Mingo Ito / NIPPON COLUMBIA CO., LTD./ Kodansha Ltd.

For an 11-year-old, Yuzu has a lot on her plate. When her mom gets sick and has to be hospitalized, Yuzu goes to live with her uncle who runs the local veterinary clinic. Yuzu's always been scared of animals, but she tries to help out. Through all the tough moments in her life, Yuzu realizes that she can help make things all right with a little help from her animal pals, peers, and kind grown-ups.

Every new patient is a furry friend in the making!

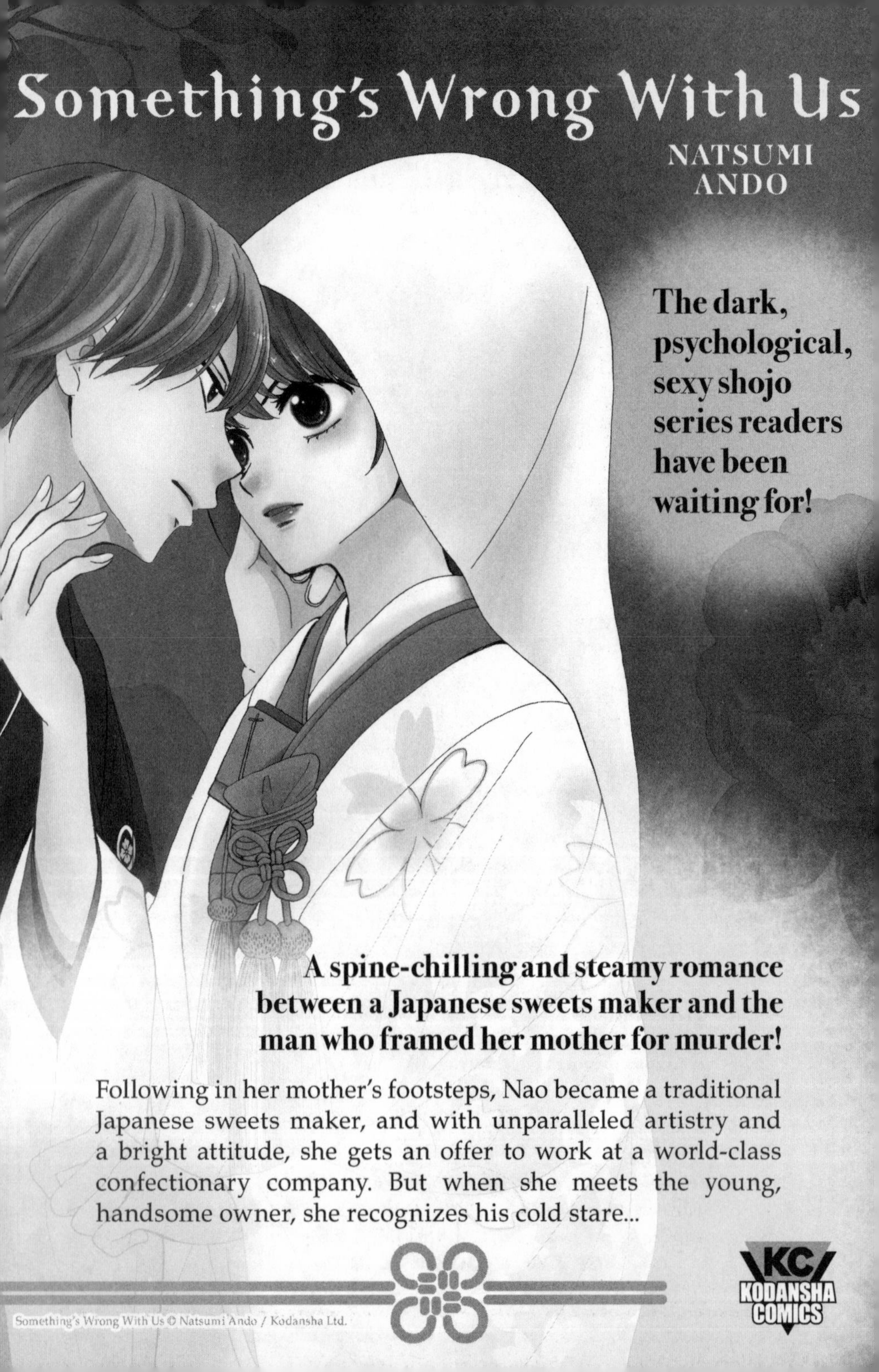
Something's Wrong With Us
NATSUMI ANDO
The dark, psychological, sexy shojo series readers have been waiting for!
A spine-chilling and steamy romance between a Japanese sweets maker and the man who framed her mother for murder!
Following in her mother's footsteps, Nao became a traditional Japanese sweets maker, and with unparalleled artistry and a bright attitude, she gets an offer to work at a world-class confectionary company. But when she meets the young, handsome owner, she recognizes his cold stare...
KC KODANSHA COMICS
Something's Wrong With Us © Natsumi Ando / Kodansha Ltd.

Young characters and steampunk setting, like *Howl's Moving Castle* and *Battle Angel Alita*

Beyond the Clouds © 2018 Nicke / Ki-oon

A boy with a talent for machines and a mysterious girl whose wings he's fixed will take you beyond the clouds! In the tradition of the high-flying, resonant adventure stories of Studio Ghibli comes a gorgeous tale about the longing of young hearts for adventure and friendship!

THE SWEET SCENT OF LOVE IS IN THE AIR! FOR FANS OF OFFBEAT ROMANCES LIKE *WOTAKOI*

Sweat and Soap © Kintetsu Yamada / Kodansha Ltd.

In an office romance, there's a fine line between sexy and awkward... and that line is where Asako — a woman who sweats copiously — meets Koutarou — a perfume developer who can't get enough of Asako's, er, scent. Don't miss a romcom manga like no other!

THE HIGH SCHOOL HAREM COMEDY WITH FIVE TIMES THE CUTE GIRLS!

"An entertaining romantic-comedy with a snarky edge to it." —Taykobon

Futaro Uesugi is a second-year in high school, scraping to get by and pay off his family's debt. The only thing he can do is study, so when Futaro receives a part-time job offer to tutor the five daughters of a wealthy businessman, he can't pass it up. Little does he know, these five beautiful sisters are quintuplets, but the only thing they have in common...is that they're all terrible at studying!

THE QUINTESSENTIAL QUINTUPLETS

negi haruba

ANIME OUT NOW!

KC KODANSHA COMICS

The Quintessential Quintuplets © Negi Haruba/Kodansha, Ltd.

◄ KAMOME ►
SHIRAHAMA

Witch Hat Atelier

A magical manga
adventure for
fans of Disney
and Studio
Ghibli!

Witch Hat Atelier © Kamome Shirahama/Kodansha Ltd.

The magical adventure that took Japan by storm is finally here, from acclaimed DC and Marvel cover artist Kamome Shirahama!

In a world where everyone takes wonders like magic spells and dragons for granted, Coco is a girl with a simple dream: She wants to be a witch. But everybody knows magicians are born, not made, and Coco was not born with a gift for magic. Resigned to her un-magical life, Coco is about to give up on her dream to become a witch...until the day she meets Qifrey, a mysterious, traveling magician. After secretly seeing Qifrey perform magic in a way she's never seen before, Coco soon learns what everybody "knows" might not be the truth, and discovers that her magical dream may not be as far away as it may seem...

KC
KODANSHA
COMICS